WESTERN WORDS
A Dictionary of the Old West

WESTERN WORDS

A Dictionary
of the
Old West

Ramon F. Adams

HIPPOCRENE BOOKS

New York

Originally published by University of Oklahoma Press.

Hippocrene paperback edition, 1998.

For information, address:
HIPPOCRENE BOOKS, INC.
171 Madison Avenue
New York, NY 10016

ISBN 0-7818-0590-2

Printed in the United States of America.

Dedicated to the old-timers who used the saddle for a workbench in making history, to the modern cowhands who are still using a saddle for their throne in upholding a tradition, and to future cowmen who will never forsake this saddle for a jalopy to help them over the rough places.

"A cowboy is a man with guts and a hoss"

INTRODUCTION

"There ain't much paw and beller to a cowboy"

THEY SAY a good range cook never misses a rock when "herding" his teams across the country. I hope that, like him, I have not missed many words from the cowman's vocabulary in compiling this lexicon. My greatest pleasure in collecting the material has been in associating with the cowboy in his native haunts. Never loquacious around strangers, he has attained the reputation of being about as talkative as a Piegan Indian. But I learned, as a small boy, that when one becomes intimate with him, he "don't depend entirely on the sign language." Among his own kind he is never "hog-tied when it comes to makin' chin music." In fact, if he accepts you, his tongue gets "plumb frolicsome."

From first youthful impressions, my interest in his speech has grown until recording it has become the hobby of a lifetime. When a tenderfoot hears this range vernacular—distinctive, picturesque, and pungent—he is as surprised as a dog with his first porcupine. After he recovers from the shock of such unconventional English, the more he listens the more refreshing it becomes, because, like a fifth ace in a poker deck, it is so unexpected.

Never having had a chance to "study the higher branches of information through book learnin'," the native cowman forged his own language. Like other men of the soil, he created similes and metaphors, salty and unrefined, but sparkling with stimulating vigor. In the early days, many men with college degrees came west, fell in love with the freedom of range life, and remained. Not bound by conventions, they were not long in "chucking" their college grammar and drifting into the infectious parlance of the cow country. I have never yet met a cowman who didn't use it naturally and unconsciously, be he educated or otherwise.

Within the cowman's figures of speech lie the rich field of his subtle humor and strength—unique, original, full-flavored. With his usually limited education he squeezes the juice from language, molds it to suit his needs, and is a genius at making a verb out of anything. He "don't have to fish 'round for no decorated language to make his meanin' clear," and has little patience with the man who "spouts words that run eight to the pound."

Perhaps the strength and originality in his speech are due to the solitude, the nearness of the stars, the bigness of the country, and the far horizons—all of which give him a chance to think clearly and go into the depths of his own mind. Wide spaces "don't breed chatterboxes." On his long and lonely rides, he is not forced to listen to the scandal and idle gossip that dwarf a man's mind. Quite frequently he has no one to talk to but a horse that can't talk back.

William MacLeod Raine told me that he once heard his friend Gene Rhodes call a man a "rancid, left-handed old parallelogram." Who but a Westerner could put so much punch into a phrase? Who but a cowman would say of a gesticulating foreigner that "he couldn't say 'hell' with his hands tied"? Or think of a better figure for hunger than "hungrier'n a woodpecker with the headache"?

"The frontiersman, like the Indian," says Edward Everett Dale, "was a close observer. He saw every detail and in speaking of something he did not describe it. Rather he painted a picture in a single apt phrase— a picture so clear and colorful that description was unnecessary. He did not tell the listener—he preferred to show him—and show him he did with one pungent, salty phrase that often meant more than could long and detailed explanation."[1]

Unlettered men rely greatly upon comparisons to natural objects with which they are familiar to express their ideas and feelings. Mental images are a part of the life of a cowman. His comparisons are not only humorous, but fruity and unfaded. One cowhand spoke of a friend who had gone into a city barbershop to experience his first manicure with, "He's havin' his forehoofs roached and rasped by a pink and white pinto filly." A certain fiery old-timer was said to be "gettin' 'long in years, but his horns ain't been sawed off."

"Calm as a hoss trough," "pretty as a red heifer in a flower bed," "soft as a young calf's ears," "useless as a knot in a stake rope," "a heart in his brisket as big as a saddle blanket," "noisy as a calf corral," and "gals in them days didn't show much of their fetlocks" are but a few of the many examples of homely comparisons cowmen create.

One of the inherent characteristics of the cowboy is exaggeration. Not only does he have a talent for telling tall tales, but he has a genius for exaggeration in ordinary conversation. In the following examples the ordinary man would be content to use the unitalicized words, but the cowman wants more strength and he adds words such as the italicized ones to gain this potency: "so drunk he couldn't hit the ground with his hat *in three throws*," "raised hell *and put a chunk under it*," "his

[1] "Speech of the Frontier," an address at the Association Banquet, Central States Speech Association, Oklahoma City, April 1, 1941.

tongue hangin' out a foot *and forty inches*," and "he'd fight y'u till hell freezes over, *then skate with y'u on the ice*."

Another pronounced trait is the pithy, yet robust humor which continually crops out in his speech. Struthers Burt writes, ". . . this closeness with nature makes the cowboy exceedingly witty. They are the wittiest Americans alive. Not wisecracking like the city man, but really witty."[2]

The cowman has always reserved control of his spelling and pronunciation, completely ignoring the dictionary. He pronounces his Spanish as it sounds to his ear, and thus new words have been created; for instance, *hackamore* (from *jáquima*) and *hoosgow* (from *juzgado*).

"Just as the cowboy 'borrowed' much of his traditional 'riggin''" from the *vaquero*," wrote S. Omar Barker, "and adapted it to his own needs, so, too, he borrowed freely from this *vaquero's* word supply, which he also adapted. He borrowed 'by ear,' of course, and so plentifully that today much typical western terminology owes its origin to Spanish, however little it sometimes resembles the original either in spelling or pronunciation."[3]

Like all other Americans, the cowman is in a hurry and employs our typical shortening of words and phrases. His grammar is rough and rugged like his hills and canyons, but his short cuts are practical. Thus he creates words such as *lariat*, from *la reata*; *chaps*, from *chaparejos*; and *dally*, from *dar vuelta*.

Yet in his actions he is not hurried, but takes time to examine small things. He gets the habit of "usin' his eyes a lot and his mouth mighty little." He catalogs each detail and stores it away in his mind for future use, squeezing out all significant items and adding their essence to his refreshing philosophy. He has a talent for "sayin' a whole lot in a mighty few words," and "don't use up all his kindlin' to get his fire started."

Not only did the cowman borrow from the Spanish, but he took what he wanted from the Indian, the trapper, and the freighter who preceded him, and from the gambler, the gunman, and others who came after him.

The terms recorded in this volume have been gathered from every part of the range. There are genuine cowmen who may disclaim ever having heard of certain ones. This can easily be true, just as throughout our country one section is unfamiliar with the colloquialisms of another. When the East-Sider ridicules the Southerner's *you-all*, he doesn't

[2] Struthers Burt, *Powder River* (New York, Farrar & Rinehart, 1938), 229.

[3] S. Omar Barker, "Sagebrush Spanish," *New Mexico Magazine*, XX, No. 12 (December, 1942), 18.

stop to think that his own *youse guys* is just as comical and ridiculous south of Mason and Dixon's line.

Different sections of the West also have their own peculiar argot. As Will James said, "A feller wrote a review of my books one time, without being asked, and he said something about my language not being true cowboy language. As I found out afterwards, that feller had been a cowboy all right enough, but I also found out that he'd only rode in one state all his life. He'd compared his language with mine and mine had been picked up and mixed from the different languages from the different parts of the whole cow country. The language of the cow country is just as different as the style of the rigs and ways of working."[4]

The Texan says *pitch;* the northern cowboy says *buck;* yet they mean the same thing. Likewise, the Texan's *stake rope* becomes *picket rope* on the northern range, and *cinch* in the North becomes *girth* when it hits the South. These are but a few examples of many that could be mentioned. California, Oregon, Utah, Nevada, and Idaho use terms rarely heard in the rest of the range country.

When Texas first went into the cattle business, it adopted the Mexican's methods and equipment—big-horned saddles, spade bit, rawhide rope, system of "dallying," and all the rest. The massacre at the Alamo stirred in Texans a fierce hatred of all things Mexican and brought changes in following the customs of the Spanish *vaquero.* The long rope and system of "dallying" disappeared, and Texas became a "tie-fast" country. The grazing bit was substituted for the spade and ring bits, and the Spanish rig gave way to the double-rigged saddle.

But the language of the Mexican had deeper roots. This the Texan kept and corrupted to suit his needs. The cattle business of California was also born under Spanish influence, but it had no Alamo, no Goliad. Today it still uses the Spanish rig, the long rope, the spade bit, and the dally. Many other Spanish customs dominate, and the language has been less corrupted.

When the Texan rode over the long trails north, he carried his customs and his manner of working all the way to the Canadian line. Montana, Wyoming, and other northern and central states adopted much of his Spanish-influenced language. In exchange, the northern cowman gave the Texan that which he had appropriated from the northern Indian and the French-Canadian, words strange to the man from the Rio Grande.

Many cowmen, yearning to see what was "on the other side of the hill," or being forced to go where they "could throw a rope without gettin' it caught on a fence post," were like a tumbleweed drifting be-

4 Will James, *Lone Cowboy* (New York, Charles Scribner's Sons, 1930), 226.

fore a wind. They scattered their language until it no longer remained a "boggy crossin'" for a cowman from another section.

Yet, even today, there are some who have never been off their home range; and to them portions of this collection will seem strange. One old-timer told me that he had never heard the word *cowpuncher* until he was an old man. Of course, it is a comparatively recent word, having come into use with the moving of cattle by train and the closing of the trails. Now the majority prefer it to *cowboy*, for the word *cowboy* has more or less borne a stigma for many years. Yellow journalists, during the trail days, spread the cowboy's reputation for woolliness far and wide. He was pictured as a demon of death and disaster. Mothers even threatened their unruly offspring with the coming of this evil one.

And so almost every cowman chooses to be called *puncher, cowhand,* or just plain *hand.* But no matter by what name he is called, the working cowhand is called "plenty early in the mornin'."

Cowhands are neither so plentiful nor so picturesque as they were in the days of the open range, and with the passing of its customs, many of their terms are becoming obsolete. This volume has been prepared to help preserve this lingo for posterity. As long as we are a nation of meat-eaters, I am not afraid that the cowboy himself will become extinct, but some of his older language may die with the passing years. However, he will create new idioms typical of the range as long as he forks a horse. Furthermore, living in the tradition of men who rode semiwild horses to work obstinate, unruly cattle, he will never become so soft that he will *pack* a lunch, wear his sleeves rolled up, and say *my gracious* instead of *goddam* when he is mad.

IN APPRECIATION

"A full house divided don't win no pots"

MANY YEARS AGO, my "roundup" of the lingo of the cowboy became so copious that I arrived at the decision to move some of it, grass finished though it was, to shipping pens, and thence to market. Riding herd over it had been a keen but solitary pleasure for nearly twenty years. It seemed to me, as it must to most cowmen, that a reasonably well filled-out herd is not for the keeping, but for the sharing. My *Cowboy Lingo*, published in 1936, was the result. Its reception was sufficiently gratifying to justify my previous course in pasturing the stuff out of sight for so long. Since its publication, many of its terms have been used in stories by writers of "westerns"; and western story magazines are reflecting current interest in the subject by conducting columns and departments on this jargon of the range, cow camp, and trail.

Letters from philologists, authors, and editors asking for more examples of this lusty speech have encouraged the preparation of *Western Words*. Yet the completed volume would not have been possible without the help of others, who contributed expressions, defined words, gave other definitions, dug up sources of phrases, and added colorful anecdotes.

First, I want to thank the host of sun-tanned, grin-wrinkled cowhands I have met upon the range and the old-timers with whom I have talked at cowmen's conventions throughout the West. They are too many to name. Besides, they are of the breed whose mention in a book would make them as uncomfortable as a camel in the Klondike. To them I can only say *muy gracias*. This volume is largely theirs, and I hope it will serve as a monument to their picturesque speech.

The authors I quote are not those "town-gaited" writers who have never been closer to a cow than a milk wagon. They have lived the life, and you may have confidence in their knowledge. I extend thanks to the following writers, each of whom I am proud to list as a personal friend: J. Frank Dobie, W. S. Campbell (Stanley Vestal), Edward Everett Dale, J. Evetts Haley, Foster-Harris, William MacLeod Raine, Agnes Wright Spring, Jack Potter, John M. Hendrix, and the late George Saunders.

I am also grateful to these writers, with whom I have corresponded and whose co-operation has been most helpful: Philip A. Rollins, Harold W. Bentley, the late Will James, Agnes Morley Cleaveland, Dick Halliday, W. M. French, Bruce Clinton, and "Don," who wishes to remain anonymous.

I am no less grateful to Eugene Cunningham, Ross Santee, E. W. Thistlethwaite, the late Will C. Barnes, and all others whom I have quoted in citations.

Particular attention is called to Don McCarthy's booklet, *Language of the Mosshorn* (The Gazette Printing Company, Billings, Montana, 1936), which I have consulted in the preparation of the present volume. Students of language will find it of high interest and value.

I especially wish to thank *Cattleman* magazine and its former editor, Tad Moses; *Western Horseman* magazine and its former editor, Paul Albert; and all the publishers who so generously allowed me to quote from books in their lists.

Last, but by no means least, I wish to acknowledge a debt of grateful obligation to Elizabeth Ann McMurray, bookdealer and lover of all literature of the West, for her continued interest, faith, and encouragement. She has been unceasing in her efforts to spur my own energies to the riding of the "final horse." Thanks are extended, also, to E. DeGolyer for his sustained and stimulating interest. Without the urging of such good friends, this volume would have perhaps been hazed into the "cut backs" until the old man with the hay hook "come along."

Rounding up this bunch of strays, driving them to the home range, and cutting them into the proper herds has been a long, hard work. The brush has been thick, the coulees rough, and the quicksands boggy. Yet all my saddlesores are healed by the thought that this bob-tail may fill some hand long after I've "sacked my saddle." You can now ride the same trail at a high lope without rope or running iron, but you'll miss the fun I had in dragging these mavericks to the branding fire.

RAMON F. ADAMS

Dallas, Texas
September 15, 1944

WESTERN WORDS

A

"A wink's as good as a nod to a blind mule"

ace in the hole

A shoulder holster, a hideout. A man's ace in the hole might take various forms, as the carrying of his gun in the waistband, in a boot-leg, or in some other unexpected place.

ación (ah-the-on')

Stirrup leather. A Spanish term sometimes used on the southern border and in California.

acorn calf

A runty calf, a weakling.

ACTION

See cut his wolf loose, get down to cases.

adiós (ah-de-os')

A Spanish word (meaning literally *to God*) commonly used in the border cattle country as an expression of friendly leave-taking equivalent to the English *good-bye, so long,* or *I'll see you later.*

adobe (ah-do'bay)

A mud brick made from clay that adheres compactly when wet. After being mixed with water and straw, it is cast into wooden molds about 18 by 6 by 10 inches in dimension. When taken from the molds, these bricks are placed in the hot sun and allowed to dry and bake. They are a common building material in the sections under Spanish influence. The word is also used in referring to a house built of adobe—usually shortened to *'dobe.* The word is also used by the cowboy in referring to anything of inferior quality. (Harold W. Bentley, *Dictionary of Spanish Terms in English* [New York, Columbia University Press, 1932], 87). The Mexican silver dollar is sometimes spoken of as a *'dobe* because the cowman holds it to be of small value.

ADVANTAGE

See hold the high card.

advertisin' a leather shop

Said of a tenderfoot dressed up in exaggerated leather "trimmin's," such as boots, chaps, cowhide vest, leather cuffs, etc. Charlie Nelms pointed out to me one dressed in hairy chaps and vest with the remark that "from the hair he's wearin' y'u'd think it's cold 'nough to make a polar bear hunt cover, and here it's hot as hell with the blower on."

afoot

Said of a man without a horse. A man afoot on the range is looked upon with suspicion by most ranchers and is not welcome when he stops for food or shelter, unless he can prove that he belongs to the country and that his being afoot is caused by some misfortune. It has always been the custom of the range country to regard a man as "a man and a horse," never one without the other. Even cattle have no fear of a man afoot, and he is in danger of being attacked. One of the old sayings of the West is, "A man afoot is no man at all." He can not do a man's work without a horse and is useless in cow work. Teddy Blue used to say, "There's only two things the old-time puncher was afraid of, a decent woman and bein' left afoot."

airin' the lungs

What the cowboy calls "cussin'," which seems to be a natural part of his language; and he has a supply of words and phrases that any mule skinner would "be happy to get a copy of." As one cowman said, "The average cowhand ain't pickin' any grapes in the Lord's Vineyard, but neither's he tryin' to bust any Commandments when he cusses. It jes' sets on his tongue as easy as a hoss-fly ridin' a mule's ear, and he can shore cram plenty o' grammar into it."

airin' the paunch

Vomiting.

air-tights

Canned goods. Today we can buy anything in cans from pie dough to potato strings, but the open-range cowboy rarely saw any canned foods other than corn, tomatoes, peaches, and milk.

albino

A horse ranging in color from a pure white with a blue, or "glass," eye to a cream too light to be considered a palomino.

alforja (al-for'hah)

A Spanish word meaning *saddlebag* or *portmanteau*. Americanized, it is a wide, leather or canvas bag, one of which hangs on each side of a packsaddle from the crosses on the top of the saddle. English modifications are *alforge, alforche, alforki,* and *alforka* (Philip A. Rollins, *The Cowboy* [New York, Charles Scribner's Sons, 1936], 155).

alkalied

Acclimated to the country; said of one who has lived in the country a long time; also of one who drinks alkaline water. Most of the men considered old-timers had been living in the country so long that, in the language of the cowboy, "They knowed all the lizards by their first names, except the younger set."

all hands and the cook

This phrase signifies an emergency. It is used when every hand is called to guard the herd, when the cattle are unusually restless or there is imminent danger of a stampede.

all horns and rattles

Said of one displaying a fit of temper. A man in this mood, as one cowboy said, "maybe don't say nothin', but it ain't safe to ask questions."

all-round cow horse

One good at performing any duty, as cutting, roping, etc.

amble

To go; to go leisurely. The cowboy very often uses this term as, "I'm goin' to amble over to the north pasture."

AMBUSH

See bushwhack, dry gulch, lay for.

amigo (ah-mee'go)

A Spanish word commonly used in the Southwest, meaning *friend, good fellow,* or *companion.*

among the willows

Said of one dodging the law.

AMOUNT

See burro load, poco.

andale (ahn'dah-lay)

The Spanish *andar* means *move, stand out of the way,* plus *le* meaning *you (thou)*. It is commonly used by Spanish-speaking cowboys as *hurry up, get a move on, get going.* Because it is easier on the vocal organs, they frequently yell this in place of longer English phrases at cattle being driven.

ANGER

See all horns and rattles, arches his back, cabin fever, dig up the tomahawk, easy on the trigger, frothy, get a rise from, get his back up, get his bristles up, haul in your neck, horning the brush, horn-tossin' mood, on the peck, on the prod, on the warpath, paint for war, red-eyed, riled, sharpens his horns, sod-pawin' mood, techy as a teased snake, wash off the war paint.

angoras

A frequently used slang name for chaps made of goat hide with the hair left on.

animal

A bull. The cowboy will use any word to avoid calling a spade a spade in the presence of ladies. In earlier times *bull* was a word unsuited for parlor use, but today we are not so modest, and we hear *throwing the bull* on every hand.

ANIMALS

See cat, cimarron, hooter, javalina, ketch dog, kip pile, lobo, medicine wolf,

4

nice kitty, otie, pack rat, painter, pikets, prairie lawyers, rooter, sachet kitten, stand, wolf, wood pussy, wooshers.

anquera (an-kay'rah)

From the Spanish meaning a round covering for the hindquarters of a horse; semilunar tailpiece of a saddle. Americans use this term as meaning the broad leather sewn to the base of the cantle when there is no rear jockey, and extending beyond the cantle.

anti-godlin

The cowboy's description of going diagonally or in a roundabout way.

anvil

When a traveling horse strikes his forefeet with his hind ones, especially if he is shod all around. See *forging*.

aparejo (ah-pah-ray'ho)

Spanish, meaning *packsaddle*. This is a form of packsaddle composed merely of a large leather pad about twenty-eight inches wide and thirty-six inches long. It is made double and stuffed to a thickness of two or more inches. Attached to it is a wide cinch and an exceptionally wide breeching which fits close under the animal's tail, like a crupper. Since it is not equipped with sawbucks like the ordinary packsaddle, kyacks can not be used with it. Anything can be packed on it, but it is especially designed for heavy, awkward loads that can not be handled on ordinary packsaddles. Today it is becoming scarce, and consequently good aparejo men are rare.

appaloosa

A breed of horse whose distinguishing characteristics are the color spots on the rump, a lack of hair on the tail and inside the thigh, a good deal of white in the eye, and pink on the nose. This particular breed was developed by the Nez Percé Indians in the Pelousé River country. There are several explanations of the origin of the word *appaloosa*. Some writers contend the word comes from the Spanish noun *pelusa* (since this feminine noun means *down which covers plants or fruits*, it is certainly not applicable); others claim the spelling is *Appaluchi*

and, with a vivid imagination, connect it with the Appalachian Mountains.

Yet it is easy to discover the correct origin of the spelling of the word. In the early days no one had occasion to write the name, and as a spoken term the two words *à Pelousé* were corrupted into *appalousy*, which, in turn, became *appaloosa*. The spelling is merely an endeavor to follow the Nez Percé pronunciation of stressing the final *e*. (F. D. Haines, "The Appaloosa, or Palouse Horse," *Western Horseman*, II, No. 1 [January–February, 1937], 8–9; "More Care in Breeding Spotted Horses," *Western Horseman*, III, No. 2 [March–April, 1938], 30–31; Robert M. Denhardt, "Peculiar Spotted Ponies," *Cattleman*, XXVI, No. 6 [November, 1939], 19–23.)

APPEAR

See bulge, show up on the skyline.

apple

A slang name for the horn of the saddle.

apple-horn

The name given the style of saddle used in the eighties. It was so named from the small horn whose top was round like an apple, compared to the broad ones of the saddles it replaced.

apron-faced horse

One with a large white streak on the forehead.

Arbuckle

A green hand. Called this on the assumption that the boss sent off Arbuckle coffee premium stamps to pay for his "extraordinary" services.

Arbuckle's

The brand of coffee so common on the range that most cowmen never knew there was any other kind. Coffee is the first thing on the fire at the cook's "roll out," long before day; and throughout the day and night, if camp is not to be moved, the pot nests on hot coals so that the hands can have a cup at the change of guard. Nothing else the cook can do will make the cowboy hold him in such high esteem as keeping the coffee hot and handy.

The old-time wagon cook loved to tell the tenderfoot his favorite recipe for making cowboy coffee. With the greatest of secrecy he would say: "Take two pounds of Arbuckle's, put in 'nough water to wet it down, boil for two hours, and then throw in a hoss shoe. If the hoss shoe sinks, she ain't ready." The cowman likes his coffee to "kick up in the middle and pack double."

arches his back

Said of an angry person, of a horse preparing to buck.

Arizona nightingale

A prospector's burro. Called this because of his extraordinary bray.

Arizona tenor

A coughing tubercular.

Arizona trigger

A cattle-trap consisting of a sort of chute going into a watering place, which is left wide open at first so that the cattle will get used to going into it. Then, when the cattle are to be caught, the chute is narrowed down at the inside so that the cattle can get in but can not get out.

Arkansas toothpick

A large sheath knife; a dagger.

armitas (ar-mee'tas)

From the Spanish *armar*, meaning *to arm* or *to plate with anything that may add strength*. Well-cut aprons, usually made of home-tanned or Indian buckskin and tied around the waist and knees with thongs. They protect the legs and clothes and are cooler to wear in summer than chaps. Their use practically passed with old-time range customs, although they are still used to some extent, especially in Southern California. (Dick Halliday to R. F. A.)

ARMS

See ace in the hole, Arkansaw toothpick, artillery, belly gun, black-eyed susan, blow pipe, blue lightnin', blue whistler, border draw, border shift, buffalo gun, buscadero belt, caught short, credits, cross draw, Curly-Bill spin, cutter, derringer, dewey, double roll, draw, equalizer, fill your hand, flame thrower, forty-five, forty-four, gambler's gun, gun, hair trigger, hardware, heeled, hide-out, hogleg, iron, Kansas neckblister, lead chucker, lead plum, lead pusher, man-stopper, meat in the pot, no beans in the wheel, old cedar, old reliable, one-eyed scribe, open-toed holster, parrot bill, peacemaker, persuader, plow-handle, road agent's spin, scattergun, Sharps, shootin' iron, single roll, six-gun, skinning knife, smoke wagon, stingy gun, talkin' iron, thumb buster, tied holster, Walker pistol, Winchester, Winchester quarantine, Worchestershire.

arriero (ar-re-ay'ro)

Muleteer, packer, a man who packs loads on pack mules.

ARRIVE

See blow in, blow in with the tumbleweeds.

arroyo (ar-ro'yo)

This is a Spanish word meaning *rivulet*. It is used almost exclusively in the Southwest, where a small stream is capable of cutting a deep channel for itself in the soft earth, and the name has come to mean a narrow gorge having precipitous walls of dirt.

artillery

Pistols, personal weapons. I heard one cowhand say of a heavily armed man, "He's packin' so much artillery it makes his hoss swaybacked."

Association saddle

The saddle adopted by rodeo associations in 1920. Its use is now compulsory at all large contests. Built on a modified Ellenburg tree, medium in height, with a fourteen-inch swell and a five-inch cantle, it has nothing about it which permits the rider to anchor himself. As the cowboy says, "It gives the hoss all the best of it." The original Association saddle was made with small, round skirts, three-quarter rigged, with a flank rig set farther back than on a regular rigged saddle. It was full basket stamped and had stirrup leathers made to buckle for quick and easy adjustment.

augur

Boss, a big talker (as noun); to talk (as verb).

augurin' match

A talking contest such as is held no-where else except in the West. In the language of the cowman, an augurin' match is "jes' a case of two loose-tongued humans a-settin' cross-legged, knee to knee and face to face, talkin' as fast as they can to see which one can keep it up the longest without runnin' out of words and wind. There's jes' a constant flow of words that don't make no sense a-tall,

both of 'em talkin' at the same time and each one's got so much to say that it gets in his way. At the start they talk fast and furious, but after an hour or so they slow down to a trot to be savin' of both words and wind. By the time it's over, neither one of 'em's got 'nough vocal power left to bend a smoke ring."

axle grease

Slang name for butter.

B

"Brains in the head saves blisters on the feet"

baa-a-ah

The cowboy's contemptuous name for sheep. If you want to start a fight, just blat this at a cowboy.

backfire

A term used in fighting prairie fires, which means to start a new fire in front of the one to be fought. This purposely set fire is controlled on the advancing side and driven toward the oncoming blaze until the two meet and burn themselves out.

back jockey

The top skirt of a saddle, being the uppermost broad leathers joining behind the cantle.

back trail

A trail just traversed (as noun); to go back over such a trail (as verb).

Badlands

A section of country with little vegetation, composed principally of buttes, peaks, and other badly eroded soil; also the cowboy's name for a red-light district.

Badlander

An inhabitant of the Badlands.

bad medicine

Bad news, a man considered dangerous. Some of these men, said one cowboy,

"Were so tough they'd growed horns and was haired over." Tom Kirk spoke of one's being "a wolf, and he ain't togged out in no sheep's wool either."

BADMEN

See bad medicine, cat-eyed, curly wolf, Daniel Boones, gun fanner, gunman, gunny, gun tipper, hired killer, killer, leather slapper, short-trigger man, wanted.

bag pannier

A flat, oblong bag of canvas or leather with a long flap, lashed to the pack-saddle to carry camp equipment.

baile

The Southwest's name for a dance, especially one conducted under Mexican or mixed auspices.

bait

Food, a meal.

bake

To ride in such a way as to overheat a horse.

baldfaced

A stiff-bosomed shirt, sometimes called *boiled;* also applied to a horse when the white on its head includes one or both eyes. Sometimes white-faced cattle are called *baldfaced.*

band

A group of horses. This word is used in referring to horses only, as either cattle, stock, or livestock are spoken of as a *herd* or *bunch* of cattle, or as a *bunch* of livestock.

bandido (ban-dee'do)

A bandit, an outlaw. Used near the Mexican border to refer to a Mexican outlaw. *Bandit* is the more common word referring to the American outlaw.

band wagon

A range-peddler's wagon, usually loaded with clothing, cinches, stirrup leathers, and other cowboy supplies.

bangtail

A mustang or wild horse. Later *bangtail* was used in the East in speaking of race horses, as, "playing the bangtails."

bar bit

A straight or slightly curved round bar for a mouthpiece, having a ring at each end for attaching the rein and headstall.

barbed brand

One made with a short projection from some part of it.

barboquejo (bar-bo-kay'ho)

A Spanish word meaning *chin strap*. A halter for the hind part of the under jaw of a horse; also a chin strap for the cowboy's hat (see *bonnet strings*). Rarely used except near the Mexican border.

bar-dog

A bartender. Many were former cowboys too stove-up for riding. A bar-dog's favorite occupation, as one cowhand said, was "yawnin' on the glasses to give 'em a polish." When he reached for your bottle and hammered the cork home with the heel of his hand, that action told you more plainly than words that your credit had run out.

barefooted

Said of an unshod horse.

barkin' at a knot

Trying to accomplish the impossible. One cowman might express the same thought with, "like tryin' to scratch yore ear with yore elbow," or another with, "like huntin' for a whisper in a big wind."

bar shoe

A horseshoe with a metal piece welded across the heel.

base-burner

Slang for a drink of whiskey.

basket hitch

A packer's knot made with sling ropes, by passing them across the bottom of the pannier and around the rear cross of the packsaddle, then bringing the loose end up under the pannier and tying it down.

basto (bahs'to)

A Spanish word meaning *a pad*. The skirt of a saddle. The word is a technical term restricted to the saddle industry and to horsemen.

batch

An unmarried man, short for *bachelor* (as noun); to live alone, to cook one's own food (as verb).

bat-wings

Chaps made of heavy bull-hide with wide, flapping wings. They have become the most popular chaps on the range because they snap on. Every cowboy lives with a pair of spurs on his heels, and when wearing the bat-wings, he does not have to pull his spurs off to shed his chaps as he does with the "shotgun" style. These chaps are commonly decorated with nickel or silver conchas down each leg.

bay

A horse of light reddish color, always having a black mane and tail.

bayo coyote (bah'yo ko-yo'tah)

The Southwest's name for a dun horse with a black stripe down its back.

bean-eater

A nickname for a Mexican.

bean-master

A slang name for the cook.

bear-sign

The cowboy's name for doughnuts.

bear-trap
The name for a certain style of saddle, a severe bit.

beast with a bellyful of bedsprings
Said of a good bucking horse. Sometimes a poor rider would let another top off his horse "to see that there ain't no bedsprings loose."

BED
See bed down, bedroll, bed-wagon, bunk, cama, crumb incubator, cut the bed, dream sack, flea-bag, flea-trap, goose hair, hen-skins, hippin's, hot-roll, lay, Mormon blanket, mule's breakfast, parkers, prairie feathers, rildy, shakedown, skunk boat, split the blankets, spool your bed, star-pitch, suggans, tarp, Tucson bed, velvet couch.

bedded
In the cowman's language, this means that a roped animal has been thrown full length with such force as to cause it to lie still.

bedding down
The forming of a herd for their night's rest—a scientific job requiring that the herd be not crowded too closely, nor yet allowed to scatter over too much territory. With a trail herd, as the sun began to sink in the west, the men in charge would carefully and gradually work the cattle into a more compact space and urge them toward some open, level ground selected for the bed-ground. If the herd had been well grazed and watered during the day, they would stop, and gradually a few would lie down to their contented cud chewing. (Will C. Barnes, "Texas Cowboy—Pioneer and Senator," *Cattleman*, XV, No. 9 [February, 1929], 27–30.) With patience the cowboys would stay with them until relieved by the men of the first guard.

beddin' out
A term often used in connection with the roundup season, as at this time the cowboy does all his sleeping in the open.

bed-ground
The place where cattle are held at night. It is the duty of the day herders

to have the cattle on the bed-ground and bedded down before dusk. The bed-ground is chosen in a wide open space when possible, away from ravines or timber, in order to avoid things which might frighten the cattle.

bed him down
To kill one; also used in speaking of putting a drunk to bed.

bedroll
The cowboy's bedroll consists of a tarpaulin seven by eighteen feet, made of No. 8 white ducking, weighing eighteen ounces to the square yard and thoroughly waterproofed. This is equipped with rings and snaps so that the sleeper may pull the flap over him and fasten it. In the bed proper will be, perhaps, two heavy quilts, or *soogans*, a couple of blankets, and a war-bag which the cowboy uses for a headrest. In such a bed placed on well-drained ground, he can sleep as dry as inside a house, even in a heavy rain. (John M. Hendrix, "*The Bed-roll*," *Cattleman*, XX, No. 4 [September, 1934], 10.)

Next to his horse and saddle, his bedroll is the cowboy's most valued possession. It serves as his safe-deposit box, and it is not what you would consider healthy for a man to be caught prowling through another's bedroll.

Such a bed is warm in winter. The "tarp" keeps out snow, sleet, and wind; and even when the bedroll is covered with snow and ice, the extra weight helps keep the sleeper warm. In the morning when he awakens, he dresses *à la Pullman* style without quitting the blankets.

For a cowhand to leave his bed unrolled and not packed for loading into the wagon when camp is to be moved is a very serious breach of range etiquette. The cook will be sure to call him names that would "peel the hide off a Gila monster." If the careless puncher commits the offense more than once, the cook is certain to drive off and leave his bed behind.

bed-slat ribs
Said of an animal in poor condition. A cowhand in New Mexico told me of a drought when "them bed-slats got so pore their shadows developed holes in 'em."

bed-wagon

A wagon used to carry bedding, branding irons, war-bags, hobbles, and corral ropes. It generally contained all that the cowboy truly valued, and was also used as a hospital to carry the injured or sick until they could be taken to town or to headquarters. Only the larger outfits carried a bed-wagon, the smaller ones piling their beds into the chuck wagon.

beef

Any cow or steer over four years of age (as noun); to kill an animal for food, to bellyache (as verb).

BEEF

See beef, beef cut, beefing, beef round-up, big antelope, jerky, slow elk, wohaw.

beef-book

A tally book in which the records of the ranch are kept. See also *tally sheet.*

beef cut

Roundup parlance for cattle cut out of a herd for shipment to market.

beefing

Slaughtering, bellyaching.

beef issue

The issue of beef for food to reservation Indians at a government agency.

beef roundup

Synonymous with *fall roundup,* for the purpose of gathering all cattle for shipment to market.

beefsteak

When used as a verb, it means to ride so that a horse's back becomes galled and sore.

beef-tea

The old-timer's name for shallow water in which cattle had stood—usually green, stagnant, and full of urine.

BEHAVIOR

See wagon manners.

bell mare

A mare with bells around her neck, which is used in some sections of the cattle country to keep the saddle horses together. Cowmen in these sections contend that the bells will warn them if the horses become frightened in the night and leave in a hurry. But most cowmen object to a bell in the remuda because it sounds too many false alarms and awakens a sleeping outfit needlessly.

belly-buster

The Texan's name for the long stick, or pole, which serves as a latch to wire gates. If you have ever tried to open one of these gates and have had this pole slip from your hand, you will know that it is well named.

belly-cheater

A slang name for the cook. Many cooks were merely cooks and not cowmen. One cowhand informed me that the cook with his outfit "didn't savvy *cow* unless it was dished up in a stew."

belly-gun

A slang name for a gun carried in the waistband of the pants instead of in a holster. The gun is naked and drawn with a single motion similar to the regulation cross draw.

belly rope

When the roper's loop slips over the shoulders of a roped animal and tightens around its belly, as the result of using too large a loop. This act is always funny to everyone except the man doing the roping.

belly through the brush

Said of one hiding and dodging the law.

belly up

Dead, to drink at a bar. Old Cap Mulhall had nothing but contempt for the younger punchers when they "raised hell" in town after a few drinks. I have often heard him utter the philosophy, "It don't take backbone to belly up to a bar."

belly-wash

A slang name for weak coffee.

bench

A plain rising above a lowland.

bench brand

A brand resting upon a horizontal

bracket with its feet downward like a bench.

bend

To turn a stampede, or general movement of animals. Used in some sections of the North.

bendin' an elbow

The act of drinking whiskey. One old rancher, who had no patience with a drinking man, used to hold to the philosophy that "a corkscrew never pulled no one out of a hole."

BEST

See nickel-plated, tops.

between a rock and a hard place

Bankrupt, in a tight.

between hay and grass

In different seasons, as in early spring, when hay is gone and grass has not come up; also meaning difficult times.

Bible

The cowboy's name for his book of cigarette papers.

Bible "Two"

The Texas Rangers' annually published fugitive list, read by them more than the real Bible.

bicycling

The act, when riding a bucking horse, of scratching with first one foot and then the other in the manner of riding a bicycle.

biddy bridle

An old-fashioned bridle with blinders.

big antelope

An animal, belonging to someone else, killed for food. It was the custom in the old days for a ranchman never to kill his own cattle for food, and many an old-timer was accused of never knowing how his own beef tasted. One ranch woman was heard to say, "I would just as soon eat one of my own children as one of my yearlings."

big augur

The big boss.

big casino

Whatever idea or physical asset that is expected to bring success (Philip A. Rollins, *The Cowboy* [New York, Charles Scribner's Sons, 1936], 80).

big fifty

A nickname for the .50 caliber Sharps rifle.

big house

The home of the ranch owner.

big jump

The cowman's reference to death. When one died, he was said to have taken the *big jump,* and a good many cowmen were "weighted down with their boots."

big sugar

Nickname for the owner of a ranch.

big swimmin'

Said of a high river.

billet

A wide leather strap looped through the tree on the off side of the saddle. Holes are punched in it to accommodate the tongue of the cinch buckle.

Bill-show

A wild west show such as Buffalo Bill's and Pawnee Bill's.

Bill-show cowboy

A show-off cowboy of the Buffalo Bill show type.

BIRDS

See chaparral bird, hooter, paisano, road runner.

biscuit

A slang name for the horn of the saddle.

biscuit-roller

A slang name for the cook.

biscuit-shooter

Another slang name for the cook, a waitress in a restaurant.

bit

A metal bar which fits into the horse's mouth. There are many kinds of bits, some of them extremely cruel when misused. Yet it is rare that a cowboy uses a bit for cruelty. His idea of a bit is that it is merely to hang in the horse's mouth. When turning to the right, for example, he does not pull the right rein; he merely moves his bridle hand a couple of inches to the right, bringing the left rein against the horse's neck. It is merely a signal. The well-trained horse turns himself; he does not have to be pulled around. Many cowboys do not use bits, but ride with a hackamore instead.

BITS

See bar bit, bit, bit ring, chain bit, cricket, curb bit, grazin' bit, half-breed bit, Kelly's, port, ring bit, snaffle bit, spade bit, stomach pump, straight bit, tool chest, war bridle.

bitch

A tin cup filled with bacon grease, and, with a twisted rag wick, used in place of a lamp or candle when either is not available; also a cowhide stretched under a wagon from axle to axle for carrying wood. See *cuña.*

bite 'em lip

When a rodeo bulldogger leans over and fastens his teeth in the upper lip of the bulldogged steer. This stunt was originated by Tom Pickett, a famous Negro bulldogger.

bit ring

The metal ring to which the reins are fastened.

bit the dust

Thrown from a horse. When Hawk Nance once got thrown, he got up to gingerly test his bones, then remarked with a grin, "I reckon I didn't break nothin', but all the hinges and bolts are shore loosened." It also means *to be killed.* This expression originated in the Indian days, and during a battle when an Indian was shot from his horse, it was said that "another redskin bit the dust."

bittin' ring

The device of fastening the rein of the bit to the belly-strap. When it is fastened thus, the horse gallops in a circle and is not likely to crash through a fence. This device helps make the horse bridle wise before the rider mounts.

blab

To clip on a calf's nose a thin board, six by eight inches in size, at the center of one of the long edges (as verb). He can graze but is assuredly weaned (Philip A. Rollins, *The Cowboy* [New York, Charles Scribner's Sons, 1936], 194). This device used for weaning (as noun). Also, as a noun, it had another meaning now obsolete. The early-day rep wore around his neck and hanging down a piece of stiff leather which was known as a blab. It bore the brand of the outfit he represented for all to see, and served as his identification card. (Will James, *Home Ranch* [New York, Charles Scribner's Sons, 1935], 118.) The word is now commonly used in the meaning of *to tell* or *loose talk.*

blab board

The full name for the weaning device.

blackballed outfit

A ranch, or outfit, barred from sending a rep to the general roundup, the term being especially applied to small ranchers suspected of being rustlers or friendly to them.

black book

The Texas Rangers' list of "wanted" men.

black chaparral

A very thorny kind of brush peculiar to the Southwest.

black-eyed susan

A slang name for a six-gun.

blackjack steer

A scrawny steer from the timbered country.

blacksmithing

Pimping or procuring for a woman of easy virtue. A polite way of giving information of such a man, as "Bill is blacksmithin' for Bertha."

blacksnake

A long whip.

black spot

What the cowboy calls a piece of shade. It is also used in another sense, as when one cowman spoke of another's reputation by saying, "His past is full o' black spots." In this characteristic cowboy manner, he let me know of the other's shady reputation.

black-strap
A slang name for molasses, thick and black.

blattin' cart
The calf wagon. See *calf wagon*.

blaze
To mark a trail (as verb); a white color on a horse's nose which goes upward to join the strip (see *star strip*), causing the whole to become a blaze (as noun).

blind as a snubbin' post
Undiscerning. One cowhand described such a person with, "He couldn't see through a bob-wire fence."

blind bucker
A horse that loses his head when ridden and bucks into or through anything.

blinder
A sack or cloth used in covering a horse's eyes when saddling or shoeing.

blinding
Covering a horse's eyes with a sack or cloth to keep him quiet enough for saddling.

blind trail
A trail with indistinct markings or sign.

blind trap
A hidden corral for trapping cattle or wild horses.

blizzard
A high, cold, searching wind, accompanied by blinding sleet and smothering snow. When riding through a blizzard, you would think, as one cowboy of my acquaintance did, that you were "ridin' on the knob o' the North Pole."

blizzard choked
Said of cattle caught in a corner or draw or against a drift fence during a blizzard.

Blocker loop
An extra-large loop, taking its name from John Blocker, a well-known roper of Texas, who originated and used this loop. It is turned over when thrown and goes over the steer's shoulders and picks up both front feet. It is started like the straight overhead loop, being taken around the head to the left. The cast is made when the loop is behind the right shoulder, the right arm being whipped straight forward across the circle it has been describing. At the same time the hand and wrist give the loop a twist toward the left. The loop goes out in front of the roper, appears to stop, stand up, then roll to the left, showing the honda to be on the side of the loop opposite its position when the throw was started (W. M. French, "Ropes and Ropers," *Cattleman*, XXVI, No. 12 [May, 1940], 17-30).

blood bay
A horse of darker red color than the bay.

blot
To deface a brand.

blow a stirrup
Losing a stirrup, an act which disqualifies the rider in rodeo contests.

blow in
To spend money, to arrive.

blow in with the tumbleweeds
To come unexpectedly.

blow out
A celebration.

blow out his lamp
A slang expression for *kill*.

blow-pipe
A slang name for a rifle.

blow the plug
Said of a horse when he does all the types of bucking seen in the rodeo arena.

blow up
To start bucking.

blue-belly
The southern cowman's name for any Yankee.

blue lightnin'
A slang name for a six-gun.

blue meat
The flesh of an unweaned calf.

blue whistler
A bullet, so called because of the blue frame of the pistol; also a norther.

BLUFF
See cold blazer, fourflusher, put the saddle on him.

boar's nest
A line camp, taking this name because its occupant is a man more interested in his duties as a cowhand than in the art of housekeeping. These camps usually consist of shacks with one or two rooms and a small corral and storage for horse feed. They are furnished with a minimum amount of equipment so that visiting prowlers will not profit. Single men who do not mind loneliness and who can eat their own cooking are usually placed in these camps. Because there is too much waste in killing a beef for one man, the principal diet of this cowboy consists of beans, lick, coffee, flour, lard, a few cans of food, and a slab of white, salt-covered "sow belly." (John M. Hendrix, "Batchin' Camp," *Cattleman*, XVI, No. 8 [July, 1934], 5.)

bob-tail guard
The first guard at night herding.

body spin
A term in trick roping. The act is accomplished by bringing a wide, spinning loop up and over the head and thence down around the body during the spinning. It can be performed from the ground or from horseback.

bog camp
A camp established close to a boggy area so that men may be handy to pull out cattle which become mired.

bogged his head
Said of a horse which puts his head between his forelegs as a preparation for bucking.

bogged to the saddle skirts
To be deeply implicated in some situation.

boggin' 'em in
A term used in rodeo riding when the rider fails to scratch his horse. See *boggin' time in*.

boggin' time in
When a rodeo contestant fails to scratch his mount.

boggy crossin'
A crossing of a stream which is full of quicksand or boggy earth; also something which one does not fully understand.

boggy-top
The cowboy's name for a pie with one crust.

bog hole
Alkali hole, mud hole, or quicksand where cattle are likely to enter for a little moisture and get bogged too deeply to extricate themselves.

bog rider
A cowboy whose immediate duty it is to rope the mired cattle and pull them to dry ground. He rides a stout horse and frequently carries a short-handled shovel, which he uses to get the bogged cow's legs clear. Placing his rope about the animal's horns, he wraps the other end around the horn of his saddle. After cinching up his saddle as tightly as the latigo straps can be drawn, he mounts and starts his horse slowly. Then inch by inch the cow is pulled to dry ground. (Will C. Barnes, "The Bog Rider," *Cattleman*, XVI, No. 8 [January, 1930], 27–28.)

As soon as this is done, the rider dismounts and "tails" up the brute. The cow usually shows her gratitude by immediately charging her rescuer. The ingratitude of a bogged cow is notorious. "As ungrateful as a cow fresh pulled from a bog-hole" is a common comparison. Bog riders usually ride in pairs, as the job is strenuous for one man.

boil over
To start bucking.

bonanza
A rich body of ore, hence, prosperity. The word is also used in referring to any unusually promising or profitable enterprise.

bone-orchard

A slang name for a cemetery.

bone picker

A man who, in the old days, gathered buffalo bones after the hunters had exterminated the buffalo; also a slang name for a buzzard.

bone seasoned

Experienced.

bone-yard

Another name for a cemetery; also a reference to an emaciated horse.

bonnet strings

Buckskin thongs hanging from each side of the brim of a hat at its inner edges, to hold the hat on. The ends are run through a bead or ring, and by pulling these up under his chin, the cowboy has a hat that will stay on during a fast ride or in windy weather. He does not care to have to ride back several miles to hunt for a hat that has blown off, for he is usually too busy to stop.

booger

To scare, to confuse.

book count

Selling cattle by the books, commonly resorted to in the early days, sometimes much to the profit of the seller.

Books

See beef book, Bible, Bible "two," black book, book count, books don't freeze, brand book, dream book, prayer book, shepherd's bible, tally sheet, wish book.

books won't freeze

A common byword in the northwest cattle country during the boom days when eastern and foreign capital were so eager to buy cattle interests. The origin of this saying is credited to a saloon keeper by the name of Luke Murrin. His saloon was a meeting place for influential Wyoming cattlemen, and one year during a severe blizzard, when his herd-owner customers were wearing long faces, he said, "Cheer up boys, whatever happens, the books won't freeze." In this carefree sentence he summed up the essence of the prevailing custom of buying by book count, and created a saying which has survived through the years.

boot

The cowman's footwear; also a horse-shoe with both heel and toe calked. The cowboy's boots are generally the most expensive part of his rigging, and he wants them high-heeled, thin-soled, and made of good leather. The tops are made of light-weight, high-grade leather, and all the stitching on them is not merely for decoration. It serves the purpose of stiffening them and keeping them from wrinkling too much at the ankles where they touch the stirrups. (John M. Hendrix, "Boots," *Cattleman*, XXXIII, No. 11 [April, 1937], 5.)

The boots are handmade and made to order. The cowman has no use for hand-me-down, shop-made foot-gear, and no respect for a cowhand who will wear it, holding the opinion that ordinary shoes are made for furrow-flattened feet and not intended for stirrup work.

The high heels keep his foot from slipping through the stirrup and hanging; they let him dig in when he is roping on foot, and they give him sure footing in all other work on the ground. Then, too, the high heel is a tradition, a mark of distinction, the sign that the one wearing it is a riding man, and a riding man has always held himself above the man on foot.

A cowhand wants the toes of his boots more or less pointed to make it easier to pick up a stirrup on a wheeling horse. He wants a thin sole so that he has the feel of the stirrup. He wants the vamp soft and light and the tops wide and loose to allow the air to circulate and prevent sweating.

When a man is seen wearing old boots "so frazzled he can't strike a match on 'em without burning his feet," he is considered worthless and without pride.

bootblack cowpuncher

A man who came from the East to go into the cattle business for the money there was in it, called this by the old-time cowman.

boot-hill

A name given the frontier cemetery, because most of its early occupants died with their boots on. The word has had an appeal as part of the romantic side of the West and has become familiar as a picture of the violent end of a reckless life. But to the Westerner boot-hill was just a graveyard where there "wasn't nobody there to let 'em down easy with their hats off." Like the old saying, "There ain't many tears shed at a boot-hill buryin'," and it is "full o' fellers that pulled their triggers before aimin'."

Boots

See boot, California moccasins, custom-mades, Justin's, mule-ears, peewees, stogies.

booze blind

Very drunk. A man with a full-grown case of booze blindness perhaps "never knowed he had a twin brother till he looked in the mirror behind the bar." Very often he got to the state where he "sees things that ain't there." Speed Carlow declared that no man "could gargle that brand o' hooch" he'd been drinking "without annexin' a few queer animals."

border draw

A cross draw made with the gun carried at or near the hip, but hanging butt forward. A quick stab of the hand across the body reaches the gun, and the continuation of the movement lifts it clear of the holster. It is called this because of its popularity with men in the vicinity of the Mexican border. (Eugene Cunningham, *Triggernometry* [New York, Press of Pioneers, 1934], 423.)

border shift

The throwing of the gun from one hand to the other and catching, cocking, and if need be, firing it without seeming to pause. (Eugene Cunningham, *Triggernometry* [New York, Press of Pioneers, 1934], 423). A very difficult stunt requiring much practice.

borrowed

Euphemism for *stolen*.

bosal

From the Spanish *bozal (bo-thahl')*, meaning *a muzzle, a temporary headstall*. A leather, rawhide, or metal ring around the horse's head immediately above the mouth, used in place of a bit.

bosal brand

A stripe burned around the animal's nose.

bosque (bos'kay)

In Spanish the word means literally *a forest*, but English-speaking men use it more commonly in referring to a clump or grove of trees.

Bosses

See big augur, big sugar, buggy boss, caporal, cock-a-doodle-doo, corral boss, foreman, head taster, old man, powders, presidente, range boss, read the Scriptures, right-hand man, rod, roddin' the spread, roundup captain, runnin' the outfit, segundo, straw boss, top screw, trail boss, wagon boss, white-collar rancher.

botch

Said of a bungled worked-over brand. A botched job is an acute mortification to most rustlers.

both ends against the middle

A method of trimming cards for dealing a brace game of faro. A dealer who uses such a pack is said to be "playing both ends against the middle," and the saying became common in the West.

bottom

Endurance, as, "This horse has plenty of bottom"; also a low ground contiguous to a stream. One of the sayings of the cow country is, "Real bottom in a good hoss counts for more than his riggin'."

boughten bag

Cowboy's name for the traveling bag used by an Easterner.

bounce

To turn animals. Not commonly used.

bow up

Said when cattle hump their backs in a storm; also used in the sense of showing fight, as one cowboy was heard to say, "He arches his back like a mule in a hail storm."

box brand

A brand whose design bears framing lines.

16

box canyon

A gorge with but a single opening, the inner terminal being against a wall of rock within the mountain mass; also called a *blind canyon.*

box pannier

A flat, narrow wooden box, usually covered with green rawhide with the hair on and lashed to the packsaddle to carry camp equipment.

Boys

See button, door knob, fryin' size, hen wrangler, pistol, put a kid on a horse, whistle, yearling.

brace game

A gambling game which the dealer has fixed so that he is sure to win. Many trusting and ignorant cowboys were victims of the crooked gambler.

bradded brand

Letter or figure having enlarged termini.

Braggarts

See flannel mouth, got calluses from pattin' his own back.

brain tablet

A slang name for a cigarette.

brand

The mark of identity burned upon the hide of an animal (as noun); the act of burning this emblem (as verb). Also slangily used to mean the deed to a saddle horse. The origin of the brand dates back to antiquity, and there has never been anything to take its place as a permanent mark of ownership. As the cowman says, "A brand is somethin' that won't come off in the wash."

brand artist

A rustler, one expert at changing brands.

brand blotter

A cattle thief who mutilates brands in order to destroy the legitimate owner's claim; also called *brand blotcher* and *brand burner.*

brand book

An official record of brands of a cattle association.

brander

The man whose immediate duty it is to place a brand upon an animal during branding. When the calf is dragged to him, he jerks the branding iron from the fire, hits the rod on his forearm to jar off the coals and slaps it on the critter's hide. Perhaps he is working away from the fire and has an assistant. Then when his iron becomes too cold to scar the hide, he yells, "Hot iron!" and another, glowing a cherry red, is brought from the fire on a trot.

Branding

See blot, botch, brander, branding chute, brand inspector, burn cattle, burn 'em and boot 'em, burnin' rawhide, burnin' and trimmin' up calves, butcher, calf on the ground, cook stove, corral branding, dotting irons, fireman, fire out, flank, flanker, hair brand, hair over, herrar, hot iron, hot stuff, iron, iron-man, irontender, Look out, cowboy!, mavericking, more straw, open-range branding, op'ra, picking a sleeper, range branded, rolling a calf, run a brand, running iron, scorcher, slappin' a brand on, slicks, snappin' turtle, tally branding, working brands, work over.

branding chute

A narrow, boarded passage into which cattle are driven and held so that they may be branded without having to be thrown.

brand inspector

A man hired by cattle associations to inspect brands at shipping points and cattle markets.

Brands

See barbed brand, bench brand, bosal brand, box brand, bradded brand, brand, brand you could read in the moonlight, burnt till he looks like a brand book, calling the brands, cold brand, connected brand, counterbrand, county brand, decoy brand, drag brand, fluidy mustard, flying brand, fool brand, forked brand, greaser madhouse, hair brand, lazy brand, map of Mexico, maverick brand, open brand, picked brand, rafter brand, road brand, running brand, set brand, skillet of snakes, sleeper brands, slow brand, stamp brand, swinging brand, tumbling brand, vent brand, walking brand, whangdoodle.

brand you could read in the moonlight

Said of a large brand, or one covering a large area of hide.

brasada

Brush country. The Spanish word is *brazada (brah-thah'dah)* from *brazo*, meaning *arm* or *branch*. This term is particularly applied in parts of Texas to the region densely covered with thickets and underbrush (J. Frank Dobie, *Vaquero of the Brush Country* [Dallas, Southwest Press, 1929], 229).

brave-maker

An occasional name for whiskey. It has been said that, "When a man has to go into a barroom to build his courage up, he mighty often has to prove it."

breachy

A cow that jumps over or breaks through fences.

breaking

Conquering, taming, and training a horse by force and fight.

BREAKING

See blinding, breaking, breaking age, breaking patter, breaking pen, broken, bronc stall, bust, choke down, curry the kinks out, ear down, gentling, hazer, Indian broke, ironing him out, kick the frost out, lady broke, let the hammer down, makin' shavetails, rough break, sacking, sacking out, smoothing out the humps, snappin' broncs, soak, three saddles, top off, uncorkin' a bronc, unrooster, whip breaking, wiping him out, work over.

breaking age

The age at which horses are usually broken, between three and one-half and four years old.

breaking brush

Said of one riding in the brush country.

breaking patter

The soothing, yet derisive talk that horse tamers use to distract the minds of

their mounts while saddling and breaking them.

breaking pen

A small corral used for breaking horses.

breaking the medicine

Overcoming an enemy's efforts to harm you, breaking a jinx.

break in two

Said when a horse starts bucking.

break range

Said when horses run off their home range.

breed

To mate animals for the purpose of reproduction (as verb); short for the West's half-breed, or person of mixed blood (as noun).

bridle

The headgear of the horse, composed of a crown-piece, brow-band, throat-latch, and, on each side, a cheek-piece. Most cowboys prefer a plain headstall. There are no buckles nor conchas down the cheeks to interfere with roping. When the cowboy ropes anything and holds it, he keeps his horse facing it so that the rope naturally runs out beside the head.

bridle chain

A short piece of chain fastened to the bit ring on one end, and to the reins on the other end. Some riders like chains because the reins do not get wet when the horse drinks, and they also keep a tied horse from chewing the reins.

bridle head

The headgear of the bridle.

bridle ring

A metal ring at each end of the bit, to which the reins are fastened.

BRIDLES

See biddy bridle, bittin' ring, bosal, bridle, bridle chain, bridle head, bridle ring, brow band, bucking rein, California reins, cheek-piece, cricket, crown piece, ear-head, fiador, freno, hackamore, headstall, horse jewelry, one-eared bridle, open reins, romal, throat-latch, tied reins, war bridle.

bridle wise

Said of a horse so trained that he can be controlled and guided in the direction desired solely by laying the bridle reins on the side of his neck.

brindle

To go; also used in describing the color of a cow, variegated with spots of different colors.

bring-'em-close glasses

Field glasses.

bringin' up the drags

In the rear. Sometimes used in speaking of a slow or lazy person.

brockled

An animal covered with splotches of various colors.

BROKE

See between a rock and a hard place, close to the blanket, didn't have a tail feather left, down to the blanket, sold his saddle.

broken

Said of a horse when he has had the rough edges taken off, but to the tenderfoot he would still seem fairly wild.

broken bit

A bit composed of two pieces of metal joined by a swivel.

bronco

A wild or semiwild horse, often contracted into *bronc*. From the Spanish *bronco*, meaning *rough, rude*. A horse usually retains this appellation until he has been sufficiently gentled to be considered reliable.

bronc belt

A broad leather belt sometimes worn by bronc fighters to support their back and stomach muscles.

bronc breaker

A man who breaks wild horses.

bronc buster

A man who follows the hazardous trade of horse-breaking as a steady business. He has to be good, even better than the man who just breaks horses, and a good one is hard to find. The best cow-hands can ride the "snuffy" ones, but won't. This is the buster's job, and he receives a few extra dollars per month. No man hired to break horses ever abuses them. He takes great pride in his work, and it is an honor to be pointed out as the rider of the rough string for a big outfit. He does his best to make good cow horses out of his charges and not spoil them. No outfit wants spoiled horses, and a man who spoiled them would last only long enough to ride one horse.

His job requires strength and skill, and he has to possess the "sixth sense" of knowing which way the horse will jump next. Once in the saddle, he does his best to keep the bronc's head up. If he is thrown, he is certain to crawl back on the animal immediately, provided he has not been crippled. To let the horse think he has won the fight gives him bad ideas. Falls have no terrors for the seasoned rider, but the thought of a foot's becoming hung in the stirrup, or of finding himself under a man-killer's hoofs worries him plenty. How to fall is one of the first things he learns. He learns how to kick free of the stirrups, to go limp and hit the ground rolling. He always knows he is going a jump or two before he actually goes.

His working years are short, and he is too old for the game at thirty. Then he has to be content to ride horses other men have gentled, the jar and lunge of the rougher ones having torn him up inside.

bronc fighter

Another name for a buster, but one which more properly fits the man who has never learned to control his own temper, and he, therefore, usually spoils the horse rather than conquers it.

bronc peeler

Another name for a rider of the rough string.

bronc saddle

A specially built saddle used in breaking horses, made with wide, undercut fork, with built-in swells, and a deep-dished cantle.

bronc scratcher

A slang name for the breaker of wild horses.

bronc snapper

Synonymous with *bronc scratcher*.

bronc squeezer

Another term for *bronc buster*.

bronc stall

A narrow enclosure where a wild horse can be tied inside with just enough room for him to stand. Once a horse is in a place of this kind he can do nothing but snort, and a man can place his hand upon him without fear of getting bitten or kicked. It is a gentling place for bad horses used at many ranches, especially where a number of horses are broken for work in harness. The cowboy seldom uses such a contrivance, but does his gentling in the middle of a bare corral, or wherever he happens to be (Will James, *Sand* [New York, Charles Scribner's Sons, 1929], 294).

bronc stomper

Another rider of the rough string, which the old-timer would describe as a "man with a heavy seat and a light head."

bronc tree

A saddle with dished cantle and swell fork, made especially for riding bad horses. Same as *bronc saddle*.

bronc twister

Still another term for *bronc buster*.

broom-tail

Range mare, a horse with long bushy tail. Usually shortened to *broomie*.

brow band

The front part of a bridle.

brown gargle

A slang name for coffee.

brush buster

A cowboy expert at running cattle in the brush. Cowboys of the plains country have a much easier time working cattle than the brush hand. The brush hand has to be a good rider because he has to ride in every position to dodge the brush. At one time or another during his ride, he is practically all over the horse, first in one position, then in an entirely different one, as he dodges. In order to dodge successfully, he has to keep his eyes open,

although thorns and limbs are constantly tearing at his face. When he comes out of the brush, he perhaps has knots on his head and little skin left on his face, but he goes right back in at the first opportunity.

The brush hand dresses differently from the plains cowboy. Compared with the romantic cowboy of fiction, he is a sorry-looking cuss. No big hats or fancy trappings for him. He is not much in the sun, and a big hat gives too much surface for the brush to grab. His chaps are never of the hair variety, and flapping leather bat-wings are likely to be snagged. He wears a strong, close-fitting, canvas jacket without a tail. If he can afford gloves, he wears them; otherwise, his skin has to pay the penalty. Some of the tougher busters claim it is "cheaper to grow skin than buy it" anyway. His saddle is a good one, though smooth and without fancy stamping to invite the hold of thorns. Every saddle is equipped with heavy bull-nosed tapaderos and these, together with his ducking-covered elbows, fend off most of the whipping brush. (J. Frank Dobie, *Vaquero of the Brush Country* [Dallas, Southwest Press, 1929], 205.)

The brush hand does practically all his work on horseback, is tireless and full of courage. No other cowman is such a glutton for punishment.

brush country

A country covered with low-growing trees and brush. The most famous section of such a country is in southwestern Texas.

Brush Country

See brush country, brush hand, brush horse, brush popper, brush roper, brush roundup, brush splitters, brush thumper, brush whacker, limb skinner.

brush hand

A cowboy of the brush country.

brush horse

This is usually a light-weight horse and has to be agile, although a big horse is better for making an opening. It requires little reining, and once it gets sight of the cow, nothing can stop it (J. Frank Dobie, *Vaquero of the Brush*

Country [Dallas, Southwest Press, 1929], 206). Like its rider, the brush horse is a brute for punishment and game as they come. The number of horses in the brush hand's mount is greater than in other mounts because the work is too hard to keep a horse at it long at a time. Between rides each horse is given a rest to allow the thorns to work out and the wounds to heal. Yet no matter how stove-up it becomes, it is always ready to break into the brush at the first opportunity.

brush popper

The most popular name for the brush hand. He knows he would never catch a cow by looking for a soft entrance; therefore, he hits the thicket center, hits it flat, hits it on the run, and tears a hole in it.

brush roper

It is said that just two things are required to make a good brush roper—a damned fool and a race horse (J. Frank Dobie, *Vaquero of the Brush Country* [Dallas, Southwest Press, 1929], 211). Nevertheless, he is without a peer when it comes to roping. He uses a short rope, a small loop, and frequently has nothing but a hind foot to dab his rope on. There is neither space nor time to swing a loop, and to avoid entanglements his cast must be made expertly at just the right moment. The plains cowboy, with his long rope and his wide, swinging loop, would be worthless in the brush country.

brush roundup

This is more of a drive than it is a roundup and is done quietly. It takes many "workings" to scare out a good percentage of the hidden cattle. The drive starts as early in the morning as possible, as cattle in the brush country can not be worked well in the heat of the day. Often these drives are made on moonlight nights because brush cattle lie in the brush and bottoms during the day and come out on the grass to feed at night.

brush splitters

Cattle of the brush country.

brush thumper

Another slang name for the man who works in the brush country.

brush whacker

A brush hand.

buckaroo

A term used in the Northwest for *cowboy*. The terms *baquero, buckhara,* and *buckayro,* each a perversion of either the Spanish word *vaquero* or *boyero,* are also used (Philip A. Rollins, *The Cowboy* [New York, Charles Scribner's Sons, 1936], 39).

buckboard

A light, four-wheeled vehicle in which elastic boards or slats, extending from axle to axle and upon which the seat rests, take the place of the ordinary springs. Instead of sides on the body, it has an iron rail, three or four inches in height, which holds in luggage or other packages carried on its floor.

buckboard driver

A mail carrier. Called this because he usually used this vehicle for his deliveries. Ranch mails, especially in the early days, were always small, no matter how infrequent their coming or how large the outfit. The owner's business involved little correspondence, and the boys' inspired less. Few with close home ties exiled themselves on the range. Many were on the scout from the scene of some shooting scrape and known by no other name than a nickname.

bucker

A horse that pitches.

BUCKERS

See beast with a bellyful of bed springs, blind bucker, bucker, cinch binder, close-to-the-ground bucker, cloud-hunter, gut-twister, high-roller, honest pitcher, killer, livin' lightnin', pile-driver, pioneer bucker, run-away bucker, show bucker, spinner, sulker, sunfisher, weaver.

bucket dogie

Sometimes stockmen purchased calves in the corn belt, or from farmers, and shipped them to their ranches to restock the range. These were called *bucket dogies.*

bucket man

A contemptuous name given the cowboy by the rustler.

buck fever

Violent nervousness; sometimes called *buck ague.*

buck hook

A blunt-nosed, up-curved piece added to the frame of the spur and used to lock in the cinch or in the side of a plunging horse.

bucking

Synonymous with the Texas term, *pitching.* See *pitching.*

BUCKING

See blow up, bogged his head, boil over, break in two, broken, bucking, bucking on a dime, buckin' straight away, casueying, cat-back, chinnin' the moon, circle buck, come apart, come undone, crawfish, crow hop, double shuffle, fall back, fence corner, fence wormin', fold up, goat, haul hell out of its shuck, hop for mama, jack-knifing, kettling, kick the lid off, moan, pinwheel, pitching, pitchin' fence-cornered, pumphandle, pussy-back, rainbowin', rearback, settin' the buck, shoot his back, slattin' his sails, straight buck, stuck his bill in the ground, sunfishing, swallowed his head, swapping ends, throw back, tryin' to chin the moon, turned through himself, turn a wildcat, unwind, walkin' beamin', waltz with a lady, warps his backbone, watchin' the op'ra, whingding, windmilling, wrinkled his spine.

bucking on a dime

Said when a bucking horse does his bucking in one spot.

bucking rein

Usually a single rope attached to the hackamore of a bucking horse. By gripping this, the rider has an aid in keeping his balance, but in contests he is not permitted to change hands.

bucking rim

A round-headed projection on the cantle of some saddles.

bucking roll

A roll of blankets tied across the saddle, just behind the fork, to help wedge the rider in the saddle and make it more difficult for the horse to throw him. Sometimes it is a leather pad, stuffed with hair, three or four inches high, and tied down on each side of the fork just behind the horn.

bucking the tiger

Playing faro. During the early days the professional gambler of the frontier carried his faro outfit in a box upon which was painted the picture of a Royal Bengal tiger. Tigers were also pictured upon his chips and oilcloth layout, and the game became known as the *tiger.*

buckin' straight away

This buck consists of long jumps straight ahead without any twists, whirling, or rearing, an easy horse for some to ride, yet poison for others. Straightaway buckers are usually big and strong and rough in their actions. Their chief stock in trade is to jump extremely high, then, as they start down, to kick high with their hindquarters. At the same time the cantle of the saddle hits the seat of the rider's pants, and the rider hits the dirt. A horse of this type usually hurts his rider when bucking him off, because he generally throws him high and hard. (Bruce Clinton, "Buckin' Horses," *Western Horseman*, III, No. 3 [May–June, 1938], 10.)

buck-nun

A recluse, a man who lives alone.

buck out

To die. Commonly used to express a tragic death.

buck out in smoke

To die in a gun battle.

buckskin

A horse of light yellowish color produced by the mixture of sand and blood bays.

buck strap

A narrow strap riveted to the leather housing of the saddle just below and on the off side of the base of the horn. Top riders have nothing but contempt for this hand hold, and of course it is barred at contests.

buck the saddle

Said when a green bronc, at the first saddling, is allowed to buck with the empty saddle while he is held by a rope.

buds

A mark of ownership made by cutting down a strip of skin on the nose of an animal.

bueno (boo-ay'no)

A Spanish word, meaning *good* or *perfect of its kind*, but during open-range days in the Southwest, it was also used as a cattle term. In this sense, it meant that the animal called thus was "good" in that it had not been claimed by anyone at the roundup, and that its brand could not be found in the brand book. Such animals were "good" pickups because they were supposed to get by brand inspectors at shipping points and market centers. (Jack Potter to R.F.A.)

buffaloed

A slangy synonym for *mentally confused, bluffed*.

buffalo gun

A heavy caliber rifle used by the buffalo hunters, usually a Sharps .50.

buffalo mange

A western name for lice, of which the buffalo hunters usually had a supply.

buffalo skinner

A man who made a business of skinning buffaloes for their hides.

buffalo soldier

The Indian's name (adopted by the cowboy) for the Negro soldier of the early frontier forts, because of his color and kinky hair.

buffalo wallow

A depression in the prairie which had been hollowed out by the wallowing of buffaloes.

buggy boss

Title given an eastern owner of a ranch, who rode around in a buggy on his inspection tour because he did not ride horseback well.

bug juice

A slang name for whiskey.

build a smoke under his hoofs

Shooting at another's feet.

building a loop

Shaking out the noose in preparation for a throw with a rope.

built high above his corns

Said of a tall person. Cowboys are strong for exaggerations. I heard one speak of another's being "so tall it'd take a steeple-jack to look 'im in the eye," and again, "so tall he couldn't tell when his feet was cold."

bulge

To appear suddenly, as, "He bulged into the road ahead."

bull-bat

A slang name for the bronc buster.

bulldog

To throw one's right arm over a steer's neck, the right hand gripping the loose, bottom skin at the base of the right horn or the brute's nose, while the left hand seizes the tip of the brute's left horn. The dogger then rises clear of the ground, and, by lunging his body downward against his own left elbow, so twists the neck of the animal that the latter loses his balance and falls. The first bulldogger was a Negro named Tom Pickett, and he astonished the cowboys of his day by dropping off a running horse on the neck of a steer and throwing the animal by hand. Others began trying it with success, but it was not until a good many years later that enough of them were present at any one rodeo to make a contest. As far back as 1910 and 1911 a single steer was bulldogged at some shows, purely as an exhibition.

bulldogger

One who bulldogs.

Bulldogging

See dogger, hoolihaning, mug, twisting down.

bulldogs

A slang name for short tapaderos.

bulled

When a cowboy speaks of an animal's *bulling* on him, he means that it balked or refused to move.

bull-head

A dehorned animal.

bull hides

A frequent name for heavy leather chaps.

bull nurse

A cowboy who accompanies a shipment of cattle on the train to their ultimate destination.

bull riding

An event at rodeos, where the contestant rides a bull equipped with bull rigging. In the early contests the rider was allowed to hang on with both hands, setting himself well back, with his feet well forward, and spurring the shoulders and neck only. Later two hands were barred, one hand had to be kept free, and finally the surcingle was abandoned altogether and a loose rope substituted.

bull riggin'

A specially made surcingle used at rodeos for riding wild bulls. It consists of a heavy leather strap, three inches wide and about two feet long with two hand holds about nine inches apart. At each end is a heavy ring to which latigos and cinch are attached as on a saddle. Not used in present-day rodeos.

bull shoes

Shoes, sometimes made of rawhide, sometimes of iron, placed on the feet of work oxen, much after the fashion of horseshoes, to keep their feet from getting sore.

bull's manse

The home of the big boss.

bull tailing

A game once popular with the Mexican cowboys of Texas. One bull would be released from a pen of wild bulls, and with much yelling a cowboy took after him. Seizing the bull by the tail, the rider rushed his horse forward and a little to one side, throwing the bull off his balance and "busting" him with terrific force. American cowboys are more humane and seldom indulge in this sport. (J. Frank Dobie, *Vaquero of the Brush Country* [Dallas, Southwest Press, 1929], 16, 19.) Bull tailing may be considered the forerunner of bulldogging, but with the increase in the value of cattle, owners frowned upon the tailing of their stock, and the sport died out.

bullwhacker

A man who drove (called *whacked*) the ox teams in early freighting days.

bull whip

A heavy cow whip, sometimes the knotted end of a rope.

bull-windy

A balky horse.

bunch

A group of cattle (as noun); to herd a group of cattle together (as verb).

bunch grasser

A range horse living upon bunch grass; also a man who lives in the foothills.

bunch ground

Occasional name for roundup grounds.

bunch quitter

A horse that has the habit of leaving the remuda and pulling for the home ranch or to parts unknown.

bunk

A built-in bed (as noun); to sleep, to sleep with another (as verb).

bunkhouse

Sleeping quarters of the cowhands at a ranch.

Bunkhouse

See bunkhouse, dice-house, dive, doghouse, dump, ram pasture, shack.

burn cattle

Said of branding.

burn 'em and boot 'em

Branding calves. After a calf is branded, it is usually booted toward its anxious mother.

burnin' and trimmin' up calves

Branding, earmarking, and castrating calves.

burn powder

To shoot.

burnin' rawhide

Branding. Used mostly with reference to rustling.

burnt till he looks like a brand book

Said of a much-branded horse. A horse with many brands shows that he has changed hands often and that he has no friends among any of his former owners. A good sign that he is untrustworthy.

burn the breeze

To ride at full speed. One cowhand, in telling of a fast ride he made, said that when he "pushed on the reins, I had that hoss kickin' the jack rabbits out of the trail."

burro (boo'r-ro)

Not *burrow*, as pronounced by many Americans. A donkey, an ass. This animal was extensively used in the early West as a carrier of freight. The word also means a stand made like the roof of a house, upon which to keep a saddle when it is not in use. Using a burro is much better than laying the saddle down or hanging it by a stirrup. If the cowhand does lay his saddle down, he lays it on its side or stands it on its head. He does not drop it on the skirts. If he hangs it up, it is usually by the horn string.

burro load

This term is often used as a unit of measure, as we use *peck* or *bushel*, especially in the hauling of firewood bought by the *burro load*.

BURY

See plant, put to bed with a pick and shovel. *See also* death.

bury the hatchet

Expression of Indian origin, meaning to cease hostilities and again become friends.

buscadero (boos-cah-day'ro)

From the Spanish *buscar*, meaning *to search for, to seek*. Used in the Southwest for a tough, gun-carrying officer of the law. Later occasionally used to mean any gunman.

buscadero belt

A belt made from four to six inches wide with a slotted flap on each hip for carrying the gun.

bushed

Exhausted, worn out; also short for *bushwhack*.

bushwhack

To ambush. One cowboy friend used to say, "Some men are bad—behind a bush."

business riding

When a rider of a bucking horse is unable to spur his mount, he hooks his spurs in the cinch, and makes it his "business" to stay on—if possible.

bust

To throw an animal violently, to break a horse.

busted cinch

Either just that, or an expression meaning *failure*.

busted flush

Plans gone awry.

buster

Short for *bronco buster*, a breaker of bad horses.

BUSTERS

See bronc breaker, bronc buster, bronc fighter, bronc peeler, bronc scratcher, bronc snapper, bronc squeezer, bronc stomper, bronc twister, bull-bat, buster, contract buster, flash rider, jinete, peeler, rough-string rider, twister.

butcher

The man, during branding, who cuts the earmarks, dewlaps, wattles, and other inerasable marks of identification on the animal's anatomy.

butte

A conspicuous hill or mountain left standing in an area reduced by erosion.

butterboard weaner

Blab for weaning a calf. See *blab board*.

butterfly

The first act in ordinary trick roping is to start the rope spinning, either in front of your person or around your head. Then the noose is enlarged and rapidly darted from side to side, vertically spinning to the right and then to the left, in a stunt called *butterfly*.

buttermilk

A motherless calf.

buttermilk cow

A slang name for a bull.

buttermilk horse

What the cowboys of some sections call a palomino.

button

The cowboy's name for a boy.

buy a trunk

An expressive western phrase meaning to *leave the country*.

buyin' chips

A gambling term; also said of one who takes part, unasked, in a dispute or fight.

buzzard-bait

A poor horse. In cowboy parlance one which "was dead but jes' wouldn't lie down."

buzzard-head

A mean-tempered range horse.

buzzard-wings

Another name for bat-wing chaps.

buzzsaw

A spur whose rowel has a few, long, sharp points.

C

"Only a fool argues with a skunk, a mule, or a cook"

caballada (cah-bal-lyah'dah)

In Spanish *ll* sounds like the English *y*; *ada* is a Spanish suffix meaning *a group of*. Thus *vaca* is *cow*, and *vacada* is *a drove of cows; caballo* is *horse*, and *caballada* is *a band of horses*. The word means a band of saddle horses wherever they may be—the extra horses, not at the time under saddle—the supply of mounts maintained by a ranch. This word is not used in referring to unbroken horses, but is reserved for those used as saddle horses. Though it is a Spanish word, the Mexican corrupted it into *cavayer* or *cav-ayah*, and the American cowboy pushed it further into *cavvieyah, cavoy* or *cavvy*.

caballero (cah-bal-lyay'ro)

Horseman. Translated literally it means a *cavalier* or *knight*. The term is usually associated with a gay and reckless cowboy who has an indifferent or devil-may-care attitude.

caballo (cah-bahl'lyo)

A horse. The word is used in light conversation, but mostly the cowboy calls his horse a *hoss*.

cabestro (cah-bes'tro)

Spanish for *halter*. The American cowboy uses this word mostly to distinguish a horsehair-rope halter, which he calls *cabestro*, from a leather one.

cabin fever

When two or more cowboys are snowed in at a line-camp and forced to spend so much time in each other's company that they become hostile to each other, they are said to get *cabin fever*.

cable

What the cowboy calls the rope he uses for a rope corral. See *rope corral*.

caboodle

Lot, aggregation, amount.

caboose

A rawhide cradle under the wagon for carrying fuel.

cabrón (cah-brone')

Spanish for *he-goat*, a person who consents to the adultery of his wife. Used in the Southwest to mean an outlaw of low breeding and principle.

26

cache

From the French *cacher*, meaning *to conceal*. Hide (used as both a noun and a verb).

cactus

Not only a thorny plant of many varieties, but also a term sometimes used in referring to the desert country.

cactus boomers

A popular nickname for wild brush cattle.

cahoots

In partnership. The cowman always *throwed in* or went *into cahoots* with another man when he entered a partnership.

cake wagon

A wagon used on modern ranches to carry cottonseed-meal cake to feed cattle.

calf crop

Calves born during the season.

calf horse

A horse used in roping, so trained that he will back away, still facing the thrown animal, to take up the slack.

calf on the ground

The flanker's call to the ropers that the calf to be branded had been thrown.

calf on the string

The roper's call that the calf to be branded had been roped.

calf roping

In this rodeo event, the cowboy, while riding a horse, must rope a calf, jump off his horse, dash to the calf, and tie it by three legs—all against time. In actual practice cowboys on roundup had to rope calves and drag them to the branding fire in much the same fashion as in the rodeo contest.

calf 'round

To loaf, to idle about. It is, in the language of one cowhand, "keepin' 'bout as busy as a hibernatin' bear."

calf roundup

Synonymous with *spring roundup* and primarily for the purpose of branding the calves born during the winter. It occurs after the grass has come, taking place in March throughout the South and on correspondingly later dates in the more northern latitudes.

calf slobbers

Cowboy's name for *meringue*.

calf wagon

A wagon used by some of the old trail drivers to pick up and haul the calves born en route. Some trailers did not carry such a wagon, and, rather than delay the herd, killed the calves or gave them to settlers if any happened to live near.

calico

A pinto horse; also the cowboy's slang name for a woman, taken from the dress material commonly worn. It was said in the old West that "calico on the range was scarce as sunflowers on a Christmas tree."

calico queen

The frontier name for a woman of the honkytonks.

California

To throw an animal by tripping it.

California buckskin

Baling wire.

California collar

A hangman's noose, taking this name from the vigilante days of California, when it was freely used to curb lawlessness.

California drag rowel

Spur whose rowels drag the ground when its wearer is afoot. It is of the Spanish California type, straight heelband, with a small button on the end to loop the spur-leather on, and the heel-chains passing under the instep to hold it in position on the boot.

California moccasins

Sacks bound about the feet to prevent their freezing.

California pants

A style of pants used on the range, usually of striped or checked heavy wool of excellent double weave.

27

California reins
Reins made of one piece of leather with no separation of each rein as with the open reins.

California rig
A one-cinched saddle on a California tree.

California skirts
When the stock saddle has round skirts, it is said to have California skirts, for these are the favorite style in that state.

California sorrel
A red-gold horse of the palomino type.

California twist
A roping term meaning to cast the rope with a single overhand twist and no twirling.

calling the brands
Ability to give brands a name. Brands have made necessary the coining of a language all their own, and though they are an enigma to the tenderfoot, the cowman is very adept at reading them.

CALVES
See acorn calf, blab, blab board, blue meat, bucket dogie, butterboard weaner, calf crop, calf roundup, calf wagon, churn-dash calf, deacon, dogie, droop-eyed, hairy-dicks, hot foot, leppy, long yearling, mug, open heifer, orejano, pail fed, poddy, rusties, sanchos, short yearling, skimmy, sleeper, slick, spike weaner, weaner, wind-belly, wrastlin' calves, yearling.

cama (cah'mah)
Spanish, meaning *bed*, and used as an occasional name for the cowboy's bedroll.

CAMPING
See sage-henning.

camping on his trail
Following someone closely.

campo santo (cahm'po sahn'to)
The Mexican name for a graveyard. *Campo* meaning *field*, and *santo* means *sacred*, literally *a holy field*. The expres-

sion is not commonly used, but is well understood in the Southwest.

CAMPS
See boar's nest, bog camp, bog hole, cow camp, dry camp, Jones' place, line-camp, sign camp.

camp-staller
A horse that refuses to leave camp in the mornings.

can
To wire a tin can to a cow's neck to prevent fence breaking; also to discharge an employee.

canned cow
Canned milk.

can openers
Slang name for spurs.

cantinesses
Saddle pockets.

cantle
The raised back of the saddle.

cantle-boarding
Riding loosely and hitting the cantle or back of the saddle.

cantle drop
The outside of the back of the cantle of a saddle.

can't hook cattle
Cattle without horns, muleys.

can't whistle
The cowboy's name for a harelipped person.

canyon
A deep valley, with high steep sides. The Spanish word originally meant a large tube or funnel.

cap-and-ball layout
A shiftless and unprogressive ranch or outfit.

caponera (cah-po-nay'rah)
From the Spanish *capón*, meaning *a castrated animal*. A herd of geldings.

caporal (cah-po-rhal')
The boss, the manager or assistant manager of a ranch.

capper
A man who frequents the gambling houses, and who, by being allowed by the dealer to win large sums, leads the unwary cowboy to buck a *brace game.*

cap rock
The escarpment of the High Plains, as the Cap Rock of the Texas Panhandle.

carajoing (cah-ray'ho-ing)
Shouting "Carajo" *(cah-ray'ho)!* An exclamation used by mule skinners, cowboys, and other outdoor workers (J. Frank Dobie, *Coronado's Children* [Dallas, Southwest Press, 1930], 362).

CARE FOR
See ride herd on.

careless with his branding iron
Said of a rustler, or one suspected of having designs on other folks' livestock.

carnival hand
A stunt rider.

CARRY
See pack.

carry the news to Mary
Said when a horse runs off with the saddle on his back.

cartwheel
A spur with a rowel having few, but long, points radiating from its axle; also what a silver dollar is sometimes called.

carvin' horse
A cutting horse.

carvin' scollops on his gun
Making *credits,* or notches on a gun to commemorate a killing.

casa grande (cah'sah grahn'day)
Literally *a large house,* but to the Spanish-American ranch life it meant the place where all the hands gathered for fun and frolic; the owner's home, used only in the Southwest.

case of slow
Said of the loser in a gun-fight, said of a man too slow in getting his gun into action.

case of worms
An animal with screwworms.

cash in
To pass from this mortal life, to die.

cash in his six-shooter
An outlaw's phrase for holding up a bank.

casueying (ka-soo'ying)
A South Texas term for *pitching,* but rarely heard in other sections.

catalog woman
A wife secured through a matrimonial bureau. Usually, as Alibi Allison said, "one o' them widders that wants 'er weeds plowed under."

cat-back
A slang term for mild bucking.

cat-eyed
Said of a badman who has to be constantly watchful to keep from being "downed" by a rival jealous of his reputation. Most men of this type make it their business to sit with their backs to the wall, facing the door. If the door is closed, they watch the knob for advance notice of an entrant. In cowboy lingo, "You'd never find 'im settin' on his gun hand."

catgut
A slang name for a rope, particularly a rawhide one.

cat
Short for *cantamount,* literally *mountain cat;* cougar.

cattalo
A hybrid offspring of buffalo and cattle, the first of which were the results of experiments by Charles Goodnight, of Texas.

CATTLE
See animal, bed-slat ribs, beef, beef cut, beefing, bend, big antelope, blackjack steer, blizzard choked, bounce, bow up, breachy, brockled, brush splitters, bueno, bulled, bullheads, bunch, buttermilk cow, cactus boomers, can, can't hook cattle, case of worms, cattalo, cattle grubs, cedar braker, coaster, cold-blooded stock, come out a-stoopin', combings, corriente, cow, cowpen herd, critter, cull, cut, cut-back, cutter herds, cutting out, day herd, dehorn, dew-claws, die

up, doctor, double-wintered, downer, down steer, drag, drift, drive, droop-eyed, droop-horn, dry drive, dry stock, duke, dust, fallen hide, feeders, fence crawler, full-ear, gentler, Goodnighting, grade up, grass-bellied, grass train, grown stuff, grubber, heavy cow, herd, herd broke, horned jack rabbit, horn-swoggling, hospital cattle, hot bloods, hothouse stock, Judas steer, just a ball of hair, kettle-bellied, kneeing, ladinos, lead steer, line-back, line breeding, lobo stripe, loco, longhorn, long yearling, marker, maverick, mealy nose, Mexican buckskin, milk pitcher, mixed cattle, mixed herd, mocho, mossy-horn, mother-up, mountain boomer, muley, mustard the cattle, necking, Nellie, night drive, night herd, on their heads, on the hoof, on the lift, open-faced cattle, open heifer, pasture count, pegging, petalta, pilgrim, pitted, pony beeves, pot-bellied, poverty cattle, prayin' cow, pure, range count, range delivery, rawhide, rough steer, run over, rusties, sabinas, scalawag, scrub, sea lions, she stuff, shootin' 'em out, shorthorn, short yearling, slick, slow elk, smoking out the cattle, snubbed, snubbed stock, Sonora reds, splitting the herd, splitting the tail, spoiled herd, springer, squeezin' 'em down, stags, stampede, stampeder, stockers, stool-and-bucket cow, straight steer herd, strays, stripper, stub-horn, stuff, surly, tailings, tailing up, take on, tenderfoots, throw out, toro, trail broke, trail count, trail herd, tullies, turn-out time, twist-horn, vaca, vacada, walkin' the fence, weedy, wet stock, white-faces, wind-belly, windies, winter kill, wrinkle-horn, Yaks, yellow bellies, zorillas.

cattle grubs

The larvae of the heel fly.

Cattle Kate

A general name for a woman connected with cattle rustling. "Cattle Kate Maxwell," whose real name was Ella Watson, was hanged with Jim Averill for cattle stealing, in Wyoming in 1889 during the Rustler's War. Though history doesn't prove her to be a thief, her name has gone down as such.

cattleman

One who raises cattle.

CATTLEMEN

See little feller, longhorn, range pirate, sharpshooter, stock detective.

cat-walk

A narrow boardwalk along the top of a shipping chute, used by the cowboy to assist in driving cattle into the cars.

caught in his own loop

Said of one who fails through some fault of his own.

caught short

Unarmed in a crisis. In the language of one cowhand speaking of an unarmed man, "He was caught short and now he's deader'n hell in a preacher's back yard."

caverango (cah-vay-rran'go)

An English corruption of the Spanish *caballerango* which means *he who cares for horses.* The cowman further shortened it to *wrangler.* See *wrangler.*

cavvy

The remuda or band of saddle horses. Used more commonly on the northern ranges. See *caballada.*

cavvy-broke

Said of a horse broken to run with the saddle horses.

cavvy man

Another name for the horse wrangler, one who keeps the saddle horses together.

cayuse (ki'yuse)

The name of the wild horse of Oregon, called this for the Cayuse Indian tribe, an equestrian people; synonymous with *mustang.* Commonly used by the northern cowboy in referring to any horse. At first the term was used for the western horse, to set it apart from a horse brought overland from the East. In later years the name was applied as a term of contempt to any scrubby, undersized horse. (Francis Haines, "The Cayuse Horse," *Western Horseman,* II, No. 2 [March–April, 1937], 11.)

cedar brakes

Broken land overgrown with scrub cedars.

cedar braker

One of the wild stock which range high in the cedar brakes.

CELEBRATION
See blow out.

CEMETERY
See bone-orchard, bone-yard, boot-hill, campo santo, grave patch.

center-fire
A name for a saddle with one cinch, this being placed near the center of the saddle; also called *single-fire, single-rigged, single-barreled,* and *California rig.* This saddle is not much good in a mountainous country as the cinch will not hold when going downhill.

chain bit
A bit made of a short piece of chain.

chain hobble
The fastening of a short chain, about two feet long, to the horse's forelegs, left loose at the other end. This method of hobbling is not commonly used, because the loose end strikes the horse's legs if he starts to run, and besides causing pain often trips and injures him.

changing mounts
This is routine work with a cow outfit during roundup and occurs several times a day. A rider may change his circle horse for his cutting horse, or a rope horse, according to the duty he is going to perform. Later, if going on night herd, he changes to his night horse. There are always a few broncs in his string, and he works them in rotation to give his other horses a rest. He uses these horses on circle, and when he puts his saddle on one of them, the changing is a thrill producer.

Since all horses of the remuda are kept away from the camp, when the riders are ready to change mounts, the wrangler drives the horses to camp where they are penned in a rope corral. Then each man ropes the mount he wants. In the early morning he usually selects the gentle horses, but on cold mornings even these have a hump in their backs. At noon his courage rises with the warmth of the sun, and he catches the wilder ones if he is riding circle.

chaparral (chah-par-rahl')
Thorny shrubs, low evergreen oaks, a clump or thicket formed by thorny shrubs.

chaparral bird
A bird with long legs, long slender body, long tail, and large powerful beak, commonly living in chaparrals. It has wings but seldom uses them, since its chief defense is speed in running. It is also called *chaparral cock* and *road runner,* the latter because it customarily runs down the trail in front of a rider as if challenging him to a race.

chaparral fox
A sly, tricky person, a sneak. One of those fellows who, in the words of Frank Ortega, you "wouldn't trust as far as y'u could throw an elephant ag'in' the wind."

chaparro (chah-par'ro)
An evergreen oak.

chapping
The act of whipping one with a pair of chaps. This is often done in rough horseplay when a group of cowboys get together for a kangaroo court. When used against someone of vile and unpopular disposition, it can be severe punishment.

chaps
An American abbreviation of the Spanish *chaparejos (chah-par-ray' hose),* meaning *leather breeches* or *overalls.* This word was too much of a mouthful for the American cowboy, so he "bit shallow" and said *chaps,* pronouncing it *shaps.*

They are skeleton overalls worn primarily as armor to protect a rider's legs from injury when he is thrown or when a horse falls upon him, pushes him against either a fence or another animal, carries him through brush, cacti, or other chaparral, or attempts to bite him; also they are proof against rain or cold. The word occurs in English dictionaries as *chaparejos,* but the Spanish word is really *chapareras (cha-par-rray'rahs).*

In spite of the movies and popular fiction, the cowhand sheds his chaps when he dismounts for ground work, for they are hot and uncomfortable to walk in. Only the hand of the brush country keeps his on, because he never knows when he is going to have to tear a hole in the brush. When the cowboy rides to town, he leaves his chaps hanging on a nail in the bunkhouse. If he does wear them, he takes them off when he arrives, and either hangs them over his saddle horn, leaves them at the livery stable, or throws them behind the bar of some saloon where he is known.

CHAPS

See angoras, armitas, bat-wings, bull hides, buzzard wings, chaps, chap string, Cheyenne cut, chigaderos, chinkaderos, chivarros, dude chaps, grizzlies, hair pants, leggin's, open-shop pants, pinto chaps, riding aprons, shotgun chaps, twelve-hour leggin's.

chap string

A short string which holds the legs of the chaps together in front at the waist. It is not so strong that it will not break when the cowboy gets "hung up" in the riding gear.

Charlie Taylor

A substitute for butter, a mixture of syrup or sorghum and bacon grease.

chase a cloud

To be thrown high from a horse.

chassé

From the French *chasser*, meaning *to go*. *Chasséd into* is commonly used as a synonym for *happened upon*.

CHEATING

See deal from the bottom, gig, gouge.

cheeking

Grasping the cheek strap of the bridle just above the bits and pulling the horse's head as far toward the saddle as possible while mounting to prevent the horse from running or bucking. If a man does not know a horse, he is sure to cheek him the first few times. Cheeking pulls the horse toward you if he starts in motion, and this has the advantage of almost swinging you into the saddle without effort. Swinging in the opposite direction would make mounting difficult. (John M. Hendrix, "Gittin' Up in the Big Middle," *Cattleman*, XXI, No. 5 [October, 1934], 5.)

cheek-piece

The side part of the bridle.

chestnut

A horse of brownish hue with neither flax nor black mane and tail; the mane and the tail are always approximately the same color as the body.

chew gravel

To get thrown from a horse.

chew it finer

A request to explain in more simple words. One cowhand I know admitted that he'd "never got past the fly-leaf of a primer," and words that "showed up as big as a skinned hoss" discouraged him.

chew the cud

To argue, to carry on a long-winded conversation. Blackie Taylor spoke of two such old "augurs" with, "Their tongues was so frolicsome their prattle sounded like rain on a tin roof, but it wasn't long till they both run out o' smart answers."

Cheyenne cut

A type of wing chap developed in Wyoming, the wing being narrower and straight. The under part of the leg is cut back to the knee, with no snaps below that point.

Cheyenne roll

Frank Meanea, a saddlemaker of Cheyenne, to create something different from the current saddles of his day, made a saddle with a leather flange extending over, to the rear, of the cantleboard, and this is called a "Cheyenne roll." (Bruce Clinton to R.F.A.) This saddle was brought out about 1870 and became very popular throughout the seventies and eighties, especially east of the Rockies.

chicken horse

Small, scrubby horse killed for dog and chicken feed as in recent years.

chicken saddle

A slang name for an unusually small saddle.

chigaderos (chig-gah-day'ros)
Another name for riding aprons or armitas. See *armitas* and *chinkaderos*.

Chihuahuas (Chee-wah'was)
Large Mexican spurs. Made in one piece with wide heel bands, the genuine Chihuahua spur is often a beautiful piece of workmanship, inlaid with silver in the most intricate designs, even to the spokes of the rowels (Dick Halliday to R.F.A.).

Chihuahua cart
A heavy wooden cart with solid wooden wheels.

chili
Not only a favorite dish of the Mexican, but also the slang name the cowboy sometimes gives the Mexican himself.

chili-eater
Another nickname for the Mexican. Commonly used to mean *low caste* or *low-brow*.

chinkaderos (chink-ah-day'ros)
Same as *chigaderos*; often shortened to *chinks*.

chinnin' the moon
Said of a horse which bucks high, or stands on his hind feet and paws the air.

Chinook
A warm wind in the Northwest from the Japan current, which melts the snow even in midwinter; also the term used for the universal Indian language understood by all tribes of the Northwest.

chin spot
When a white snip on the horse's face increases in size to include part of the lower lip, it is called a *chin spot*.

chip-box
Place where dung fuel is kept; also called *chip pile*.

chip wagon
A two-wheeled cart used in the early days on the range to carry cow chips when wood was scarce.

chivarras (chee-vah'rras)
From the Spanish *chiva, female goat,* and another name for leggins or chaps, more commonly those made of goat skin.

choke-bored pants
A name given the flare-hipped, tight-kneed riding breeches of the Easterner.

choke down
To subdue an animal by choking with a rope.

choke rope
A rope placed around the horse's neck, used by many old-time Wild West show riders. When the horse lowers his head to buck, the rope slips down near his jaws. With a firm grip on the rope, the rider rears back against it, thus more or less choking the horse down, as well as steadying himself in the saddle and therefore making the ride much easier.

choke strap
The derisive reference to a necktie, something for which the cowboy has little need.

choke the horn
To catch hold of the saddle horn during the riding of a bucking horse. If a rider concentrates on holding to the horn instead of trying to ride with his whole body, the horse will soon have him "knockin' a hole in his vest with his chin." George Phillips, the old "foothill filosopher," once described such a rider with, "His head got to poppin' back and forth, lookin' like every jump it would pop plumb off, back and forth, forth and back, jes' like he was sayin' how-de-doo, how-de-doo."

cholla (chol'lyah)
A particularly spiny species of cactus. It grows to a height of six or eight feet and has many stumpy branches which are easily detached, and on this account has a most vicious reputation for embedding itself in passers-by.

choosin' match
The selection of mounts on a ranch. The choice rotates according to seniority with the firm, and each puncher chooses his string from the remuda of the ranch. His choice is final, and even the foreman respects it.

33

chopper

A man employed in cutting out cattle.

chopping horse

A slang name for a cutting horse.

chouse

This word, as used by the cowboy, means to handle cattle roughly, to make them nervous, to annoy them and stir them up unnecessarily.

chuck

The cowboy's name for food.

CHUCK

See air-tights, Arbuckle's, axle grease, bait, bear-sign, belly-wash, black-strap, boggy top, brown gargle, calf slobbers, canned cow, Charlie Taylor, chuck, chuck wagon chicken, cow grease, cut straw and molasses, dip, district attorney, doughgods, fancy fluff-duffs, fried chicken, frijoles, grub, grub-pile, grub-stake, gun-wadding bread, hen-fruit stir, horse-thief's special, hot rock, huckydummy, immigrant butter, jerky, John Chinaman, Kansas City fish, larrup, lick, lining his flue, long sweetenin', machinery belting, man at the pot, Mexican strawberries, moonshine, mountain oyster, muck-a-muck, music roots, nigger-in-a-blanket, padding out his belly, pig's vest with buttons, pooch, poor doe, potluck, prairie strawberries, sea plum, sinkers, skid grease, slow elk, soft grub, son-of-a-bitch-in-a-sack, son-of-a-bitch stew, sop, sourdoughs, sourdough bullet, sourdough keg, sow bosom, splatter dabs, spotted pup, staked to a fill, state's eggs, Supaway John, swamp seed, Texas butter, throat-ticklin' grub, trapper's butter, wasp nests, whistle-berries, wool with the handle on.

chuck-box

Bolted to the rear of the chuck wagon is the chuck-box. It has a hinged lid that, when let down and supported by a stout leg, forms a wide shelf or table. This is the cook's private property and woe unto the nervy puncher who tries to use it for a dining table. Occasionally this privilege is granted to the wrangler, who generally eats after all the others have finished and are changing horses, but never to a rider.

Convenient drawers are made for plates, cups, and knives and forks. Others are stored with coffee, bacon, beans, and other chuck. Also in every chuck-box the cook has a drawer for a few simple remedies such as liniment, pills, salts, quinine, and calomel; and he might sneak in a bottle of whiskey for his personal use in case of "snake bites." See *chuck wagon.*

chuck-eater

A man from the East who came west to learn ranch work. The cowboy contends that about all the help he renders is to make the chuck disappear.

chuckle-headed as a prairie dog

Contrary, undiscerning.

CHUCK HOUSE

See cook house, feed-bag, feed-rack, feed-trough, grub house, mess house, nose-bag, swallow-and-git-out trough.

chucking the Rio

Said of a cowman of the Northwest affecting the dress and manners of the Southwesterner.

chuck-line rider

This appellation is applied to anyone who is out of a job and riding through the country. Any worthy cowboy may be forced to ride chuck-line at certain seasons, but the professional chuck-line rider is just a plain range bum, despised by all cowboys. He is one who takes advantage of the country's hospitality and stays as long as he dares wherever there is no work for him to do and the meals are free and regular. See *grub-line rider.*

chuck wagon

The mess wagon of the cow country. Usually made by fitting at the back end of an ordinary farm wagon a large box which contains shelves and has at its rear a lid that, hinged at the bottom and armed with legs, makes, when lowered, a serviceable table.

In the open-range days the chuck wagon was the most widely known and most talked of institution in the cattle country. Nothing added more to the harmony of the cowboys' life than a well-appointed chuck wagon. It furnished a complete index to the good or bad management of the ranch.

Once a hand has thrown his bedroll into the wagon, he has pledged allegiance to the brand for which it stands, and he will fight for it until he leaves it. He may cuss the cook, the company, and everything connected with it, but he had better not hear an outsider say anything against it.

The life of the cowboy away from headquarters has always centered around the chuck wagon. It is his home, his bed and board; it is where he gets his fresh horses, and it means fire, dry clothes, and companionship; it is his hospital and office, his playground and social center. At night it is his place of relaxation, where he spins his yarns, sings his songs, smokes his cigarettes at leisure, and spends the happiest years of his life.

CHUCK WAGON

See chuck-box, chuck wagon, crumb castle, cuña, Dutch oven, fly, groanin' cart, growler, jewelry chest, long-eared chuck wagon, mess wagon, pie-box, pie wagon, possum-belly, round pan, sheet, sourdough keg, squirrel can, the wagon, Which way's the wagon?, wreck pan.

chuck-wagon chicken

Cowboy's slang name for fried bacon.

churn-dash calf

One, although belonging to a milk cow, which has not the full benefit of the mother's milk.

churn-head

A hard-headed horse, one with no intelligence.

churn-twister

The cowboy's contemptuous name for a farmer.

chute

A narrow, fenced lane, usually connecting one corral with another; also a narrow passage designed for loading cattle into cattle cars, or passing them through into dipping vats.

chute crazy

Said of a horse which rears, backs, and otherwise shows extreme nervousness when placed in a rodeo chute.

CHUTES

See branding chute, cat-walk, chute, snappin' turtle, squeezer.

CIGARETTES

See Bible, brain tablet, dream book, fill a blanket, makin's, prayer book, quirly, shuck.

cimarron (the-mar-rone')

Spanish, meaning *wild, unruly*. The Mexican uses it for an animal, horse, bovine, or even human, which, deserted by all its friends, runs alone and has little to do with the rest of its kind. Literally, it signifies one who flees from civilization and becomes a fugitive or wild person.

cinch

From the Spanish *cincha (theen'chah)*, meaning *girth*. This is a "broad, short band made of coarsely woven horsehair or sometimes of canvas or cordage, and terminating at each end with a metal ring" (Philip A. Rollins, *The Cowboy* [New York, Charles Scribner's Sons, 1936], 126). Together with the latigo, it is used to fasten the saddle upon the horse's back.

CINCHES

See billet, cinch, cinch ring, flank girth, flank rigging, girth, latigo, rear cinch, rear girth, scratcher cinch, tackberry buckle, tarrabee, trunk strap.

cinch binder

A horse which rears on its hind legs, loses its balance, and falls backward.

cinch ring

A metal ring at the termination of the cinch for fastening the cinch, by means of the latigo, to the saddle ring.

cinch up

(As verb, and never merely *cinched.*) The act of fastening the saddle upon the horse's back by drawing the cinch up tight with the latigo straps.

circle buck

The bucking of a horse in long, rapid, and evenly timed leaps in a circle of thirty or forty feet, the horse leaning inward toward the center of the circle.

circle horse

A horse used on circle during the roundup. The wilder horses are used for this task. They do not have to be specially trained, but they do have to be tough and have bottom. See *on circle*.

circle rider

One of the horsemen, who, on roundup, widely separate into small parties, starting miles from a chosen holding spot, then ride toward it, driving slowly before them all cattle encountered (Philip A. Rollins, *The Cowboy* [New York, Charles Scribner's Sons, 1936], 221).

circular story

Wherein the cowboy tells a long story for the benefit of the tenderfoot, rambling on until seemingly he has reached the end, but starting at the beginning and continuing in a circle. There is a "sell" at the bottom of every tale the cowboy tells the tenderfoot. If this "pilgrim" doesn't "bite," the cowboy keeps talking, but sooner or later the greener usually pulls the cork under, and then there's "a heap o' hilarity in camp."

I remember a puncher who told one for the benefit of an old man from the East, and after this tale-teller had talked " 'til his tongue hung out like a calf-rope," the old man said, "Would you mind talking a little louder? I'm hard of hearing."

In a case of this kind the teller of the yarn feels "as helpless as a dummy with his hands cut off," and "might as well been talkin' Chinee to a pack-mule."

claim jumper

One who unfairly and unlawfully appropriates a homestead or mine claim from the prior and rightful owner.

claw leather

To catch hold of the saddle horn during the riding of a bucking horse.

claybank

A horse, of yellowish color, produced from the mixture of the sorrel and the dun.

clean his plow

To whip a man. One puncher, in telling of a fight he heard in the bunkhouse when passing it, said, "It sounded like they was shoein' a bronc inside." And when he went in to see what the trouble was, he found both fighters so skinned up "their own folks wouldn't know 'em from a fresh hide."

clean straw

What the cowboy calls clean sheets.

clear footed

Said of a horse which is able to dodge successfully gopher holes, etc.

clipped his horns

Said of one who has been placed in a disadvantageous position, to make one harmless.

clogs

A hobble made by taking forked sticks about an inch and one-half or two inches in diameter and about two feet long and lashing them with rawhide thongs on the front legs of a horse. Used principally in the brush country.

close to the blanket

A gambler's term meaning that the one spoken of is about broke, or has lost all his money but a small amount.

close-to-the-ground bucker

This type of horse is very quick in his actions, and though bucking very hard, he never gets very high off the ground. He kicks sideways with his hindquarters and seems to be trying to explode and disintegrate. He shakes his head from side to side, and with ever quick-changing movements he hurls his body through the air, doing everything possible to confuse his rider. With his fast and violent actions it seems no task for him to befuddle the rider and cause him to lose his sense of timing and direction. Very frequently the rider loses track of his mount entirely and finds himself gathering a handful of something he does not want. (Bruce Clinton, "Bucking Horses," *Western Horseman*, III, No. 3 [May-June, 1938], 28.)

close herd

To herd cattle in a compact group; also cheek-to-cheek dancing.

close seat

A steady and firm seat in the saddle.

CLOTHES

See baldfaced, barboquejo, bonnet strings, boot, bronc belt, California moccasins, California pants, Cheyenne cut, choke-bored pants, choke strap, chucking the Rio, collar and hames, conk cover, cow riggin', custom-mades, flag at half mast, fried shirt, full war-paint, fumadiddle, hair case, hard-boiled hat, John B., Levis, lid, low-necked clothes, mail-order catalog on foot, mule-ears, nickel-plated, peewees, pots, slick up, spraddled out, Stetson, stove-pipes, Sunday-go-to-meetin' clothes, teguas, totin' stars on his duds, unshucked, visiting harness, war bonnet, wipes, woolsey.

clothesline

A slang name for rope.

cloud-hunter

A horse which rears wildly, vaults upward, and paws frantically with his forefeet.

cloudin' the trail

Hindering one in his endeavor to accomplish something, deceiving.

coaster

One of the longhorned cattle from the coast country of Texas.

coasting on the spurs

Riding with the spurs locked in the cinch or under the horse's shoulders.

cocinero (coh-the-nay'roh)

The Spanish word for *cook*, shortened to *coosie* by the American cowboy. See *coosie*.

cock-a-doodle-doo

A humorous name for the foreman of a ranch.

cocklebur outfit

A small ranch, a "one-hoss" outfit, a "seedy" outfit.

cocktail guard

The last watch before daylight. It is the one despised by all herders because it is at a time when men most love to sleep. Before the watch is over, it is morning, the cattle are beginning to move, and the other cowboys are eating their breakfast and getting hot coffee.

However, this term is used differently in various sections of the range. Some sections call the period of first guard, from six to eight o'clock, *cocktail*.

coffee cooler

A frequent name for a prospector, a loafer or bum.

coffee grinding

The incorrect way of taking dallies. It means that the rope is wound clockwise on the saddle horn instead of counterclockwise. See *dally*.

coffin

The cowboy's name for a trunk.

coffin varnish

A slang name for whiskey.

coil

Another name for rope.

cold blazer

To bluff.

cold-blooded stock

Cattle or horses without pure or *hot blood*, not thoroughbreds.

cold brand

A hair brand. See *hair brand*.

cold deck

To take unfair advantage.

cold-footed

Cowardly. With the Westerner's contempt for cowardice, one cowhand of the desert country informed a group of natives who had proved their meekness that they "shore had cold feet for such a hot country."

cold jawed

Said of a hard-mouthed horse.

cold trail

Vernacular for old markings in following a trail.

collar and hames

Aside from being a part of harness, it is a slang term for a stiff collar and a necktie.

comb

To spur a horse to make him pitch.

comb his hair
To hit one over the head with the barrel of a gun. After one had had his "hair parted" in this manner, he was, in the language of one cowman, apt to "sleep as gentle as a dead calf."

combings
The final cattle driven in from the circle on roundup.

come along
A rope halter made so that it will tighten if the horse refuses to follow, but will loosen if the animal obeys.

come apart
Said when a horse starts bucking.

come a-smokin'
To come shooting.

comeback
A ready retort. Many cowmen have a genius for repartee.

come out a-stoopin'
Said when a cow comes out of a corral in a crouching run.

come undone
To buck.

COME UPON
See jump.

comin' grass
Approaching spring. A philosophy of the range land is, "No matter how hard the winter, spring always comes."

Committee saddle
Another name for the Association saddle adopted by modern rodeo officials. See *Association saddle*.

community loop
A slang expression to convey the idea that the roper threw an extra-large loop or noose.

compadre (com-pah'dray)
A Spanish term, meaning *close friend, partner, companion,* or *protector*. Frequently used by cowboys in the southern country.

COMPLAIN
See kick like a bay steer.

complex spin
A roping term which signifies the spinning of two nooses, one horizontal and the other vertical, or both alike, operated separately, one in each hand.

compressed hay
Humorous name for dried cow chips used for fuel.

concha (con'chah)
A shell-shaped ornament of metal. Literally the Spanish word means *a shell*. In the language of the cowboy it means a small, semi-flat, circular metal disk, usually made of silver. It is used for decorative purposes, attached to chaps, saddle skirt, brow band of the bridle, belt, or hatband.

CONFUSED
See buffaloed, got his spurs tangled up.

conk cover
Cowboy slang for hat.

connected brand
One which combines two or more letters or figures so that they run together.

contest saddle
Same as Committee saddle.

contract buster
A man who makes his living by his ability to sit a bucking horse. He does most of his work at so much per head and finds employment on the smaller ranches which are unable to maintain a first-class rider throughout the year. He travels through the country from ranch to ranch, breaking horses as he goes, and will ride anything that wears hair.

conversation fluid
Whiskey. Some Westerners drink only enough to "gather a talkin' load," but there are others who can't stop "'til they get floored or frenzied."

converter
A preacher.

cookie
If ever there was an uncrowned king, it is the old-time range cook. He had to be good to qualify as a wagon cook because he had to be both versatile and resourceful. He was the most important in-

dividual in camp, and even the boss paid him homage. He was conscious of his autocratic powers, and his crankiness is still traditional.

The present-day range cook follows this tradition. He can absolutely be depended upon to have three hot meals a day, rain or shine, cold or hot, that are good to eat and in sufficient quantity that, no matter how much company drops in, there will be plenty to go round. Through necessity his equipment is limited; yet this does not seem to hinder his speed. One day he may be trying to cook in the rain with a scant supply of wet wood; on another he may have difficulty keeping the wind from scattering his fire, blowing the heat away from his pots or sand in his food, yet he works without discouragement. The outfit must be fed on time.

He has many duties to perform. He is stakeholder when bets are made, arbiter to settle quarrels, and doctor for both man and beast, concocting some sort of dosage from his assortment of bottles. He acts as father-confessor and listens to complaints; he is banker for those who have loose change that might slip out of their pockets during rough cow work. He may do a little laundry work so that one of "his boys" might call on a near-by "nester gal," or help another mend a torn garment. If he keeps the coffee on a bed of hot coals so that any hand can help himself at all times, his shortcomings, if any, are overlooked. He has to be a good packer in order to stow things in his wagon so that they stay tied down; he has to be able to repair his wagon to keep it rolling; and he is the first to grab a shovel in case of a tragedy.

Though the boys kid him and cuss his crankiness, they certainly will not concede this privilege to an outsider. If he is clean, they will tolerate the poor quality of his bread.

Almost any cook likes to talk, and while the boys eat, he squats against the rear wheel of the wagon and entertains himself and them by discussing everything from the weather and women to politics and poker. If he is a good cook, the boys do not interrupt him. (John M. Hendrix, Editorial, *Cattleman*, XX, No. 12 [May, 1934], 5.)

cookie pusher
A waitress in a restaurant.

cooking mutton
Setting a sheep range afire to destroy sheep, as was occasionally done in range wars between sheep men and cowmen.

COOK
See bean-master, belly cheater, biscuit roller, biscuit shooter, cocinero, cookie, cook's louse, coosie, dinero, dough-belly, dough-boxer, dough-puncher, dough-roller, dough-wrangler, flunky, greasy belly, grub spoiler, grub worm, gut-robber, old woman, pothooks, pot rustler, Sallie, sheffi, sop an' 'taters, sourdough, swamper.

cook shack
The kitchen, especially when a separate building.

COOK'S IMPLEMENTS
See cook's louse, Dutch oven, flunky, gouch hook, lizard scorcher, pothook, round pan, squirrel can, swamper, wreck pan.

cook's louse
The cook's helper.

cook stove
A slang name for the branding iron.

cool your saddle
Dismount and rest from riding.

coon-footed
Said of a horse with long and very low pasterns.

coosie
Borrowing from the Spanish, the Southwest cow country called the cook *cocinero*, and from this came the common nickname *coosie*.

copper
In faro, betting a card to lose by placing upon one's stake a small copper disk provided by the dealer. The word came to mean *to bet against, to nullify a rival's plan by instituting an opposite and opposing action*.

corn freight
Goods shipped by mule teams; so

called because corn had to be carried to feed the mules. This reduced carrying space and thus increased cost, but the method was much speedier than bullteam freight. Customers requiring speed demanded that goods come by *corn freight*. See *grass freight*.

corona (co-ro'nah)
Spanish, meaning *crown*. The cowman uses it to mean a shaped pad placed under the skirt of the saddle.

corpse and cartridge occasion
A gun battle. The aftermath of some of the early western gun battles, as one cowman said, "looked like beef day at an Injun agency."

corral (cor-rahl')
Spanish, meaning *yard* or *enclosure;* commonly pronounced *kr-rall'* by the cowman. As a noun, it means an enclosure or pen, a circular pen built of stout, horizontal wooden rails which are supported by posts set firmly in the ground. The rails are lashed to the posts with green rawhide, which contracts when dry, thus making the entire structure as strong as iron. The corral is circular so that the animals can not dodge into corners or injure themselves by crowding into them. Used as a verb it means to drive stock into a corral.

corral boss
The man in charge of the stock and corrals on a dude ranch. It is his duty to assign horses to dudes.

corral branding
Branding calves in a corral may not be so picturesque as branding in the open, but it is easier on men, cattle, and horses. Having no herd to hold, every man can take part in the branding. The actual work is done in the same manner as branding in the open, but before reaching the pens, the steers and dry cows are worked out. When the pens are reached, the mother cows are cut back outside, where they bawl until the calves are turned out to relieve their anxiety and receive their sympathy.

corral dust
Lies, windies.

CORRALS
See Arizona trigger, belly-buster, blind trap, breaking pen, corral, crowding pen, op'ra house, road house, rope corral, round-pen, snubbin' post, squeezer, trap corral, water trap, wing fence.

corrida (cor-ree'dah)
The Spanish use this word to mean *expert, artful*. The cattleman uses it to mean a *cow crowd*, an outfit of cowhands. It is from the verb *correr*, which means *to run*, thus to the cowman, an expert at running cattle.

corriente (cor-re-en'tay)
To run. From the Spanish, literally it means *current* and is adopted by the southwestern cowboy to signify inferiority, when referring to the quality of cattle (Harold W. Bentley, *Dictionary of Spanish Terms in English* [New York, Columbia University Press, 1932], 129).

corus
The covering of a saddle, at first made of two pieces of leather stitched together through the middle, with a hole cut for the fork and a slit for the cantle. It was worked and shaped to fit the tree, and, after the rigging was in place, was slipped down over the saddle and buckled or laced in front of the horn.

cotton-patch loop
An extra-large loop.

cottonwood blossom
Said of a man hanging from the limb of a tree.

couldn't drive nails in a snow bank
Said of an ignorant person.

couldn't find his saddle seat with a forked stick
Said of one riding in an extremely rough country.

couldn't ride nothin' wilder'n a wheel-chair
Said of one with no riding ability.

couldn't teach a settin' hen to cluck
Said of an ignorant person.

could outhold a warehouse

Said of a lucky person, especially a winner at gambling.

coulee

A dry creek. Used in the North as a synonym for the Southwest's *arroyo*, it is a French word for what an Easterner would call a ravine, and means a deep cut in the earth's surface, its sloping sides covered with brush.

counterbrand

When a brand is superseded, by purchase or by discovery that the wrong brand has been placed upon an animal or that the brand has been put in the wrong place, the custom is for the brander to burn a bar through the original brand, put his own brand above or below it, and also on that part of the animal where it properly belongs, if the correct mark is differently situated. Later in the cattle industry, counterbranding was done by repeating the undesired brand and placing the new one upon the animal where it belonged; and the use of the bar through the discarded brand was discontinued. (Philip A. Rollins, *The Cowboy* [New York, Charles Scribner's Sons, 1936], 240.) See *vent brand*.

county brand

A brand, used only in Texas, consisting of a letter or group of letters for each Texas county, and unlike other brands, always placed upon the animal's neck (Philip A. Rollins, *The Cowboy* [New York, Charles Scribner's Sons, 1936], 240). This brand was intended to make stealing more difficult, as the rustler would now have to see that his doctored brand was recorded in the county of the county brand or alter that brand also.

COURAGE

See gravel in his gizzard, gritty as fish eggs rolled in sand, knows how to die standin' up, more guts than you could hang on a fence, sand.

COURTING

See cut a rusty, dropped his rope on her, gallin', ride herd on a woman, rotten loggin', settin' the bag.

covered his back with his belly

Said when one was forced to sleep in the open without blankets. Such a situation is also spoken of as, "usin' his back for a mattress and his belly for a blanket."

covered his dog

When the roundup captain has gathered all the cattle in a given region, he is said to have *covered his dog*.

covering

Getting the drop.

COWARDLY

See booger, buck fever, cold-footed, down in his boots, gunshy, his tail draggin'.

cow

The cowboy's generic term for everything from a sucking calf to a ten-year-old bull.

cowboy

This word seems to have originated in Revolutionary days when a group of Tory guerillas roamed the region between the lines in Westchester County, New York, and called themselves by this title. I have never been able to discover why they gave themselves this title since they had nothing to do with cows.

The next men we find calling themselves by this name are a bunch of wild-riding, reckless Texans under the leadership of Ewen Cameron, who spent their time chasing longhorns and Mexicans soon after Texas became a republic. To the Mexicans they became the symbol of calamity.

Then came the real cowboy as we know him today—a man who followed the cows. A generation ago the East knew him as a bloody demon of disaster, reckless and rowdy, weighted down with weapons, and ever ready to use them. Today he is known as the hero of a wild west story, as the eternally hard-riding movie actor, as the "guitar pickin'" yodeler, or the gayly bedecked rodeo follower.

The West, who knows him best, knows that he has always been "just a plain, everyday bow-legged human," carefree and courageous, fun-loving and loyal, uncomplaining and doing his best to live up to a tradition of which he is proud. He has been called everything from a cow poke to a dude wrangler, but never a coward. He is still with us today and will always be as long as the West raises cows, changing, perhaps, with the times, but always witty, friendly, and fearless.

cowboy change

In the early West paper money was unknown, gold and silver coins being the only money used. A silver fifty-cent piece was the smallest coin in circulation, but it was sometimes necessary to make change to the value of dimes and quarters. For this the standard sizes of cartridges were used, and they became known as *cowboy change.*

cowboy of the Pecos

In the old days the saying, "He's a cowboy of the Pecos," had a broad meaning. The Pecos River drained a wild empire. There was no law west of it. Its brackish waters were shunned by the buffalo and even the coyotes. The country was hot, birdless, and infested with snakes. The Lincoln County War was fought in the territory drained by it, and its name became a symbol for toughness (J. Frank Dobie, *Vaquero of the Brush Country* [Dallas, Southwest Press, 1929], 292).

In one sense *cowboy of the Pecos* might mean that the one spoken of was exceptionally expert as a cowboy and rider; in another, it might mean he was a rustler. But in either sense, he was sure to be salty and efficient. There is an old saying that "When a badman dies, he either goes to hell or to the Pecos." Another saying is, "Once a cowboy has watered on the salty Pecos, he'll always return."

Cowboys

See bill-show cowboy, bog rider, bootblack cowpuncher, bronc breaker, bronc buster, bronc fighter, bronc peeler, bronc scratcher, bronc snapper, bronc squeezer, bronc stomper, bronc twister, brush buster, brush hand, brush popper, brush roper, brush thumper, brush whacker, buckaroo, bucket man, bull-bat, bull nurse, buster, caballero, carnival hand, chuck-line rider, circle rider, contract buster, corrida, cowboy, cowboy of the Pecos, cow crowd, cowhand, cow nurse, cow poke, cow prod, cowpuncher, cutter, dally man, drag rider, flanker, flank rider, flat-heeled peeler, floating outfit, gate horse, grub-line rider, gunnysacker, hand, heel squatter, hillbilly cowboy, hold-up man, horseman, jinete, knothead, lead men, leather pounder, light rider, limb skinner, line rider, lone ranger, mail-order cowboy, makin' a hand, mavericker, miller, mill rider, nursey, outrider, outside man, peeler, pliersman, point rider, pothole rider, pumpkin roller, puncher, ranahan, ranchman, range bum, ranny, rawhider, renegade rider, rep, rough-string rider, saddle slicker, saddle stiff, saddle tramp, saddle warmer, saint, scissor-bill, sheepdipper, skim-milk cowboy, snubber, Sooners, stray man, swing rider, tail rider, tally hand, tally man, three-up screws, trail hand, tullies, twister, vaquero, waddy, white-water bucko, windmiller, windmill monkey.

cow bunny

Wife or sweetheart of a ranchman.

cow camp

Cowboy's headquarters on a roundup, a place where a group of cowmen have gathered to work cattle.

cow chips

Dried cow droppings. A popular fuel in the early days on the plains, where timber was scarce. It was hard to get a fire started with them, but when dry, this "prairie coal" made a hot one. However, it soon burned out and required replenishing. It also made as much bulk in ashes as there was in fuel, and the ashes had to be carried out as often as the fuel was put in the stove. In cold weather it was claimed that the constant exercise of carrying in fuel and carrying out ashes was what kept the fire-tender warm, rather than the heat from the fire.

Many of the old-time cooks in the early days had nothing else to cook with, and although this fuel gave off a peculiar odor when burning, it did not affect the food. When cow chips were damp, it was hard to make a fire with them, and a certain old range cook claimed that in one season he "wore out three good hats tryin' to get the damned things to burn."

cow crowd

An outfit or unit of cowboys.

cow folks

Persons engaged in the cow business for a long time or brought up in it.

cow geography

Scratching in the sand with a stick to give directions to another for reaching a certain section of the range or other destination.

When two friendly riders meet on the trail, they stop and sooner or later swing off their horses to loosen the cinches and give their bronc's backs some air. Then, squatting on their bootheels, they will fish around for a cowboy fountain pen and paper, which are a broomweed stalk and plenty of loose dirt to draw in. Jesse Evans used to say, "A cowhand kin jes' talk better when he's a-scratchin' in the sand like a hen in a dung heap." They can always make a picture of some brand, and show how one brand could be worked into another. Perhaps some nester with a pretty daughter has squatted in a certain valley, and directions will be drawn for getting there. Then with a swipe of the hand the cowboy can have a clean slate and start another lesson in cow geography.

cow grease

A slang name for butter.

cowhand

One working with cattle. On the range this is the most common term used by the cowboy himself when referring to one of his profession. Usually the one word *hand* is used.

cow-hocked

A horse whose hind legs almost touch at the hocks, and spread at the pastern joints, like those of a cow.

cow horse

A good cow horse has to possess strength and intelligence, both well trained. He has a natural instinct for sensing direction and detecting danger, both day and night. He is game and brave and will drop dead in the performance of his work if need be. He is well adapted to his place, tough, and inured to the hardships of his life. His lightness of foot and quickness of motion fit him for the work better than any other type of horse.

He soon learns his rider, and they work together. Of necessity he is sure-footed and always has an eye for the trail. He must have good feet, good limbs, heart, and lungs, so that he might have endurance; and above all, he must have good sense.

cow hunt

The primitive forerunner of the roundup; also called a *cow work, work,* and *cow drive.*

cowman

One who raises cattle.

cow nurse

One whose duty it is to look after sick or crippled cattle, which are kept in a separate herd.

cowpen herd

The cowboy's name for the small herd of the "little feller."

cow poke

A slang name for the cowboy.

cow pony

Occasionally a Westerner uses this term in speaking of his horse, but it is used mostly by Easterners and writers who have never lived in the West. The cowman usually calls him a *hoss,* and *cow hoss* is the universal term for him, not *cow pony.*

cow prod

Another slang name for the cowboy.

cowpuncher

A more recent title of the cowboy, derived from the metal-pointed prod-pole employed to urge cattle into stockcars. While *punching* is thus the accepted term for herding livestock, it ordinarily is restricted to cattle, the term *herding* being used in connection with horses. A cowpuncher might *punch* or *herd* cattle, but colloquial English makes him *herd* horses and will not let him *punch* them. The term is usually shortened to *puncher.*

(Philip A. Rollins, *The Cowboy* [New York, Charles Scribner's Sons, 1936], 40.)

cow riggin'

Clothes, or costume, worn by the cowman when working. As one cowboy said, "Y'u'd have to be some persuader to get a puncher to shed his cow riggin' for any of that gearin' of the shorthorn."

cow savvy

Knowledge of cattle and the cattle business.

cow skinner

A frequent name for a severe winter storm.

cow talk

Said when two or more cowmen get together and talk about cattle. Jack Potter once started a letter to me on a certain date, but when I finally received it, his excuse for the delay was that a friend came by his house and "started talkin' cow and I followed him off."

cow town

In the early days, a town at the end of the trail, from which cattle were shipped; later applied to towns in the cattle country which depended upon the cowman and his trade for their existence. Many an old-time cowboy had to leave one of those trail towns in a hurry, as one said, "without waitin' to kiss the Mayor good-bye."

cow whip

A long whip used more to pop than to lash cattle.

cow wood

Dried cow chips.

coyote (co-yo'tay)

Pronounced by the Westerner *ki'yote*. A prairie wolf much smaller than the timber wolf. It is very shy and has never been known to attack man unless mad or suffering with rabies. The word is also used for a man who has the sneaking and skulking characteristics of the animal.

coyote dun

A dun horse with a dark stripe running down the back, sometimes into the tail, and often marking the legs.

coyotin' 'round

Sneaking.

coyotin' 'round the rim

Touching a subject on the edges, as in a conversation or speech.

crawfish

Said when a horse pitches backward.

crawl your hump

To start a bodily attack upon you.

crease

One method used in capturing wild horses. The act consists of shooting with a rifle so that the bullet grazes only the cords in the top of the animal's neck just in front of the withers, about an inch or so deep, close to the spinal column. This causes a wound which temporarily paralyzes a nerve center connected with the spinal cord and the brain and knocks the horse down. He is thus stunned long enough for the hunter to tie him down before he recovers. Success with this method calls for expert marksmanship and an abundance of luck. From talks with old horse hunters and through other records, I find that this method was very rarely successful, and that for every horse captured in this way, fifty were killed.

credit

A notch carved upon a gun to commemorate the killing of a victim. Outlaws and gunmen of the wild bunch who killed for the sake of brag followed this custom, but no man of principle wanted to remember the men he had killed.

CREDIT

See jawbone, on tick.

cremello

A type of albino horse with cream-colored coat, pink skin, and blue, "china," eyes.

cribber

A horse that has the habit of gnawing on wood such as hitch racks or stall partitions.

cricket

A little roller inserted in the bit to make a chirping noise, giving the horse something with which to amuse himself with his tongue and creating a music the cowboy loves to hear.

critter

By this word the cowboy means *cow*, and the word *cow* stands for cattle in general. If the feminine gender is spoken of, it is designated as "she stuff," or if an individual is pointed out, the sex is designated as "that two-year-old heifer" or "that line-backed steer."

crock-head

An unintelligent horse.

crop

An earmark made by cutting one-half of the ear off smoothly straight from the upper side.

crop-eared

Descriptive term for any animal with ears shortened by freezing or sunburn.

croppy

A bad outlaw horse with his ears cropped for identification as such.

cross-buck

A packsaddle, named this from its similarity to the woodcutter's cross-buck sawhorse. It consists of two short, parallel planks connected at each end by a short wooden cross. Of necessity it has two cinches and is used to carry equipment or freight.

cross canyon

A canyon bisecting another canyon.

cross draw

Made with a gun carried at the hip but hanging butt forward, on the opposite side from the hand making the draw.

cross hobble

To hobble one front foot to the hind one on the opposite side. This method is dangerous to a nervous horse because it throws him into a panic. If this happens, he will fight the hobbles, throw himself, and be injured.

crossing

The ford or crossing of a river.

crow bait

Anything poor, but usually refers to a horse.

crowding pen

A small corral used for branding grown cattle.

crow hop

When a horse jumps about with arched back and stiffened knees at a pretense of bucking.

crown piece

The top part of the bridle, a strap passing over the top of the horse's head.

crumb castle

A slang name for the chuck wagon.

crumb incubator

Slang name for the cowboy's bed.

crying room

Headquarters of a rodeo. The office where alibis are offered and disappointments aired.

cuidado (coo-e-dah′do)

A Spanish shout of warning sometimes used in place of the English *look out* or *take care.*

cuitan (coo-e-tan′)

An Indian pony. The first coastal Indian tribe to see a horse called him an *e-cu-i-ton,* and the later trade jargon or Chinook named him *qui-tan,* and from this the present word is derived.

cull

A scrubby animal.

cultus

Mean, worthless; from the Indian.

cuña (coo′nyah)

Spanish, meaning *cradle.* This is a green hide stretched to the running gear of the wagon. The head and forelegs are lashed toward the front of the wagon, the sides to the sides of the bed, and the hind legs to the rear axle. It is tied lower behind to make it easier of access, and while drying, the whole is filled with rock or something heavy to make it bag down, thus increasing its carrying capacity. It is used to carry wood or other fuel and is called the *coonie, possum belly,* or *bitch.*

curb bit

One with an upward curve, or port, in the center of the mouthpiece. One of the most widely used bits in the cattle country.

curled him up

Denoting that the one spoken of was killed.

curled his tail

A slang expression meaning to get either man or animal on the run.

Curly-Bill spin

A gun spin, more commonly known as *road agent's spin.* In some localities it takes this name because Curly Bill Graham used it to kill Marshal Fred White when the latter attempted to arrest him in Tombstone, Arizona. See *road agent's spin.*

curly wolf

A tough character.

curry him out

To rake a horse across his sides with spurs.

curry the kinks out

To break a horse, to take the meanness out.

Cussin'

See airing the lungs, private cuss words.

custom-mades

Made-to-order boots.

cut

A group of cattle separated from the main herd for any definite purpose, as for shipping or for branding.

cut a big gut

To make one's self ridiculous.

cut a rusty

To do one's best, to do something clever, to court a girl.

cut a shine

To perform an antic.

cut-back

One of cattle rejected on roundup for any reason, a cull.

cut-bank

A precipitous hillside or jump-off. Cut-banks constituted one of the dangers in the path of herders trailing longhorns up from Texas. They are caused by the wind's whipping around some point and eroding the soil until precipitous banks, sometimes yards high, have been formed. There is no way of detecting them in the dark, and more than once the mangled bodies of a man and a horse have been found at the bottom of one after a stampede.

cut 'er loose

A bronc rider's signal to release his mount, given when he is ready to start his ride.

cut for sign

To examine the ground for tracks or droppings, the two signs.

cut his picket-pin and drifted

Said of one who left for parts unknown of his own free will and not under compulsion.

cut his suspenders

Said of one who leaves one place for another, to leave the country.

cut his wolf loose

Said of a man drinking, shooting, or on any other kind of a "tear." One of the favorite stunts of the old-time cowboy was riding his horse into a saloon.

A story used to be told in New Mexico about the time three or four young punchers rode their horses into a saloon when one of those overdressed eastern drummers happened to be at the bar partaking of his after-dinner refreshment. Being considerably jostled by one of the horses, he complained bitterly to the bartender.

This bar-dog, an old stove-up former cowpuncher, glared at him a minute and came back in characteristic style with, "What the hell y'u doin' in here afoot anyhow?"

Perhaps he didn't appreciate all that livestock in the saloon, but he appreciated even less complaints coming from an outsider.

cut horse
Short for cutting horse.

cut in
To drive stragglers or wandering cattle back into the herd from which they had strayed.

cut of cows with calves
This cut is made on roundup by segregating all cows with calves in a separate cut preparatory to branding.

cut straw and molasses
Poor food.

cutter
A slang name for the pistol, one engaged in cutting out cattle, a good cutting horse; also the man who cuts earmarks during branding.

cutter herds
Bunches of cattle held about a hundred miles apart along the trail by cowboys hired, as in roundup season, to cut trail herds for several different ranchmen.

cut the bed
To share one's bed with another.

cut the deck deeper
A request to explain more fully or more clearly.

cut the trail
The act of halting a herd of cattle for an inspection. The trail-cutter causes the herd to be driven past him in a thin line so that he might identify any animal which does not properly belong to this particular herd.

cutting gate
A wide, swinging gate so arranged that it can be operated with a long ex-

tension by a man sitting on top of the fence. It is used like the switch of a railroad track to shunt cattle into one of several pens which it serves.

cutting horse
A horse highly trained for cutting out cattle. A good cutting horse is the top-ranking and most talked-of horse in cattle work. This coveted title comes only after years of training and experience, and the rider who can boast of such a horse is the envy of his comrades and the pride of the entire outfit.

When a good cutting horse begins his work, he is made to understand which animal is to be cut. He works quietly until the animal is urged to the edge of the herd. Naturally the cow tries to remain with her companions, and here is where the cutting horse proves his worth. A good cutter is both mentally and physically alert, possesses speed and action, and knows how to use them. He must spin and turn faster than the cow; and it takes an expert rider to stay on, for he must anticipate the horse's turnings to keep from getting spilled. All the work must be done in such a manner as to excite the herd as little as possible.

While the horse needs no assistance from his rider, an unskilled rider will certainly hinder the work of the horse. The work of a good cutter under an equally good rider is a joy to watch.

cutting out
The act of riding into a herd of cattle, selecting the animal to be cut, and keeping it on the move away from the herd and toward the cut being formed. It is hard and exciting work, but it gives both horse and rider the opportunity to prove their worth.

cutting the herd
Inspecting a trail herd for cattle which do not properly belong in it.

D

"You never know the luck of a lousy calf"

dab
A slang word used in speaking of roping, as "dabbed his rope on."

dabble in gore
Said of one becoming entangled in shooting scrapes.

dally
To take a half-hitch around the saddle horn with a rope after a catch is made, the loose end being held in the roper's hand so that he can let it slip in case of an emergency, or take it up shorter. Also called by the slang names of *daled, vuelted, dale vuelted,* and *dolly welter,* each derived from the Spanish phrase *dar la vuelta (dar-lah-voo-el'tah),* which means *to take a turn or twist with a rope.*

The American cowboy uses the nearest English sound, *dolly welter,* and this brings to mind a story told by S. Omar Barker of a tenderfoot roper who made a lucky catch and was immediately advised from all sides to "take your dolly welter," but he retorted that he "didn't even know the gal." Later the expression was shortened to *dally,* which is now the most common term.

dally man
One who uses a dally in roping. He makes his catch with a free rope and takes his turns around the saddle horn. He needs a longer rope than the *tie man,* one who ties his rope to the saddle horn, because he can't throw it all out, but has to have some left to make his turns.

dally your tongue
A command to stop talking.

DANCE
See baile, heifer brand, hoe-dig, shakin' a hoof, shindig, stomp.

danglers
Little, inch-long, pear-shaped pendants loosely hanging from the end of the axle of the spur rowel (Philip A. Rollins, *The Cowboy* [New York, Charles Scribner's Sons, 1936], 116), whose sole function is to make music that the cowboy loves to hear; also called *jinglebobs.*

Daniel Boones
A contemptuous title given the long-haired pseudo scouts and would-be badmen.

dashboards
What the cowboy sometimes derisively calls another's feet. Most cowboys take great pride in the smallness of their feet. If you want to "get a rise" out of one, just tell him that his feet "look like loading chutes" or accuse him of carrying most of his weight "on the spur end."

daunsy
Moody, downcast. One of the West's philosophies is, "The man who wears his chin on his instep never sees the horizon."

day herd
To stand guard over cattle in the daytime while they graze.

daylightin'
Riding so that daylight can be seen between the rider's seat and the saddle.

deacon
A small, runty calf.

deadfall
A drinking or gambling establishment of bad repute, an obstruction, especially of fallen timber.

deadline
The dividing line between a neutral and hostile or prohibited area. Used often in keeping sheep off certain cow ranges. In early days the Nueces River in Texas was called the *Sheriff's Deadline* because the numerous outlaws would not let a sheriff cross west of it.

deadman

Made by twisting a half-dozen strands of barbed wire into a cable which is passed around the top of the post of a fence and then around a large rock sunk deeply into the ground.

dead man's hand

Throughout the West the combination of aces and eights is known as the *dead man's hand*. This superstition was handed down from the time Jack McCall killed Wild Bill Hickok in Deadwood, South Dakota, while he sat in a poker game holding this hand.

dead mouthed

Said of a horse's mouth which has become insensitive to the bit.

deadwood

To get the drop on an enemy, to gain advantage over someone, control over, as to have the *deadwood* on one.

deal from the bottom

To cheat.

dealing brace

Using crooked faro boxes or manipulating cards so that the dealer is sure to win. These sure-shot games are practiced by the lowest class of gamblers.

DEATH

See big jump, buck out, cash in, curled him up, die-up, empty saddle, fried gent, gone over the range, got a halo gratis, grass is wavin' over him, hung up his saddle, kicked into a funeral procession, land in a shallow grave, last roundup, lay 'em down, long trail, misty beyond, no breakfast forever, pass in his chips, sacked his saddle, sawdust in his beard, shakin' hands with St. Peter, stiff, take the big jump.

DECEIVE

See cloudin' the trail, throw dust.

decorate a cottonwood

Said of a hanging.

decoy brand

A small brand placed on an animal's belly, used by some ranchers to trap rustlers. Choice animals would be otherwise unbranded to tempt the thief, but the ruse was rarely successful since the rustler was suspicious and as smart as the rancher.

decoy herd

A small herd of cattle used in snaring wilder animals. It is also used in starting a cut of cattle.

DEFEAT

See holler calf rope, put a spoke in his wheel, took the slack out of his rope.

dehorn

To remove horns from cattle (as verb); a hard drinker, especially one inclined to fight when drunk (as noun).

democrat pasture

The closing of a gap across a rimrock or canyon to form a pasture.

democrat wagon

A light spring wagon used on a great many ranches.

derringer

A small, short-barreled pistol with a large bore, capable of delivering a heavy blow at short range. This weapon was popular as a hide-out weapon from the early 1870's to the close of the century, especially among gamblers and bunco men. See *hide-out gun*.

desert canary

' The West's name for a burro.

desert rat

A veteran prospector of the desert country, usually without a mine or any other property.

DETERMINED

See hell in his neck.

dew-claws

The small, horny projections just above the back side of the hoof on cloven-footed animals.

dewey

A slang name for a six-shooter.

dewlap

A mark of ownership made on the underside of the neck or brisket of an animal by pinching up a quantity of skin and cutting it loose, but not entirely off.

When the wound is healed, it leaves a hanging flap of skin. Some marks are slashed up and called *dewlaps up*, others are slashed down and called *dewlaps down*.

dew wrangler

One who herds horses in the morning.

diamond hitch

A method of roping a pack on a pack animal. Wherever pack animals are used to carry loads, the diamond hitch is in common use. It produces upon the top of the pack, when completed, the figure of a diamond. An ordinary knot is tied, but a diamond hitch is always spoken of as "throwed," because a rope of forty or fifty feet is thrown back and forth across the animal as the hitch is made.

diarrhea of the jawbone

Said of one talking too much, running off at the mouth.

dice-house

A slang name for the bunkhouse.

didn't have a tail-feather left

Said of one cleaned at a gambling table or otherwise completely broke.

didn't keep his twine on the tree

A phrase meaning that the one spoken of was a rustler and did not keep his rope on the saddle horn where it belonged.

die in a horse's nightcap

To be hanged.

die-up

The wholesale death of cattle during blizzards and droughts over a wide range of territory. These die-ups are dreaded by all cattlemen, but welcomed by skinners who own no cattle. Ambitious skinners, not satisfied with the natural death of cattle, began, during the now-famous die-up in Texas, killing them for their hides, and this led to "skinning wars" (J. Frank Dobie, *Vaquero of the Brush Country* [Dallas, Southwest Press, 1929], 24).

diggers

A slang name for spurs.

diggin' for his blue lightnin'

The act of drawing a gun.

DIGGING

See gophering.

dig out the bedroll and drift

A command which informs one that he has been fired.

dig up the tomahawk

To declare war, to start trouble. When a cowboy "pulls his hat to a fightin' angle," it is a warning of things to come.

dinero (di-nay'ro)

Spanish, meaning *coin* or *money*. Used in this sense by the cowman, but also as a name for the cook.

dinner plate

A humorous name for the old broad-horned Spanish saddle, which, in the cowboy's language, had a horn "big 'nough to play a game of seven-up on."

dip

Strong antiseptic to kill ticks, lice, or scab on cattle or sheep, the cowboy's name for pudding sauce.

dirtied his shirt

Said of a rider thrown from a horse.

DISADVANTAGE

See clipped his horns, cold deck, hamstring, his leg tied up, horns sawed off, put a spoke in his wheel, shorten his stake rope, took the slack out of his rope.

DISGUSTED

See lookin' for a dog to kick.

dish

Seat of the saddle, and according to its depth it is spoken of as being "shallow dished" or "deep dished."

DISTANCE

See two whoops and a holler.

district attorney

Another name for the *son-of-a-bitch stew*. When the law began its westward march and started to question and clamp down on the cowboy government of the happy, carefree days, the blame for this cramping of liberties was placed upon lawyers. This caused the riders of the range to feel somewhat resentful toward the law, and soon they began calling this dish *district attorney*. The implication is obvious. See *son-of-a-bitch stew*.

ditch rider

An irrigation patrolman who turns water into laterals and watches for breaks in ditch banks.

ditty

A new tool, or contrivance, or practically anything unfamiliar to the cowboy is called a *ditty*.

dive

Another slang name for the bunkhouse; also a low saloon. I think it was Charlie Russell who said of such a saloon that it "would make all the other dives in the West look like a ladies' finishin' school," and I heard another cowman speak of one as a place "where a rattlesnake would be ashamed to meet his mother."

'dobe wall

A wall made of adobe, or sun-dried brick (as noun); to stand one against an adobe wall and execute by shooting (as verb). Llano Pierce once spoke of a friend in Mexico being " 'dobe walled into Kingdom Come."

doctor

To cut the knee tendon of a wild longhorn so that he can walk but can not run.

DOCTOR

See pill roller, saddlebag doctor, sawbones.

dofunnies

The cowboy's name for the useless little trinkets he carries in his war-bag.

dog fall

Throwing an animal with its feet under it.

dog fight

The name cowboys give to a fist fight. The early cowman felt that such combats were beneath his dignity. As one said, "If the Lord had intended me to fight like a dog, He'd a-give me longer teeth and claws."

dog-house

Another slang name for the bunkhouse.

dog-house stirrups

A slang name for the old, wide, wooden stirrups of the early range. It was claimed that they had enough lumber in them to build a dog-house.

dogger

One who bulldogs.

dogie

A scrubby calf that has not wintered well and is anæmic from the scant food of the cold months; also spelled *dogy* or *dobie*. It is, in the language of the cowboy, "a calf that has lost its mammy and whose daddy has run off with another cow." Although the word is used commonly in the West and is understood by all cattlemen, there has, in recent years, been some controversy over its origin. One version is that, during trail days, when it was discovered that the northern range was good cow country, especially for fattening beef, there arose a demand for young animals. It became the usage to call these *dogies*, especially yearling steers, to distinguish them from steers that were fat enough for market. Another version is that the term originated in the eighties after a very severe winter had killed off a great many mother cows and left a number of orphan calves. Grass and water were too heavy a ration for these little orphans, and their bellies very much resembled a batch of sourdough carried in a sack. Having no mother whose brand would establish ownership, and carrying no brand themselves by which they might be identified, these orphans were put into the maverick class. The first to claim them was recognized as the owner, no matter where they were found. One day on roundup a certain cowman who was trying to build up a herd, drove a bunch in from along the river.

"Boys, there's five of them dough-guts in that drive and I claim ever' damn one of 'em!" he yelled excitedly.

During that roundup all orphans became known as *dough-guts*, and later the term was shortened to *dogie* and has been used ever since throughout cattle-land to refer to a pot-gutted orphan calf. This term has recently become popular through western songs, yet too great a percentage of singers call it *doggie*, as if they were singing of a pup. The word is sometimes used by the cowboy to mean laced shoes.

dogieman
A small rancher or nester who gets his cattle from outside farm districts.

doll-babies
The wooden pegs used in making hair ropes.

don't know sic 'em
Ignorant. I have heard many unique references to ignorance such as, "He's got no more sense than a little nigger with a big navel," "He don't know 'nough to pack guts to a bear," "He don't know dung from wild honey," and many others. Ted Logan referred to a man with, "His head's so holler he's got to talk with his hands to git away from the echo."

don't travel like a colt no more
Said of one getting old and stove up.

door knob
A title sometimes given a small boy. One who, in cowboy lingo, still "had the growin' itch."

dotting irons
Primitive forerunners of the stamp branding irons. Unlike the stamp iron, which is applied with one application, the dotting irons are made in three separate parts, one a bar, one a small half-circle, and the other a large half-circle, so that by using various combinations a number of different brands can be made (J. Evetts Haley, *Charles Goodnight, Cowman and Plainsman* [Boston, Houghton Mifflin Company, 1936], 18).

double barrelled
A two-cinched saddle; also called *double fire* and *double rigged*.

double hobble
A short strap with leather cuffs at each end, fitted so that the cuffs can be buckled about the two forelegs to keep a horse from straying.

double over-bit
An earmark made by cutting two triangular pieces in the upper part of the animal's ear.

double roll
Accomplished by spinning two guns forward, one on each trigger finger, cocking and releasing the hammer as it comes under the web or lower part of the thumb. It is more of a stunt than a practice.

double-shuffle
A sudden shift in the gait of a pitching horse.

double under-bit
Same as double over-bit except that the cuts are made on the lower side of the ear.

double-wintered
Said of cattle driven up from Texas and held in the North for two winters to mature them into prime beef.

dough-belly
A slang name for the cook.

dough-boxer
Another slang name for the cook.

doughgods
A slang name for biscuits.

dough-puncher
Still another name for the cook.

dough-roller
Yet another name for the cook.

dough-wrangler
Another slang name for the cook.

downed
Killed.

downer
A cow, which, after a drought or a hard winter, is too weak from undernourishment to stand. Every time she attemps to move faster than a walk she falls and has to be tailed up again.

John Hendrix tells this story concerning downers:

"There was an old cowman down in the Brady country a good many years ago, who got all his 'downers' up one frosty morning, and, while they were steadying down, rode over the hill to skin one he felt pretty sure had died during the night. Just after he rode over the hill he heard gun shots back in the direction of the cattle he had just left. Loping back, he saw three friends from town hunting blue quail around his stack yards.

' "For God's sake don't shoot around here, fellers,' he cried, riding up to them.

" 'Why, Lige, you told us last fall we were welcome to hunt out here whenever we wanted to. Besides, we're not going to shoot any of your cattle.'

" 'I know you're not, fellers,' replied the cowman. 'That's not the idea, but when you shot awhile ago fifty-five head of my old 'Nellies' tried to run and fell down, and I'm too danged weak in the back to tail 'em many more times today.' " (John M. Hendrix, "Feedin'," *West Texas Today* [March, 1937], 7.)

down in his boots
Said when one becomes frightened, a coward, a person, in cowboy parlance, "as yeller as mustard without the bite."

down in the Skillet
A reference to the Panhandle country of Texas.

down steer
Reference to an animal off its feet in a loaded stockcar.

down to his last chip
Said of one financially broke.

down to the blanket
Said of one almost "cleaned out."

drag
The rear of a column of cattle on the trail. It holds the footsore, the weak, the young calves, the weary, and the lazy; also called *tail*. The cattle themselves are called *drags*, and this term is also sometimes applied to lazy humans. The average cowhand has little use for a lazy person, and his descriptions of one are rather high-flavored. I heard Hunk Bouden speak of one with, "The hardest work he ever done was take a long squint at the sun and a quick squat in the shade." Wishbone Wilson spoke of a man being so lazy "he had to lean ag'in' a buildin'

to spit," and Curly Hicks said of another that he "didn't do nothin' but set 'round all day on his one-spot."

drag brand
One with a bottom projection which angles downward to some degree.

draggin' her rope
Said of a woman who is trying to catch a husband. Jack Davis used to say such a woman "might have a short rope, but she shore throwed a wide loop."

draggin' his navel in the sand
Leaving in a hurry. Bill Keith, in describing to me a friend running on foot, said, "He was hobbled with a pair o' hairy chaps, but he couldn't have made better time if he'd been stripped to the buff."

drag it
To leave. Usually used with reference to going under compulsion.

drag rider
One whose duty it is to follow the drags. This is the most disagreeable job of cattle driving because one has to ride in the dust kicked up by the entire herd, and contend with the weak and lazy critters until his patience is sorely tried. While the other riders may be singing in the pure air up ahead, there is no music in the soul of the drag rider, and he is using his vocal powers to cuss beneath the neckerchief he keeps tied over his nose and mouth. He is also often called the *tail rider*.

draw
A shallow drain for rainfall; also the withdrawal of a gun, as in the phrase "quick on the draw."

DRAWING A GUN
See border draw, border shift, case of slow, covering, cross draw, Curly-Bill spin, diggin' for his blue lightnin', double roll, draw, fill your hand, hip draw, leather slapping, reach, road agent's spin, shoulder draw, single roll, skins his gun, throw down.

dream book
An occasional name for a book of cigarette papers.

dream sack

A sleeping bag.

DRESS

See advertisin' a leather shop, full war paint, fumadiddle, low-necked clothes, Some deck is shy a joker., spraddled out, spread the mustard, Sunday-go-to-meetin' clothes, swallow-forkin'.

dressed in a hemp four-in-hand

Said of one being hanged.

drift

The marching of cattle in large numbers away from a particular locality, either to avoid the local conditions or to seek better conditions elsewhere. The term is more commonly used when cattle wander aimlessly before a winter storm, though a drift might occur in summer as the consequence of a stampede or the result of a lack of water or grass because of a drought. Drifts usually happen only with cattle, for horses have enough sense to avoid them, and to find shelter for themselves. (Philip A. Rollins, *The Cowboy* [New York, Charles Scribner's Sons, 1936], 209.)

drift fence

A fence built by ranchmen to keep cattle from drifting too far away from their home range. These fences ran east and west for indefinite distances to turn the drift when cattle drifted south by the thousands with the blizzards coming from the north.

The drift fence on the open range was unlawful because the land was government land and public range, but the cowman felt that such a fence was a matter of necessity. Yet in severe winters it often proved to be a death trap for cattle.

DRINKING

See alkalied, belly up, bending an elbow, booze blind, cut his wolf loose, dehorn, educated thirst, freightin' his crop, gypped, hear the owl hoot, high lonesome, h'ist one, kept the double doors swingin', lay the dust, lookin' down the neck of a bottle, paintin' his nose, paint the tonsils, ridin' out of town with nothin' but a head, roostered, rust the boiler, somebody stole his rudder, stay out with the dry cattle, talkin' load, usin' his rope arm to h'ist a glass, walkin' whiskey vat, wearin' calluses on his elbows.

drive

The moving of cattle on foot from one location to another (as noun); the act of moving cattle (as verb).

DRIVE

See haze.

droop-eyed

Said of a calf when a rustler cut the muscles which supported its eyelids so that it could not see to follow its mother.

droop-horn

An animal with drooping horns.

dropped his rope on her

Said when a man married.

drop stirrup

A heavy, leather strap below the stirrup to enable the rider to mount more easily. Used by women riders.

dry camp

To camp without water.

dry drive

To drive without water for the cattle.

dry gulch

To kill, to ambush, to assassinate.

dry-lander

A farmer of irrigated land.

dry stock

Denotes, regardless of age or sex, such bovines as are giving no milk.

dry storm

A sandstorm.

dude

A city-bred person, usually an Easterner, who comes west for fun and thrills.

dude chaps

Fancy chaps, as are worn by dudes and actors, in which a real cowboy would not be seen.

dude ranch

A ranch, which, as in recent years, has been converted into a place of recreation for Easterners for a profit.

Dudes
See dude, dudette, dudine, dudolo, dude ranch, dude wrangler, S. A. cowboy, swivel dude.

dudette or dudine
A female dude described by the cowboy as a young lady who comes west to marry a cowboy.

dude wrangler
A man who serves as a guide to the guests at a dude ranch, usually some former cowboy out of a riding job.

dudolo
A Westerner who makes his living by sponging off dudes and dudines. Fortunately rare in the West.

duffer
A codger, a useless fellow.

dugout
A rectangular pit dug into the ground, usually on a hillside, covered with a framework of timber and turf elevated three or four feet above the ground. Dugouts were very common in the early West as first and temporary residences. As the old saying goes, "It's a dwelling whose front yard took in considerable territory."

dugway
A place on the steep bank of a stream which has been graded down to let cattle and wagons enter or leave a stream.

duke
A nickname for a bull.

dulce (dool'thay)
Spanish for *sweet, honeyed.* In the Southwest, it is common to hear a young man refer to his sweetheart, "girl," or "lady friend" as his *dulce.*

dump
Another slang name for the bunkhouse.

dumped
An expression for being thrown from a horse.

dust
To throw dust into the eyes of a charging steer or cow, to go; also short for *gold dust,* meaning *money.*

dusted
Thrown from a horse.

dutch oven
A very thick, three-footed skillet with a heavy lid. It is used for cooking much of the cowboy's food, but especially biscuit. It is placed over hot coals with more coals put on the lid, thus browning the food on both sides.

dying with throat trouble
Said of a hanging. It is hard to get a range man to talk of a hanging, nor will he admit having had anything to do with one. It is a stern and solemn matter and not subject to jests nor popular mention.

dynamite
A common name for cheap whiskey.

E

"Man's the only animal that can be skinned more'n once"

eagle-bill
A slang name for a tapadero, leather stirrup covering, taking this name from its shape.

ear down
The act of distracting a horse's attention by holding his head down by the ears while the rider mounts. Sometimes the man doing the earing will catch the tip of the ear that is above his hand with his teeth. This will cause the horse to stand very still to avoid pain.

ear-head
A headstall made in two pieces, with a loop for the right ear, one buckle on the left cheek, and no nose-band, throat-

latch, or brow-band. The bit ties in with buckskin strings. This type of headstall is used only on broken horses.

early bouten
An occasional name for a greenhorn.

earmark
Certain ownership cuts made in the ears of cattle (as noun); the act of making these cuts (as verb).

EARMARKS
See buds, crop, crop-eared, dewlap, double over-bit, double under-bit, earmark, full ear, grub, jingle-bob, jug handle, mark, marker, over-bit, over-hack, over-half-crop, over-round, over-slope, over-split, seven over-bit, seven under-bit, sharp, slick-ear, split, steeple-fork, swallow-fork, swallow-tail, under-bit, under-hack, under-half-crop, under-round, under-slope, under-split, wattle.

easy on the trigger
Excitable, quick to anger.

eatin' drag dust
Said of one riding in the drag dust of a trail herd; also used in the sense of being humiliated.

EATING
See entries under chuck.

eatin' gravel
Being thrown from a horse. Sometimes said to be "eatin' gravel without stoopin'."

educated thirst
Said of a man who drinks champagne and fancy mixed drinks. Very few of the early western saloons carried stocks of fancy liquors. In his drinking the cowman did not belong to the "garden variety." When he got drunk, he wanted everybody to know it, and all usually did if they were in the same town. The liquor served in the average frontier bar would, in the words of one cowman, "draw a blood-blister on a rawhide boot"; and Zeb Fisher declared that the bartender of a certain saloon "served a free snake with ever' drink."

elbow room
The old-time, open-range cowman felt that he was being crowded if a neighbor settled within fifty miles of him, and he complained of not having "elbow room."

empty saddle
A horse showing up at the ranch carrying an empty saddle has a great significance in the cattle country. There is much anxiety concerning the rider because it signifies he is either dead, hurt, or left afoot, perhaps far from home, which in itself might also mean tragedy. As Will James said, "To range folks, such a sight [a horse coming home with an empty saddle] hints to a serious happening." (Will James, *All in a Day's Riding* [New York, Charles Scribner's Sons, 1933], 216.)

entitled to a warm corner
Said of one who has faithfully performed his duties and has grown old in service.

epizootic
The cowboy's name for distemper, a catarrhal disease common among horses.

equalizer
A slang name for a pistol. It is a common saying of the West that "a Colt makes all men equal."

ESCAPE
See leg bail, Mexican standoff.

ewe-necked
This term applies to a horse having a long, thin neck like that of a ewe.

exalted
Hanged. Almost any cowman is, in the words of one, "too proud of his Adam's apple to want to be exalted."

excuse-me-ma'am
A bump in the road.

EXPERIENCE
See hair off the dog, wrinkles on his horns.

EXPLAIN
See chew it finer, cut the deck deeper, ride over that trail again.

eyeballer
A meddler.

The Odds Looked About Even *

Flatboat on River, Fort in Background (Fort Union)

(all artwork is by Charmes M. Russell, courtesy of the Montana Historical Society)

The Geyser Busts Loose

Old-Man Saw a Crane Flying Over the Land

Looks at the Stars

Rawhide Rawlins, Mounted

Mountains and Plains Seemed to Stimulate a Man's Imagination

About the Third Jump Con Loosens

Like a Flash They Turned

In the Old Days The Cow Ranch Wasn't Much

Pete Had a Winning Way with Cattle

F

"The man that always straddles the fence usually has a sore crotch"

FAILURE

See busted cinch, busted flush, caught in his own loop, hard wintered, His saddle is slippin'., Like a steer, I can try.

fair ground

To rope an animal, throw the rope over its back while still running, then throw the animal violently to the ground, where it usually lies long enough to be hog-tied.

fall back

When a bucking horse attempts to stand erect on its hind feet, looses its balance, and falls backward; also called a *rear back.*

fallen hide

The hide of a dead cow or steer whose death is from natural causes.

fall roundup

Synonymous with *beef roundup,* occurring in the fall of the year.

falls out of bed

Said of a horse which pulls back on the halter rope.

fancy fluff-duffs

Anything fancy from food to finery. At some of the range dances the ranch women would make doughnuts, bake pies, and other fluff-duffs "jes' to let the boys know they wasn't eatin' at the wagon."

fanning

This word in used in two senses in the West. To fan with the hat means waving it or slapping it against a horse's sides while riding a bucker. Using the hat in this manner serves as a balance such as the pole of a tightrope walker. When a rider loses his hat, he is usually not long in following it to the ground.

To fan with a gun, the person fanning grips it in one hand and with rapid passes with his other hand knocks back and releases the hammer. Fanning is done mostly in western fiction, although there are men who can use this method of shooting. Ordinarily a man might fan for practice and pastime, but he seldom resorts to it when his life is at stake. The trick is interesting in theory but is of doubtful practical value. When a large-caliber gun is shot, the recoil after each shot causes it to buck up into the air. Though it is possible to work an unloaded gun very rapidly in this way, in actual shooting the gun will not stay still to be slapped, at least not long enough for accuracy.

fannin' on her fat

Slapping a horse's side with a hat.

fan-tail

A wild horse, a horse with a long bushy tail.

FARMERS

See churn-twister, dogieman, dry-lander, fodder forker, fool hoe-man, granger, hay shoveler, hay slayer, home-sucker, juniper, kaffir-corner, lint-back, mover, nester, nesting, plow chaser, sod-buster, soddy, squat, squatter, sunpecked jay, two-buckle boy.

father the herd

To get a herd bedded down for the night.

feather-headed

Light-headed, with no brains.

FEED

See post hay, stack, stack yard, staked to a fill, standin' feed.

feed-bag

A morral, a slang name for the mess-house.

feeders

Cattle which are shipped or driven to the corn belt for fattening before marketing; also men who feed these cattle.

57

feeding off his range

Said of a meddler. According to the western code no one questions a stranger. If he rides for the aimless pleasure of going places and seeing things, that is his own business. If he chooses to explain his reason for traveling, the cowman will listen, but if his reason is one which he dares not tell, that still is his business.

feed lot

A small enclosure for feeding cattle.

feed-rack

A rack built for hay or other foodstuffs; also a slang name for the messhouse.

feed-trough

Another slang name for the eating house.

fence corner

A style of bucking in which the horse zigzags much as the frontier rail fence.

fence crawler

An animal which can not be kept in a fenced pasture.

fence cutter

One of the men, who, during fence-cutting wars of the cattle country, cut fences; usually nesters and small ranchers fighting the larger ranch owners.

fence lifter

A very hard rain, when, as Peewee Deewees used to say, "The weather gets plumb wholesale."

fence rider

A later-day cowboy who keeps barbed-wire fences in repair; also called a *fencer*. He rides leisurely along the fence, following a narrow, ever-deepening trail that has been cut by many preceding trips. During his journey he watches for broken or loose wires, fallen posts, missing staples, water gaps that may have washed deep enough for cattle to use in getting under the fence, open or tampered-with gates, and all other things which affect the security of the fence.

He carries a pouch, usually a boot-top sewn at the bottom, full of staples, a hammer or hatchet, a pair of wire cutters, and a coil of stay wire. With these he can repair any damage he finds. (John M. Hendrix, "The Fence Rider," *Cattleman*, XX, No. 11 [April, 1934], 5.)

FENCES

See belly-buster, cutting gate, deadman, drift fence, fence cutter, fence rider, fence stretcher, fence wagon, furrow fence, silk, Texas gate, wing fence.

fence stretcher

A tool for pulling the fence wire tightly from post to post. A roll of wire may be attached to a wagon which stretches the wire by its progression.

fence wagon

A wagon to haul tools and material for the building and repairing of fences.

fence wormin'

Said when a horse bucks fence cornered. See *fence corner*.

fenders

The heavy leather shields sewn to the stirrup leathers.

fiador (fee-ah-dore')

From the Spanish verb *fiar*, meaning *to answer for* or *go surety for*. It is a looped cord ordinarily made of braided horsehair, passing from the front of the bosal upward and over the top of the horse's head; sometimes, in corrupted form, called *theodore* (Philip A. Rollins, *The Cowboy* [New York, Charles Scribner's Sons, 1936], 151).

fiddle

A slang name for a horse's head. The rider strives to keep a bronc from putting "his fiddle between his feet."

fiddle foot

Said when a horse prances around; also when a person drifts or has "itching feet."

FIGHTING

See buying chips, clean his plow, comb his hair, crawl your hump, dig up the tomahawk, dog fights, fighting wages, fort up, hang up his hide, lock horns, pistol whip, powder burnin' contest, pull in his horns, sharpen his hoe.

fightin' the bits

Said of a horse which throws its head

around when reined; also used with reference to an impatient or restless person.

fightin' wages

Money drawn for work where there is fighting to be done, such as range wars or organized rustler troubles. Under such conditions the pay is much higher than ordinary cowboy wages.

figure eight

A loop thrown so as to catch the forelegs of an animal in the lower part of the *8* while his head is caught in the upper part. This is done by throwing the straight overhead loop at an animal passing to the left, so that the honda will hit him just behind the left ear, the loop going out in front and dropping over his head. The sudden stopping of the loop when it hits the animal at the honda causes the loop to fold across, and it is then up to the animal to get his forefeet into the lower part of the loop. (W. M. French, "Ropes and Roping," *Cattleman*, XXVI, No. 12 [May, 1940], 17–30.)

fill a blanket

To roll a cigarette.

filly

A young female horse, a slang name for an unmarried woman.

fill your hand

To draw a gun.

final horses

In rodeo contests the hardest ones to ride and used for the final decisions on championships.

FIRED

See dig out the bedroll and drift, put his saddle in the wagon, set down.

fireguard

Made by plowing two parallel sets of furrows about fifty yards apart with four furrows in each set. The grass between the sets is purposely burned by men who are trailed by water-laden wagons. To a cowman a burned-out range is a sad sight and truly, as one said, "looks like hell with the folks moved out."

fireman

The man who attends the branding fires and keeps the irons hot.

fire out

This term is sometimes used instead of *vent*, but it means the same process of barring out a brand. See *vent brand* and *counterbrand*.

FIRES

See backfire, fireguard, fried gent, hell stick, no breakfast forever.

fire-water

Indian term for whiskey. Derived from the custom of traders in demonstrating the alcoholic content by throwing a little of the liquid on the fire to let it burn. Unless this was done, the Indian did not trade, fearing to be cheated. (W. S. Campbell [Stanley Vestal] to R.F.A.)

first rattle out of the box

An expression denoting prompt action.

fish

The yellow oilskin slicker that all old-time cowboys kept neatly rolled and tied behind the cantles of their saddles took this name from the picture of its trademark, a fish. The cowboy might carry it until he wore it out and never need it, but let him leave it at the wagon for half a day and he was certain to get soaked to the hide. According to cowman philosophy, "A wise cowhand'll have somethin' besides a slicker for a rainy day," but few of them did.

If the cowboy is riding a bronc that might pile him, and he is riding a slick-fork, he will tie this slicker behind the fork of his saddle to a bucking-roll to help wedge him in. Some riders, when riding a spooky horse which they are interested in training, tie the slicker behind the cantle so that it nearly touches the ground on the left side. Of course the horse tries to kick it to ribbons, but he soon gets used to it and quits trying to stampede. Through this training the horse gets so that he does not spook at other boogers that are just as harmless. (Will James, *All in a Day's Riding* [New York, Charles Scribner's Sons, 1933], 14.)

The cowboy also uses his slicker for a pack cover. If he has something he wants to keep dry when swimming a river, he rolls it up in the slicker tied on his saddle. It is also a handy place to carry food or a bottle if he is traveling a distance and ranches are far apart.

It is made to turn water, but is not good for keeping out cold. I know one rider who was caught in a sudden norther without a coat. He came back to the ranch wearing his slicker as an emergency covering, but by the time he had put his horse up and reached the house, he was as "blue as a whetstone." Loud in his condemnation of slickers as overcoats, he finished by saying, "If I'd had *two* of the damned things on, I'd a-froze plumb to death."

five beans in the wheel

No Westerner carries more than five cartridges in the cylinder of his gun. The hammer is always down on an empty chamber. He does this for safety, because of the hair-trigger adjustment. Men who know guns have too much respect for them to take unnecessary chances, and a man who carries six cartridges in his gun is looked upon as a rank pilgrim. As the cowman says, "If y'u can't do the job in five shots, it's time to git to hell out o' there and hunt a place to hole up."

five-eighths rig

A saddle with the cinch between the three-quarters and the center-fire. Neither the five-eighths nor the seven-eighths are commonly used.

fixin' for high ridin'

Preparing to leave the country in a hurry, and when a man does so, "He don't stop for no kissin'." Also said of one doing something which will get him into trouble.

fizzy

A range horse with a bushy tail, a variant of *fuzzy* or *fuzz-tail*.

flag at half-mast

This is said of a cowboy when his shirttail is out, and he wouldn't be a cowboy if he didn't work with it out half the time.

flag his kite

To leave in a hurry.

flame thrower

A slang name for a six-gun.

flank

This word used as a verb means that the one doing the flanking catches the rope with his left hand just against the neck of the calf to be flanked, or against the ear on the opposite side of him, then slaps his hand into the flank on the corresponding side. By a jerk upward and a pressure of the knees against the calf's side when it makes the next jump, the cowboy sends the calf's feet outward, and it comes down on its side (J. Evetts Haley, *XIT Ranch* [Chicago, Lakeside Press, 1929], 158). This is practiced in branding the smaller calves and in calf-roping contests.

flanker

One engaged in flanking; usually flankers work in pairs.

flank girth

Always pronounced *girt*, meaning in Texas the hind cinch.

flank rider

A rider, in trail work, who stays about one-third of the distance of the length of the column of cattle behind the swing riders, and two-thirds of the distance behind the point riders.

flank riggin'

A flank strap from the rear of the saddle, going far back on the flank of the horse. This device makes a horse buck, and, though most horses used in bucking contests buck without it, the flank rigging makes them "turn the works loose." See *scratcher cinch.*

flannel mouth

A person who talks much, a person who talks nonsense, a braggart. Doc Strawn used to tell of a braggart who "had more lip than a muley cow" and invariably "bragged himself out of a place to lean ag'in' the bar." Strong men never talk freely of what is in their hearts. There is no need; they understand.

flash rider

A bronc buster who takes the first rough edges off unbroken horses.

flat-heeled peeler

An amateur cowboy, a farmer turned cowboy.

flea-bag
Slang for sleeping bag.

flea bitten
Said of a white horse which is covered with small brown freckles.

flea-trap
A slang name for the cowboy's bedroll.

FLESH
See beef plumb to the hocks, get rid of his leaf-lard, put on tallow, shore had tallow.

fling-line
A rope used as a lasso.

flip-cock
To fan a gun.

floating outfit
Five or six men and a cook kept by the larger ranches riding the range in the winter months to brand late calves and ones which had escaped the roundup.

flower rowel
The rowel of a spur shaped like the petals of a daisy.

fluidy mustard
The enigmatical name given by the cowboy to an odd-looking brand, brought into the district from the outside, and having no numerals, letters, or familiar figures by which it might be called.

flung him away
An expression meaning thrown from a horse. One cowhand described a friend's being thrown with, "He went sailin' off, his hind legs kickin' 'round in the air like a migratin' bullfrog in full flight."

flunky
The cook's helper.

fly
A sheet which is stretched at the end of the chuck wagon to make shade and shelter for the cook.

flying brand
One whose letter or figure has wings.

flying mount
Leaping from the ground into the saddle without the use of the stirrups.

fodder-forker
What the cowboy calls a hay hand or farmer.

fogging
Traveling at speed.

fold up
Said when a horse starts bucking.

folks on his mother's side wore moccasins
Meaning that the one spoken of is a half blood. Often said of the offspring of the squaw men.

FOLLOWING
See campin' on his trail, ridin' into his dust, trailing.

following the tongue
During trail days drovers set their direction by the North Star. At night, after locating this star, the wagon tongue was pointed in the direction to be traveled the next day. This was called following the tongue.

FOOD
See entries under chuck.

fool brand
One too complicated to be described with a brief name.

fool hoe-man
A contemptuous name for a farmer.

forefooting
Roping an animal by the forefeet. The roper approaches the critter from the left side, and a medium-sized noose is thrown over the animal's right shoulder and a little ahead, in position to receive one or both feet as they reach the ground. The noose is given an inward twist as it is thrown which causes the upper side of the noose to flip backward against the animal's knees, ready for the catch.

foreman
A man hired by the ranch owner to manage the detailed affairs of his ranch.

forging
Said when a horse strikes his front shoes with the toes of his hind ones. See anvil.

fork

The front part of the saddletree which supports the horn (as noun); to mount a horse (as verb).

forked brand

One with a V-shaped prong attached to any part of a letter or figure.

form-fitter

A saddle with a high horn and a cantle made to fit a man's form.

fort up

To barricade one's self for a siege.

forty-five

A common name for a .45-caliber gun.

forty-four

A .44-caliber gun.

forty-niner

A title given any man who went to the California gold rush of 1849.

fourflusher

A bluffer, an incompetent person posing as competent.

four-up driver

A driver of four teams or spans of horses.

fox-fire

A phosphorus light seen on the horns and ears of cattle during electrical storms.

fraid-hole

A wind cave or cyclone cellar.

freak

The cowboy's name for a grumbler or unwilling worker; also a saddle of unusual pattern.

free grass

The open range of the early days; also called *free range*.

free ranger

A man, who, during the early days of the barbed wire fence, was opposed to those wire barriers. Such opposition started wire-cutting wars on many ranges.

FREIGHTING

See corn freight, grass freight.

freighting his crop

Said of a man eating or drinking heavily.

freno (fray'no)

This term means most often a bit, but it can mean the whole bridle, with the bit included.

fresh horse

A horse which has had a few month's rest and has gained a good amount of flesh and sometimes a very "bad heart" since last ridden (James H. Cook, *Fifty Years on the Old Frontier* [New Haven, Yale University Press, 1923], 37).

fried chicken

A sarcastic name for bacon which has been rolled in flour and fried.

fried gent

A man caught in a prairie fire.

fried shirt

A stiff-bosomed one.

FRIEND

See amigo, compadre.

frijoles (free-ho'lays)

Dried Mexican beans, a staple in the diet of the range country.

frog walk

Said of a horse using straight, easy hops.

from who laid the chunk

Action or quality of superlative degree. A common expression of speed is, "He burned the breeze from who laid the chunk."

from soda to hock

In faro *soda* is the first card exposed face up before bets are made. The last card in the box is said to be *in hock*. In the West the expression *from soda to hock* became common as meaning *from beginning to end* or *the whole thing* as the East uses *from soup to nuts*.

front jockey

The leather on the top of the skirt of the saddle, fitting closely around the horn.

frothy

Angry.

fryin' size

Said of a youth; also of a man of short stature. I once asked a "shorty" of the range why he was so continuously in a good humor. Nothing seemed to anger him. His answer was, "I can't afford to get mad. My size won't let me whip nobody."

FUEL

See chip box, compressed hay, cow chips, cow wood, lump oil, prairie coal, prairie pancakes, squaw wood, surface coal.

full-ear

A calf or yearling, as yet unbranded, with no earmark.

full grown in body only

Said of a simple-minded or foolish person.

full-rigged

A saddle whose tree is entirely covered with leather.

full-seat

When the seat of the saddle is entirely covered with leather.

full-stamp

A saddle covered with fancy stamped designs. These hand-tooled saddles are not merely to satisfy a rider's ego. The rough indentations cause a friction between the leather and the rider's smooth trouser legs, allowing him to sit tight in the saddle without the tiresome cramping of his legs that would result from riding a fractious horse with a smooth saddle.

full war-paint

The cowboy's best "Sunday-go-to-meetin' clothes."

fumadiddle

A western term for fancy dress. *Faradiddle* and *fofaraw* are also used in this sense. These unusual words have been used in the West since the early trappers and scouts. No authority on record seems to know their origin. *Fofaraw* is probably from *fanfaron,* meaning *showy trifles, gaudy finery,* and other gewgaws. *Faradiddle* and *fumadiddle* are perhaps corrupted variants.

fumble

To bungle an attempt at drawing a gun. As one cowhand said, "He reached and fumbled, and it was a fatal weakness."

furrow fence

A furrow plowed around one's holdings. Kansas recognized this as constituting a fence and passed trespass laws to prosecute anyone crossing these furrows. Also during the late trail days furrows were plowed on each side of the cattle trails to keep drovers within certain bounds.

fuste (foos'tay)

A saddletree, a Mexican saddle, a packsaddle. In Spanish the word means *wood* or a *saddletree.* American cowboys frequently use the word to distinguish the Mexican saddle from the American cowboy saddle. The Mexican uses less leather on his saddle than the American, therefore the American looks upon the Mexican saddle as being made principally of wood. The *fuste* has a flat horn and a low cantle and is noted for its ability to make a horse's back sore, therefore it is not tolerated by the American. (Harold W. Bentley, *Dictionary of Spanish Terms in English* [New York, Columbia University Press, 1932], 137–38.)

fuzzy

Range horse; sometimes called *fuzz tail.*

G

"Polishin' your pants on saddle leather don't make you a rider"

gaboon
A spittoon in a western saloon, made of a plug-tobacco box filled with sand or sawdust.

gad
Slang name for a spur.

gaff
To spur a horse.

gallin'
Courting a girl. It is told of one cowhand on the Pitchfork ranch that when he went gallin', her "old man had to pour water on the porch steps to keep 'im from settin' there all night."

gal-leg
A spur with a shank in the shape of a girl's leg.

galves
Slang name for spurs.

gambler's gun
A derringer, a .41-caliber gun carrying a blunt-nosed bullet; called this because of its popularity with early-day gamblers.

GAMBLING
See both ends against the middle, bucking the tiger, close to the blanket, copper, could outhold a warehouse, dealing brace, dead man's hand, didn't have a tail feather left, from soda to hock, guns on the table, in the door, ivories, keeping cases, keno, lay 'em down, layin' down his character, open a snap, pass the buck, piker, saddle-blanket gambler, sweatin' a game, There's a one-eyed man in the game., tinhorn.

gate horse
A cowboy stationed at the corral gate for any purpose.

gather
Cattle brought together by the roundup.

gelding
A horse which has been castrated.

gelding smacker
A slang name for a saddle.

general work
A term sometimes used in referring to a roundup.

gentler
An animal used to *neck* to a wilder one to subdue the latter until he becomes more tractable; also a term sometimes used for a horsebreaker. See *necking*.

gentling
Breaking and taming unbroken horses.

get a rise from
To make a person angry.

get-away money
What a rodeo contestant is lucky to have after the show to make his way to the next one.

get down to cases
To confine one's activities to the matter in hand.

get his back up
To get into a fighting mood.

get his bristles up
Another expression for the above.

get his hog back
Recovering something that has been taken from one (William MacLeod Raine to R.F.A.).

get rid of his leaf lard
To reduce in flesh.

get the bacon
To succeed in one's efforts.

get the bulge on
To get the drop or advantage with a gun.

get the drop

To get one at a disadvantage before he can draw his own weapon.

GETTING THE DROP

See covering, deadwood, get the bulge, get the drop.

getting up the horses

Driving the saddle horses from the range or pasture to camp or headquarters.

ghost cord

"A thin string tied about the horse's tongue and gums, and thence passed below the lower jaw and up to the rider's hand" (Philip A. Rollins, *The Cowboy* [New York, Charles Scribner's Sons, 1936], 152). It can be an instrument of extreme torture, and is used by some busters to inflict punishment for bucking. Ghost cords are of many forms. Some men have a secret style all their own and guard its nature jealously. Most ranchers frown upon the breaker who uses a ghost cord, as it has a tendency to make an outlaw of the horse.

gig

To cheat, to swindle, to use the spurs.

giggle talk

Foolish speech.

gimlet

To ride so that the horse's back becomes sore.

gin around

To chase around, to chase cattle unnecessarily.

girth

The Texan's name for a cinch; always pronounced *girt*.

git-up end

What the cowboy humorously calls the rear end of a horse. It is this end upon which he lays the quirt when he wants him to go.

GIVE-AWAY

See tip his hole card.

Give 'im air!

A cry given by the rider of a bad horse to his helpers when he is ready to start his ride.

GIVING DIRECTIONS

See cow geography.

glory rider

One who rides an outlaw for the satisfaction of trying to conquer the beast.

goat

A bucking term for half-hearted pitching.

Go

See amble, andale, anti-godlin, brindle, buy a trunk, chasséd, cut his picket pin and drifted, cut his suspenders, draggin' his navel in the sand, drag it, dust, fixin' for high riding, flag his kite, fogging, high-tail, hit the breeze, hit the trail, hive off, humped his tail at the shore end, Jingle your spurs!, keep your moccasins greased, lean forward and shove, leavin' Cheyenne, leg bail, light a shuck, looksee, made a nine in his tail, makin' far apart tracks, pasear, pull stakes, punch the breeze, rattle his hocks, roll his tail, roll the cotton, roll your wheels, slope, tail out, take to the tall timbers, take to the tules, throw dust, vamoose.

go-devil

A taut wire which stretches from the top of the bank of a stream to an anchorage in mid-stream and carries a traveling bucket for the water supply.

go-easter

A carpetbag, bought at a store for a trip.

goin' down the rope

When a roper approaches his catch holding the taut rope as he goes, he is said to be *goin' down the rope.*

goin' like the heel flies are after him

Traveling with great and sudden speed. This phrase originated from the fact that cattle, when attacked by heel flies, run frantically to get into a bog or water.

goin' over the withers

A roping term which requires the roper, rope tied to saddle horn, to ride up close abreast of the animal to be caught, lean over the animal's back, and throw the loop about the forefeet. The catch being made, he spurs his horse square away from the victim, tripping it and completely turning it on its back.

gold colic

A desire to find gold, desire to make money.

gone over the range

A reference to death, deceased.

gone to Texas

An old saying dating back to the days when Texas developed the reputation for producing and harboring outlaws and is used as a synonym for *at outs with the law*.

Many men left their real names behind when they crossed Red River. Names were not important in the early West, and most cowboys were known only by a nickname. As one cowman said, "The West don't care by what you call yourself. It's what you call others that lets you stay healthy."

Many of the early cowboys, if they saw a stranger approaching the ranch, would ride up a draw out of sight until they made sure that the rider did not stop for a visit. The more "sheriff-looking" the visitor the more stimulating the effect on the cowboy's rate of speed.

While attending a rodeo in Las Vegas, New Mexico, I heard an old former sheriff telling one of his cronies about a certain man who had "been out of Texas long 'nough to tell his right name."

good comeback

A quick and efficient retort.

good enoughs

Horseshoes purchased by the keg in various sizes ready to put on the horse's feet cold. These are used where there is no blacksmith to make a perfect fit for each individual.

good Indian

The frontier held every live Indian to be a bad one, so that when one spoke of a *good Indian*, he meant a dead one.

good lay

A well-managed ranch.

Goodnighting

A definition of this term can best be given in the words of J. Evetts Haley: "One of his [Goodnight's] most talked-of discoveries was made on the Goodnight Trail in 1867. When being trailed or worked, stock cattle have a tendency to get in heat, and upon starting with a herd of cows, Goodnight always put in a number of bulls. The trail is doubly hard on them, and after their testicles had been banged and bruised between their legs for several hundred miles, they sometimes died. He lost two on the Pecos drive, and another, a big dun bull from South Texas, had swelled and was about to die. Goodnight roped and threw him and got down to cut him, thinking he might recover. As he got out his knife, and thought how he could hardly spare another bull, an idea struck him.

"He called to a hand to bring him a piece of grass rope, then quite rare, from the wagon. He pushed the dun's seeds up against his belly, and cut off the entire bag. He unraveled a piece of the rope, and having no needle, took his knife, punched holes in the skin, and sewed up the wound like an old tow sack. Within a week, instead of being dead, that bull was in the lead of the herd giving everything trouble, and his voice was as coarse as ever. Thereafter Goodnight practiced the operation generally upon his old bulls on the range, almost doubling, he believed, their period of use. Of course, as he said: 'It does not make a young bull of an old one, but it does enable the old one to do a great deal of work.' "

Throughout the Southwestern range country this operation is known as *Goodnighting*. (J. Evetts Haley, *Charles Goodnight, Cowman and Plainsman* [Boston, Houghton Mifflin Company, 1936], 446.)

good whittler

A good cutting horse.

goose

To spur.

goose drownder

A cloudburst, a very heavy rain.

goose hair

The cowboy's name for feather-stuffed pillows.

gooseneck
A spur with a long shank shaped like a goose's neck, the rowels fitting in its mouth.

gophering
Digging for something. I once heard a cowman characterize a certain old prospector by saying he'd "been gopherin' in them hills as far back as an Injun could remember."

got a halo gratis
Sometimes said of one killed.

got callouses from pattin' his own back
Said of a braggart.

gotch ear
Where ticks have undermined the supporting cartilages of an animal's ear, causing it to droop.

got his spurs tangled up
Said of one confused or mixed up.

gouch-hook
A pot-hook used by the cook for lifting the heavy lids of his cooking utensils.

gouge
To cheat, to swindle.

Go 'way 'round 'em, Shep.
This phrase is used as a warning of danger, or of something to be avoided. If the danger is great, there is often added the phrase, "There's seven black ones and a coulee." The sheep man judges the size of his flock by the number of black sheep in it. Seven black ones indicate a large flock, and any Westerner knows the dangers of riding off the rim of a coulee.

grabbin' the apple
Catching the saddle horn while riding.

grabbin' the brandin' iron by the hot end
Taking a chance, getting the worst of something.

grabbin' the nubbin'
Catching the saddle horn.

grabbin' the post
Another term for the same act.

grade up
To improve the breed in cattle.

grain fed
Said of a horse regularly fed on grain. Grain feeding makes for harder muscles and greater endurance than grass feeding; consequently, work horses doing heavy work are usually grain fed.

granger
Farmer. This term is used principally in the Northwest, the Southwest's term being *nester*.

grapevine telegraph
The mysterious way news traveled on the frontier.

grapplin' irons
A slang name for spurs.

GRASS
See comin' grass, green up, prairie wool, standin' feed.

grass-bellied
Pot-gutted.

grass-bellied with spot cash
Rich, to have plenty.

grassed him
Said when a horse has thrown his rider.

grass freight
Goods shipped by bull team, called this because the motive power could eat their way to and from market. Grass freight was much slower, but much cheaper than freight hauled by mule teams. See *corn freight*.

grass huntin'
Being thrown from a horse.

grass is wavin 'over him
Said of a dead person.

grass money
Money paid Indians for grazing rights on Indian land (W. S. Campbell [Stanley Vestal] to R.F.A.).

grass train
Ox trains of the early freighters, called this because oxen could live on grass, when horses and mules had to have grain.

gravel in his gizzard
Courage. Said of a brave man.

grave patch

A slang name for a cemetery.

graveyard shift

The midnight to two A.M. shift of night herding.

grazin' bit

A small bit with a curb in the mouthpiece. It is a good all-round light-weight bit, does not punish a horse, and is used now in most states east of the Rockies.

grazing permit

A permit issued by the government to stockmen, allowing them an allotted number of cattle or sheep to be grazed on a specified area at a fixed price per head.

greaser

A Mexican, particularly one of low caste. The American uses it as a term of disrespect or insult.

greaser madhouse

An occasional name for the intricate brands of the Mexican.

greasy belly

Another slang name for the cook.

greasy-sack outfit

A small ranch outfit which carries its commissary pack in a sack on a mule in lieu of a chuck wagon.

greasy-sack ride

When a group of riders are sent, without a chuck wagon, to scour the rough country for cattle, they carry their food in small cotton bags, and these trips are known as *greasy-sack rides*.

great seizer

A humorous name for a sheriff.

greener

A tenderfoot; also called *greenhorn*.

green pea

Another name for a tenderfoot.

green up

Said of spring when the grass begins to get green.

grissel-heel

An old-timer, especially one "sot" in his ways. Chuck Evans spoke of a certain one's being "so obstinate he wouldn't move camp for a prairie fire."

gritty as fish eggs rolled in sand

Said of one possessing courage.

grizzlies

The name sometimes given chaps made of bear skin with the hair left on.

groanin' cart

A term sometimes used in speaking of a heavily loaded chuck wagon.

grounding

Cowboy term for letting the bridle rein touch the ground; the horse then stands without tying.

grout

A solid wall of mortar and gravel.

growler

A slang name for the chuck wagon.

grown stuff

Full-grown cattle.

grub

A cruel earmark, made by cutting off the entire ear smooth with the head, sometimes resorted to by rustlers to destroy the original earmark; also food.

grubber

An animal which noses about the roots of the loco weed to eat them is called this and said to be *grubbin' loco*.

grub house

A slang name for the cook shack.

grub-line rider

Synonymous with *chuck-line rider*; sometimes shortened to *grub-liner*. Visiting from one ranch to another is one way a man can live in the winter. Some cowboys chose this way to spend the winter for the sake of variety, and if such riders were not too plentiful, they were welcome. People who had been shut in all winter were glad to see new faces, and these riders brought news from the outside.

grub-pile

A meal; often the call to meals.

grub spoiler

Another slang name for the cook.

grubstake

To furnish provisions (as verb); provisions (as noun). When one grubstakes another, it is usually with the understanding that he is to share in the profits of the outcome of whatever enterprise the recipient embarks upon (Philip A. Rollins, *The Cowboy* [New York, Charles Charles Scribner's Sons, 1936], 34).

grub worm

Another slang name for the cook.

grulla (grool'lyah)

A mouse-colored horse. From the Spanish *grulla*, meaning *a crane*. A bluish-gray animal. In the Southwest the term is often used in referring to horses of this color. Such a horse is produced from a mixture of liver chestnut, mahogany bay, and some blacks. These horses are also called *smokey* and *mouse* duns.

guest of honor at a string party

A man who has been hanged. Chick Coleman spoke of one whose "neck was too damned short and they took 'im out to stretch it."

gullet

The curved portion of the underside of the fork of the saddle.

gully-washer

A very hard rain. After such a rain, in cowboy parlance, it was usually "wet 'nough to bog a snipe."

gun

The name for a pistol. The rifle, with the exception of the buffalo gun was never called a gun, but *Winchester, rifle, .30–.30*, from the caliber of the gun, or the slang name *Worcestershire* (Philip A. Rollins, *The Cowboy* [New York, Charles Scribner's Sons, 1936], 57).

gun-fanner

One who fans his gun when shooting. The real fighter has nothing but contempt for the gun-fanner, and the fanner has small chance to live when pitted against the man who takes his time and pulls the trigger once. By "taking his time" is meant only that split-fraction of a second that makes the difference between deadly accuracy and a miss. The muscles are fast, but there is a mental deliberation.

gunman

A man specially trained in the use of the pistol, and one ever ready to demonstrate this skill in blazing gunplay. The word soon became so pliant as to take into account the character of the man under discussion and became synonymous with *killer*.

gunman's sidewalk

The middle of the street, so that he could see from all sides and not run into an ambush.

GUNMEN

See cat-eyed, gun fanner, gunman, gunman's sidewalk, gunny, gun shark, gun tipper, gun wise, hell on wheels, leather slapper, lookin' for someone, Mexicans don't count, packs his gun loose, quick-draw artist, short-trigger man, thumber, trigger is delicate, trigger itch, two-gun man, wore 'em low.

gunnin' for someone

Said of one seeking an enemy to shoot.

gunny

A gunman who has for hire his services as a killer.

gunnysacker

During some sheep wars the sheep men called the cowman by this name because he raided their sheep camps wearing a gunnysack over his head.

gun-shark

One expert in the use of a gun.

GUNS

See artillery, belly-gun, big Fifty, black-eyed susan, blow-pipe, blue lightnin', buffalo gun, cutter, derringer, dewey, equalizer, five beans in the wheel, flame thrower, flip-cock, forty-five, forty-four, gambler's gun, gun, hairtrigger, hardware, Henry, hideout gun, hog-leg, iron, lead chucker, lead pusher, long Tom, man-stopper, meat in the pot, needle-gun, no beans in the wheel, old cedar, Old Reliable, one-eyed scribe, parlor gun, parrot-bill, peacemaker, persuader, plow-handle, saddle scabbard, scatter-gun, Sharps, shootin' iron, six-gun, sleeve-gun, slip gun, smoke wagon, stingy gun, talkin' iron, thumb buster, Walker pistol, Worchestershire.

gunshy

Cowardly. I heard one cowboy say, "When I see a coward with a gun I git plumb skeered." Charlie Russell in *Trails Plowed Under* spoke of another's being "as gunshy as a female institute."

gun slinging

Slang for the act of shooting.

guns on the table

Fair play.

gun-tipper

One who shoots through the end of his holster without drawing his weapon. The holster works on a swivel.

gun-wadding bread

The cowboy's name for light bread.

gun wise

Said of one with a thorough knowledge of guns.

gurglin' on a rope

Said of one hanged.

gut-hooks

A slang name for spurs.

gut lancers

Another slang name for spurs.

gut-robber

Just another of the cook's many nicknames.

gut shot

Said of one shot in the stomach.

gut shrunk

Having been without food for a considerable time.

gut-twister

A bucking horse of ability.

gut-warmer

A slang name for whiskey.

gypped

In more settled communities when one hears the term *gypped* used, it calls to mind a time when one had, in the past, been talked out of some hard-earned money by a stock salesman or a confidence man. To the cowboy the term has an entirely different meaning. Many of the creeks and rivers running through the country in which he works are heavily impregnated with gypsum, or other alkaline salts.

Drunk in moderate quantities, if it is fairly cool, the water causes no ill effects, but drunk in large quantities during the summer months when it is tepid and the drinker is hot from the branding pen or dusty roundup, the water produces the effect similar to that suffered by the small boy who has eaten freely of green apples, only much worse. No matter how old the old-timer, or how much of the water he has consumed in the past, he is never immune to gypping. He knows it, but if thirsty enough, will drink water wherever it is found, regardless of mineral or other content, even though it has the effect of the famed croton oil. (John M. Hendrix, "Cow Camp Sanitation," *Cattleman*, XXI, No. 11 [April, 1935], 5–6.)

H

"It's the man that's the cowhand, not the outfit he wears"

hacienda (ah-the-en'dah)

A Spanish noun meaning *a landed estate*, usually the homestead of the owner, devoted to stock raising.

hackamore

A halter. Corrupted from the Spanish *jáquima* (*hah' ke-mah*). The American cowboy pronounces his Spanish "by ear." When he first heard the word *jáquima*, he pronounced it *hackamer*, as it sounded. Gradually it became *hackamore*, as it is found in the dictionary today. (S. Omar Barker, "Sagebrush Spanish," *New Mexican Magazine*, XX, No. 12 [December, 1942], 19.)

It is usually an ordinary halter having reins instead of a leading rope. More commonly it consists of a headpiece something like a bridle with a bosal in place of a bit, and a brow-band about three inches wide that can be slid down the cheeks to cover the horse's eyes, but it has no throat-latch.

had a bilious look

Said of anything not in first-class condition.

had his hair raised

Said of one scalped by Indians.

had his pony plated

The cowboy often uses this expression to signify that he had his horse shod.

hair brand

A brand made by holding the branding iron against the animal just long enough to burn the hair, and not the hide (as noun). The hair grows out, effacing the signs of the brand, and the rustler can then put his own brand on the animal. To brand in this manner (as verb). (J. Evetts Haley, *XIT Ranch* [Chicago, Lakeside Press, 1929], 126.)

hair case

The cowboy's slang name for a hat.

hair in the butter

A delicate situation.

hair lifter

A frontier name for an Indian on the warpath; also a dangerous and exciting incident.

hair off the dog

Said when a man has gained experience.

hair over

Said of a brand when the hair grows back over it.

hair pants

A general classification of chaps with the hair on.

hairpin

Used as a verb, it means to mount a horse.

hair pounder

A nickname for a teamster.

hair rope

A rope made of horsehair. This rope is never used as a reata. It kinks too easily and is too light to throw. Hair ropes are used for hackamore tie-ropes, and used in this way are called *mecates*. See *mecate*.

hair-trigger

A gun is said to have a hair-trigger when its mechanism has been filed to produce an explosion with the slightest touch upon the trigger.

hairy-dick

Unbranded animal, especially a calf.

halfbreed bit

A bit that has a narrow wicket-shaped hump in the middle of the mouth-bar, within which a "roller," or vertical wheel with a broad and corrugated rim, is fixed (Philip A. Rollins, *The Cowboy*

Western Words

[New York, Charles Scribner's Sons, 1936], 148).

half-pint size
Something small.

half-rigged saddle
One with a triangle of leather tacked on for a seat.

halter broke
Said of a horse trained to run with the remuda; broke to lead.

halter puller
A horse with the habit of pulling back on the halter rope.

hammerhead
An unintelligent horse.

hamstring
The severing of the Achilles tendon of an animal, thereby rendering it helpless to control its leg. Wolves often bring down their victims by hamstringing them. Also used figuratively as to foil one's plans, or place one at a disadvantage.

hand
A measurement used in speaking of the height of a horse. A hand is four inches. Thus a fifteen hand horse is sixty inches, the measurement being taken from the ground to the top of his withers. Also the most common term in the cow country for a cowboy, shortened from *cowhand.*

hand-and-spit laundry
What the cowboy calls a laundry run by a Chinaman who "sprays a feller's best Sunday shirt with his mouth for a sprinklin' can."

handbill roundup
In the early eighties the Wyoming Stock Growers' Association took in such a vast territory that it sent out notices of dates for the start of the roundups by handbills. From this the cowboy dubbed them *handbill roundups.*

handle
Sometimes used in speaking of the saddle horn.

hang and rattle
To stick to the finish.

HANGING
See California collar, cottonwood blossom, decorate a cottonwood, die in a horse's nightcap, dressed in a hemp four-in-hand, dying with throat trouble, exalted, guest of honor at a string party, gurglin' on a rope, hemp committee, hemp fever, human fruit, hung up to dry, lookin' through cottonwood leaves, lookin' up a limb, lynchin' bee, mid-air dance, necktie social, playin' cat's cradle with his neck, ridin' under a cottonwood limb, rope croup, rope meat, stiff rope and a short drop, strangulation jig, string up, telegraph him home, Texas cakewalk, use him to trim a tree.

hang up his hide
To put one out of commission.

hankerin' to sniff Gulf breeze
Said of a "wanted" man "rollin' his tail south," and making for the Mexican border.

HAPPY
See singin' with his tail up, tail over the dashboard.

happy hunting ground
The white man's term for the Indian's hereafter.

hard-boiled hat
The cowboy's name for a derby, something he could not always resist using for a target.

hard money
Coin, the only kind of money seen in the early West.

hard-mouthed
Said of a horse that does not respond to the bit.

hard-tail
A mule.

hard to sit
Said of a good bucker.

hardware
A common name for a gun. I heard one cowhand speak of a heavily armed man with, "He's packin' 'nough hardware to give 'im kidney sores."

hard-winter bunch

Men whose favorite pastime is talking of the particularly hard winters through which they have passed.

hard wintered

The range man often uses this term when referring to anyone who seems to be in hard circumstances, as, "He musta hard wintered some by the looks of his outfit."

hassayampa

A liar, or one incapable of telling the truth. The name is derived from the old legend that anyone drinking from the Hassayampa River in Arizona could never again tell the truth.

hasta la vista (ahs'tah lah vees'tah)

A Spanish term, frequently used in the cattle country where Spanish is spoken, as a friendly parting equivalent to *I'll see you later*.

hatajo (ah-tay'ho)

From the Spanish *hatajar, to divide into flocks or small herds*. A train of pack animals, commonly mules, used in transporting merchandise, especially in mountainous regions where other modes of transportation are impossible.

HATS

See bonnet strings, conk cover, hair case, hard-boiled hat, John B., lid, pots, Stetson, war bonnet, woolsey.

haul hell out of its shuck

Said of a good bucker; also of a person raising a disturbance.

haul in your neck

A command to cease your aggressiveness.

hay burner

A slang name for a horse, usually one kept up and fed hay and grain instead of being turned out to pasture.

hay crib

Log walls without a roof enclosing hay stacks.

hay shoveler

One who feeds cattle from hay stacks in winter; a farmer.

hay slayer

A hay hand.

haywire

Crazy, muddled, twisted up. When a Westerner removes baling wire from hay, he twists it into crazy shapes before throwing it away, thus keeping stock from becoming entangled in it. From this practice the expression originated.

haywire outfit

An inefficient outfit or ranch.

haze

To drive slowly.

hazer

A man who assists the buster in breaking horses. His duty, especially when the horse is broken outside the corral, is to keep the animal turned so that his bucking will not take him too far away.

haze the talk

To lead or turn a conversation into certain channels.

head and heel

The event at rodeos where one roper catches the steer by the head and another ropes the hind feet, both putting the animal down against time.

head-and-tail string

A practice of mule packers on the trail of tying the halter rope of each animal to the tail of the animal preceding it to keep the train in single file.

head catch

The act of roping an animal by the head instead of by the feet.

head 'em up

To put a leader, a steer which leads the others, in the direction the drover wishes the herd to go.

head for the settin' sun

Synonymous with *on the dodge*. In early days every lawbreaker headed west for the unsettled frontier where there was a longer distance between sheriffs.

headlight to a snow storm

Said of a very black Negro.

headquarters
The house of the ranch owner, the business office of the ranch.

headstall
The headgear of a horse, that part of the bridle which encompasses the head.

head taster
The ranch manager.

heart-and-hand woman
A wife obtained through a matrimonial agency. The name originated from the old magazine, *The Heart and Hand*, published by a matrimonial bureau. The cowboy's simple soul believed all the descriptions. Hell, wasn't it printed?

Often a bachelor cowboy started his "letter courtship" out of curiosity, through desire to receive news from the outside, or just for a joke. In time he very often discovered he had committed himself and found himself driving a buckboard fifty miles to meet a ladylove whom he had never really intended to see in his home corral. When she stepped off the train, he sometimes discovered that his little joke had backfired because "the photograph she'd sent didn't show up all the blemishes." Many a woman of this kind was a widow of the grass variety, but, as the cowboy would say, "She didn't let none of it grow under her feet."

hear the owl hoot
To have many and varied experiences, to get drunk.

heating his axles
Said of one running swiftly on foot. Ranicky Reynolds described such a runner as "shore heatin' his axles and doin' his best to keep step with a rabbit."

heavy cow
A cow carrying an unborn calf.

heel
To rope an animal by the hind feet. Never used on horses.

heeled
Armed.

heel fly
A small fly which stings cattle on the tender part of the heel, driving them frantically to water or bog holes to escape punishment.

heel-fly time
A dreaded season in the cattle country, from the middle of February to the middle of April, when the insects are at their worst.

heel squatter
The cowboy is sometimes called thus because it is a common practice for him to rest by squatting upon his heels. This is not a comfortable seat for the layman, but the cowboy will squat comfortably on his boot-heels to eat his meals when out on the range, to spin his yarns, and, in fact, he is always ready "to take comfort in a frog squat."

hefty
Said of anything large. I heard one cowhand say, in describing a large man, "For weight and size he'd take first prize at a bull show." Another conveyed the same thought with, "He's as wide as a barn door and long as a wagon track."

heifer brand
To tie a handkerchief around a man's arm to designate that he is to play the part of a female at a dance where there are "not 'nough ladies to go 'round." He is then said to dance "lady fashion," and his reward is being allowed to "set with the ladies" between dances. This privilege, however, quite often makes him feel "as out o' place as a cow on a front porch."

Sometimes a playful puncher ignores the white emblem of womanhood and gets pretty rough, but these volunteer "females" can take it and pay back with interest.

hell bent for trouble
Seeking fights or making oneself otherwise obnoxious.

he'll do to ride the river with
This expression is about the highest compliment that can be paid a cowman. It originated back in the old trail days when brave men had to swim herds across swollen, treacherous rivers. The act required level-headed courage, and

as time passed, this phrase meant that the one spoken of was loyal, dependable, trustworthy, and had plenty of sand.

hell-for-leather
In great haste.

hell in his neck
Said of a determined man.

hellin' 'round town
Going from place to place in town seeking trouble. This was done mostly by the younger men. Older and more settled ones held the theory that "pullin' up the town to look at its roots don't help its growth none," and that "only a fool spends his time makin' the town smoky."

hell on wheels
This expression originated during the building of the Union Pacific Railway in 1867. As the rails were laid westward, the honkytonks, gambling hells, and harlots were loaded on flat cars and moved to the new terminal. All the deserted town's hell was then on wheels to "pull their freight." The term was also sometimes used in speaking of the old-time gun fighters. Clee Taggart described them as "them longhairs who done their damndest to fertilize the cow country's reputation for bein' wild and woolly."

hell stick
What the cowman sometimes called the sulphur match so common on the range in the early days, because when struck it really gave him a "whiff of hell."

hell wind
A tornado.

hell with the hide off
Extremely troublesome.

hemp
A slang name for rope.

hemp committee
A name sometimes given to vigilantes, a group of self-appointed law enforcers bent upon a hanging.

hemp fever
A hanging. The victim was sometimes spoken of as being "given a chance to look at the sky."

hen-fruit stir
Pancakes.

Henry
An early repeating breech-loading, lever-action rifle first used by the Union Army in the Civil War. This type of rifle never became popular as a military weapon, but was used to some extent upon the frontier.

hen-skin
Comfort stuffed with feathers.

hen wrangler
A name given a chore boy when one is employed upon a ranch.

herd
A bunch of cattle (as noun); to bunch cattle or horses and keep them bunched (as verb).

herd broke
Said of cattle when they become accustomed to traveling in a herd.

HERDING
See all hands and the cook, bedding down, bed-ground, bob-tail guard, close herd, cocktail guard, day herd, father the herd, graveyard shift, herd, herd broke, killpecker guard, locate, loose herd, night guard, night herd, night herder, off herd, parada, relief, rustle, singin' to 'em, standing night guard, wastin' 'em.

herrar (er-rar')
A Spanish verb meaning *to brand* or *mark with an iron*.

hide-out
A shoulder holster.

hide-out gun
An auxiliary weapon, usually short barreled, so that it could be hidden upon one's person.

hide with a stovepipe hole
A hide from which the brand has been cut, leaving a hole. It resembles nothing so much as a tent canvas with a stovepipe hole in it. Rustlers and meat thieves em-

ploy this means to hinder identification of the animal.

There was a certain outfit whom Old Man Barnes, of the Booger F, suspected of beefing his cattle. He was always complaining about their "half-solin' their insides with his beef." I happened to be with him one day when we rode into their camp just after supper.

"See there," said Barnes to me, "ever' damn one of 'em settin' there pickin' Booger F gristle out of his teeth right now."

HIDING

See cache.

high heel

A cowboy expression meaning that the one spoken of is forced to walk.

high-heeled time

A common expression to convey the cowboy's idea of a good time with fun and frolic.

high-line rider

Outlaw. He usually rides the high country to keep a lookout for any sheriffs or posses.

high lonesome

A big drunk.

high-low

A trick-roping term meaning a body spin which repeatedly raises and lowers the noose from the ground to the limit of the operator's reach above his head.

high-roller

A horse which leaps high into the air when bucking; also called a *high-poler*. This horse, while not quite so fast as others, is extremely rough and goes after his rider with a cool and deliberate aim that seldom fails to disqualify him. Also, in rodeo work, this type of horse pleases the customers, for he puts on a great show, and his actions are easily followed.

high-tail

To depart suddenly and uncermoniously.

hillbilly cowboy

One working for an outfit which ranges pretty well in to the sticks.

hill rat

A prospector of the hill country.

HINDER

See cloudin' the trail.

hip draw

When the gun is worn on the hip, usually slanting forward with the butt turned to the rear, and is unlimbered with a swift down and up movement.

hippin's

Underbedding.

hip shooting

Firing a gun without raising it above the level of the waist. When firing at close range, accuracy is not needed, sights are unnecessary, and the gun is shot by instinctively pointing it at an adversary and firing as soon as it clears the holster.

hired killer

A gunman who leases his services to a less courageous man to remove an enemy.

His calves don't suck the right cows.

Said of a rustler.

His cinch is gettin' frayed.

Said of one who has worn out his welcome. An unwanted person might be described as being "welcome as a polecat at a picnic," "welcome as a rattler in a dogtown," "pop'lar as a tax collector," or "folks go 'round 'im like he was a swamp."

His cows have twins.

Said of one suspected of stealing cattle.

his leg tied up

Said of one at a disadvantage. The expression originated from the custom of tying up the leg of a green bronc to shoe or saddle him. Shoeing some of the western horses is a ticklish experience. After completing such a job, Jake Wheeler, of the Horsecollar, declared that he "tacked iron on ever'thing that flew past." I remember one cowhand, kidding another from away back in the hill country, telling us that they "had to tie his leg up to give 'im a haircut" when he came to town.

His saddle is slippin'.
Said of one losing his efficiency, said of one telling a tall tale.

his tail draggin'
Said of a coward; also of one discouraged.

His thinker is puny.
Said of a weak-minded person. Such a person is said to be "off his mental reservation."

h'ist one
To take a drink.

hitchin' bar
A hitchrack.

hit the breeze
To travel, to depart.

hit the daylight
Said when the horse ridden in a contest comes out of the chute.

hit the trail
To leave, to travel.

hive off
Another expression meaning *to leave* (William MacLeod Raine to R.F.A.).

hobble
A leather cuff to buckle about each of the forelegs of a horse above the pastern joints, the two cuffs being connected with a short swivel chain (as noun). Most men get the same result with a wide band of cowhide, or a diagonally cut half of gunnysack. The act of applying these cuffs to horses (as verb). They are only applied, however, at a camp, for at the ranch, if the horse is not placed in a corral, he is turned loose (Philip A. Rollins, *The Cowboy* [New York, Charles Scribner's Sons, 1936], 141-42). When a rider camps at night, he wants to be able to find his horse in the morning. With hobbles on, the horse can move about with a certain amount of freedom and find grazing, but he will be unable to get very far because he can travel only at a slow walk.

hobbled stirrups
Stirrups connected with a strap or rope passing under the horse's belly. They have the advantage of furnishing a form of anchorage during bucking, but are held in contempt by the real rider, and barred at rodeos. Though hobbled stirrups practically tie a rider into the saddle, they are extremely dangerous, for if the horse falls, the rider has no chance to free himself quickly. In the cow country a man who rides with hobbled stirrups is considered "plumb loco," and is certainly not a top hand.

HOBBLES
See chain hobble, clogs, cross hobble, hobble, hobbled stirrups, Scotch hobble, sideline.

hobble your lip
Advice to quit talking so much.

hoe-dig
A dance; also called *hoe down*. Any old-timer will tell you that "Dancin' in them days wasn't jes' wigglin' 'round and shakin' yore rump."

hogback
Said of a horse with roached back, the opposite of swayback; a narrow ridge with steep sides leading from a high to a lower level.

hoggin' rope
A short rope used in hog-tying; also called a *hoggin' string* and *piggin' string*.

hog-leg
A popular name for the Bisley model single-action Colt, but later slangily applied to any big pistol of the frontier type.

hog skin
What the cowboy sometimes calls the small eastern riding saddle.

hog-tie
Rendering an animal helpless after it is thrown by tying its two hind legs and a front one together with a short piece of rope. The ties are made with half hitches and the rope used is a small soft one about three feet long. On one end is a loop which the man doing the tying slips on the foreleg of the down animal. Standing behind the animal, with one knee on it to help hold it down, he then sticks his foot under and behind the hocks

and boosts the hind legs forward, at the same time drawing the hoggin' string under and around both hind feet. This puts the two hind feet on top, pointing forward, and the forefoot below, pointing back. With two or three turns and two half-hitches the animal is thoroughly tied. Horses are never hog-tied.

hokey-pokey
Putting carbon disulphide ("highlife") on an animal. It puts the brute into a frenzy.

holding spot
The location selected for stopping and working a herd on roundup.

hold of the jerk-line
To be in control.

hold the high card
To have the advantage over another.

hold-up man
A robber; also a man stationed at crossroads, on a hill, or at critical points to keep a herd from leaving the trail.

hole up
To keep indoors in bad weather; also used in the sense of an outlaw hiding out, yet prepared to defend his liberty.

holler calf rope
To give up, to surrender, to acknowledge defeat, to declare one has had enough.

hombre (om'bray)
Man. Generally applied by Americans to one of low character, or in conjunction with such adjectives as *bad, tough,* etc.

homeless as a poker chip
Said of a restless person, one with a wanderlust, one who never remained long in one locality.

home range
The territory with which certain cattle are acquainted and where they belong.

homestead
A claim (as noun); to live and prove up this claim (as verb).

home-sucker
The cowman's name for the homeseeker who came west to farm.

honest pitcher
A horse which starts pitching as soon as mounted and tries by every device to unseat its rider. Some horses will make no effort to pitch until they get their riders off guard, then before the riders are aware of the horses' evil intentions, they find themselves on the ground. These latter horses are not classed as honest pitchers.

honda (on'dah)
A knotted or spliced eyelet at the business end of a rope for making a loop; sometimes a metal ring is used, though some men claim that metal objects might possibly blind an animal, and they will not "set" to keep the struggling brute from freeing itself. Hondas tied in the rope itself should be protected with a piece of slick leather sewed about the upper end of the loop so that the rope will not burn through it. (W. M. French, "Ropes and Roping," *Cattleman,* XXVI, No. 12 [May, 1940], 17-30.) The term is Spanish, meaning *eye,* and originally had reference to the receptacle in a sling for holding a stone or other article to be thrown.

honkytonk
A low saloon, dance hall, or other place of amusement.

honkytonk town
The towns at the end of the old cattle trails came under this classification, as their business districts were composed largely of saloons and honkytonks. Such towns were "tough" and, as the cowman would say, a "bad place to have your gun stick."

hood
The man who drives the hoodlum wagon, most generally the night-hawk.

hooden
A cabin where bachelor cowboys sometimes sleep during bad weather.

hoodlum wagon
A slang name for the bed-wagon.

hoofed locusts
The cowboy's occasional name for sheep, because it is claimed that their sharp hoofs kill the grass down to the roots.

hoof-shaper

A slang name for a blacksmith, or horseshoer.

Hook 'em cow!

The war cry of the branding corral and a phrase of encouragement at every rodeo.

hooks

A slang name for spurs.

hook up

To harness horses to a wagon or buggy. The verb *harness* is never used in the cow country.

hooley-ann

A roping term. This throw can be made either from the ground or on horseback. The roper carries the loop in his hand, and when the chance presents itself, he swings one quick whirl around in front of him toward the right, up over his head, and releases the loop and rope in the direction of the target. As it comes over, it is turned in a way to cause it to flatten out before it reaches the head of the animal to be roped. It lands straight down and so has a fair-sized opening.

It is a fast loop and is strictly a head catch, being especially used to catch horses in a corral. It is thrown with a rather small loop and has the additional virtue of landing with the honda sliding down the rope, taking up the slack as it goes. (W. M. French, "Ropes and Roping," *Cattleman*, XXVI, No. 12 [May, 1940], 17–30; Duff Green to R.F.A.)

The rope has not been slung over the horse's head, for to sling it so would cause even the steadiest old horse to become excited. Using the hooley-ann, half a dozen men can rope mounts at the same time without exciting the horses. (John M. Hendrix, "Roping," *Cattleman*, XXII, No. 1 [June, 1935], 16, 17.)

hooligan wagon

A wagon used on short drives to carry fuel and water in a country where these commodities are scarce.

hoolihaning

The act of leaping forward and alighting on the horns of a steer in bulldogging in such a manner as to knock the steer down without having to resort to twisting him down with a wrestling hold. This practice is barred at practically all recognized rodeos. Also to throw a big time in town—to paint the town red.

hoosgow

The cowboy's name for jail, now used throughout the country. From the Spanish *juzgado (hooth-gah'oo)*, meaning *tribunal* or *court of justice*. The Spanish *j* is always pronounced like the English *h* and a *d* between vowels is breathed rather than pronounced.

hooter

Short for hoot owl.

hop for mama

To buck.

hoppin' dog holes

Said of a cowhand riding in the prairie dog country.

hop-skip

Hopping into and out of a vertical noose while keeping it spinning.

horn

That part of the saddle above the fork. Its technical name, *pommel*, is never used by the cowman.

horned jack rabbit

A name sometimes given the longhorn by the old-time cowmen because it was all horn and speed.

hornin' in

Meddling, intruding. One of the cowman's codes is, "Never interfere with nothin' that don't bother you."

horning the brush

Angry, or displaying aggressiveness.

horns sawed off

Said of one rendered helpless, to take the fight out of one.

horn string

A leather or buckskin string, fastened to the horn of the saddle and used for securing a rope to it.

hornswoggling

The dodging and wriggling movements of a roped steer, by means of which he throws off the rope. The steer thus hornswoggles the cowboy from whom he escapes.

horn-tossin' mood
Angry.

HORSE COLORS
See albino, baldfaced, bay, bayo coyote, blaze, blood bay, buckskin, calico, chestnut, chin spot, claybank, cremello, flea bitten, grulla, Indian pony, moros, nigger horse, overo, paint, palomilla, palomino, piebald, pinto, race, roan, sabino, skewbald, snip, sock, sorrel, star, star strip, stew ball, stocking, tobiano, trigueño, zebra dun.

horse jewelry
Fancy riding paraphernalia.

horse man
One who raises horses.

horseman
A mounted person, or one skilled in horsemanship.

HORSEMEN
See horse man, horseman.

horse pestler
The herder of the saddle horses, wrangler.

horseplay
Tricks, pranks, and practical jokes by which the cowboy displays his peculiar and rough sense of humor.

HORSE RIGGING
See bridle, come along, corona, fiador, ghost cord, hackamore, headstall, horse jewelry, jerk line, martingale, morral, nose-bag, ribbons, sacking, saddle, saddle blanket, surcingle, tapaderos.

horse rustler
Another title for the wrangler.

HORSES
See anvil, appaloosa, apron-faced horse, band, bangtail, barefooted, bell mare, bone-yard, bottom, breaking age, break range, bridle wise, bronco, broomtail, brush horse, bucker, buck the saddle, bull-windy, bunch grasser, bunch quitter, buttermilk horse, buzzard-bait, buzzard-head, caballado, caballo, calf horse, California sorrel, camp-staller, caponera, carry the news to Mary, carvin' horse, cavvy, cavvy-broke, cayuse, choosin' match, chopping horse, churnhead, chute crazy, circle horse, clearfooted, close-to-the-ground bucker, cold jawed, coon-footed, cow-hocked, cowhorse, cow pony, coyote dun, crease, cremello, cribber, crock-head, croppy, crow bait, cuitan, cut horse, cutter, cutting horse, dead mouthed, ear down, epizootic, ewe-necked, fall back, falls out of bed, fan-tail, fiddle, fiddle foot, fightin' the bits, filly, final horses, fizzy, forging, fresh horse, frog walk, fuzzy, getting up the horses, git-up end, good whittler, gotch ear, grain fed, grounding, grubber, gut twister, had his pony plated, halter broke, halter puller, hammerhead, hay burner, high-roller, hog back, hokeypokey, huntin' a horse, Indian broke, Indian pony, individual, jerked down, jerk-line string, jigger, jiggle, jughead, killer, knothead, last year's bronc, lead span, loco, loggin', long horse, manada, man-killer, mesteño, mockey, moon-eyed, mount, mule-hipped horse, mustang, navvy, neck-reiner, nicking, nigger brand, nigger-heeled, nigger horse, night horse, night mare, notch in his tail, off side, oily bronc, one-man horse, Oregon puddin' foot, owlhead, pack train, pecker-neck, peg pony, pestle-tail, pie-biter, plug, pole team, potros, puddin' foot, puller, pumpkin skins, quarter horse, range horses, rat-tailed horse, raw one, remuda, remudera, ridge runner, rockin' chair horse, rope horse, rope shy, rough string, runaway bucker, sabinos, saddle band, saddler, salado, salty bronc, scalawag bunch, seraglios, set back, set fast, shavetail, short horse, shotgun cavvy, show bucker, smokes his pipe, smooth, smooth mouth, snake eyes, snatch team, snorter, snorty, snub horse, sobre paso, soft, sop and 'taters, spoiled horse, spooky, squaw horse, stampeder, steer horse, stick horse, stock horses, strays, string, stud bunch, stump sucker, sugar eater, suicide horse, stock horse, strays, string, stud swimming horse, swing team, tail pulling, tender, toothing, turn a wildcat, turned the cat, twitch, walkin' down, walkin' sticks, wall-eyed, wassup, watermelon

under the saddle, weedy, wet stock, wheel horse, whey-belly, whittler, wild bunch, willow tail, winter horses, witches' bridle, work horses, wring-tail, yakima.

HORSESHOES
See bar shoe, boot, bull shoes, good enoughs, had his pony plated, hoof-shaper, Indian shod, shoe, slipper.

horse-thief's special
The cowboy's name for a dish made of boiled rice and raisins.

horse wrangler
See *wrangler*.

hospital cattle
Weak stock that have not wintered well.

hot blood
A thoroughbred.

hot foot
To burn a calf between the toes with a hot iron as done by some rustlers to keep the calf from following its mother.

hothouse stock
A contemptuous name given by old-timers to the newly introduced Hereford cattle.

Hot iron!
The call of the brander when he wants a freshly heated iron.

hot lead
Bullets fired from a gun.

hot rock
A slang name for a biscuit.

hot-roll
The cowboy's bedroll.

hot rope
One that slips through one's hands until it burns the flesh.

hot shot
A device used in a rodeo chute to make the tamest horse buck when ridden by a greenhorn. It is an electrical charge, the points of which are directed to hit the horse on the shoulders. It is guaranteed to get results.

hot stick
A charged rod used in stockyards to prod cattle.

hot stuff
A slang name for heated branding irons; also a slang expression for something good or extraordinary.

HOUSES
See adobe, big house, bull's manse, bunkhouse, casa grande, cook shack, dice-house, dive, dog-house, dump, feed-bag, feed-rack, feed-trough, grub house, headquarters, hooden, jacal, Jones' place, mess house, nose-bag, parlor house, ram pasture, shack, swallow - and - get - out trough, white house.

hubbing
Driving a wagon so that the hubs will strike gateposts or other objects.

huckydummy
Baking powder bread with raisins.

huggin' rawhide
Sticking to the saddle.

hull
A slang name for the saddle.

human fruit
The body of a man hanging from a tree after a lynching.

humped his tail at the shore end
Said of man or animal leaving in a hurry.

hundred-and-elevens
Spur marks on a horse's sides.

hundred-and-sixty
A homestead, commonly of 160 acres.

HUNGER
See gut shrunk, narrow at the equator, Spanish supper.

hungry loop
When one throws a rope intent on a catch.

hung up his saddle
Said of one who had retired from the cattle business, or one too old to ride; also a reference to death.

hung up to dry
Said of one hanged.

hunker
To sit, or squat upon one's heels. The cowboy rarely used a chair; he saved it "for company."

huntin' a horse
A common excuse for one's presence or absence not easily explained; also a frequent alibi for being on another's range (Agnes Morley Cleaveland, *No Life for a Lady* [Boston, Houghton Mifflin Company, 1941], 67). Old man Johnson had a pretty daughter and a certain Mill Iron puncher used to drop by when he thought the old man was not at home. One day he was surprised to find the old man sitting on the front porch.

"Have y'u seen a little sorrel mare with our brand 'round here?" stammered the surprised cowhand with this threadbare excuse.

"Go right on into the parlor; y'u'll find 'er a-settin' on the sofa," grinned the old man, jerking his head toward the front door. That horse-hunter didn't fool him. He had been young once himself.

hunting leather
Catching hold of the saddle horn during a ride.

hymns
What the cowboy calls the songs he sings to cattle. They are usually religious tunes accompanied with profane words and as "hymns" would surely shock the clergy.

All cowboys are not good singers. There are many who "couldn't pack a tune in a corked jug" and sound as if they are "garglin' their throats with axle grease, or givin' the death rattle." An old cowhand I knew only as Cut-bank used to say, "They lost their voices explainin' to so many different judges how they'd come to have their brands on somebody else's cows."

I

"Success is the size o' the hole a man leaves after he dies"

Idaho brain storm
A twister, a cylindrical sandstorm.

IGNORANCE
See couldn't drive nails in a snow bank, couldn't teach a settin' hen to cluck, don't know sic 'em, full grown in body only, needs a wet nurse.

I'll shoot through the water barrel and drown you
During the old Kansas cow-town days full water barrels were placed at convenient places along the street for use in case of fire. In those wild times gun battles were plentiful and gunfighters and innocent bystanders alike ducked behind these water barrels for safety. More than one man got a good wetting by having a bullet come through the barrel he was hiding behind. From this the phrase became a common expression in the West as a threat.

immigrant butter
Gravy made from bacon grease, flour, and water.

Indian bread
This was a tasty strip of fatty matter starting from the shoulder blade and extending backward along the backbone of a buffalo. When scalded in hot grease to seal it, then smoked, it became a tidbit the buffalo hunter used as bread. When eaten with lean or dried meat it made an excellent sandwich.

Indian broke
Said of a horse trained to allow the rider to mount from the right, or off side, instead of the left, or nigh side.

Indian haircut

Said of a scalping. This was one haircut the cowman tried to avoid. In his own words, "It calls for a certain amount of hide, and no puncher wants to see his hair danglin' from an Injun's belt." When the government tried to make farmers of the Indians, Charlie Russell used to offer the criticism that "an Injun never raised nothin' but hell an' hair."

Indian pony

What the old-timers of the Southwest called a paint or pinto horse. He was a favorite with the Indian because of the savage's love of color.

Indian shod

Done by cutting a piece of rawhide and covering the entire hoof with it, fastening it on with thongs. When dry, it formed to the foot and made a tough, lasting foot protection.

INDIANS AND INDIAN TERMS

See beef issue, cuitan, fire-water, folks on his mother's side wore moccasins, good Indian, grass money, had his hair raised, hair lifter, happy hunting ground, Indian bread, Indian haircut, Indian pony, Indian side of a horse, Indian sign, Indian signboard, Indian up, Indian whiskey, lost his hair, lost his topknot, muck-a-muck, navvy, off the reservation, powwow, send up a smoke, siwash, skookum, skull cracker, smoke signal, Supaway John, teepee, voucher, wickiup, wigwam, yakima.

Indian side of a horse

The right side, because the Indian mounts from that side, while the white man mounts from the left.

Indian sign

Indication that Indians had been in the neighborhood. To put the Indian sign on someone meant to hex or curse him with some kind of witchcraft; also to get him where you want him (W. S. Campbell [Stanley Vestal] to R.F.A.).

Indian signboard

The bleached shoulder bone of a buffalo commonly seen upon the plains in the early days. The Indians painted messages on these bones.

Indian up

To approach without noise. Commonly used with reference to sneaking.

Indian whiskey

A cheap whiskey used by early Indian traders. Teddy Blue, who claims it was invented by Missouri River traders, gives the following recipe for making it: "Take one barrel of Missouri River water, and two gallons of alcohol. Then you add two ounces of strychnine to make them crazy—because strychnine is the greatest stimulant in the world—and three plugs of tobacco to make them sick —because an Indian wouldn't figure it was whiskey unless it made him sick— five bars of soap to give it a bead, and half-pound of red pepper, and then you put in some sage brush and boil it until its brown. Strain this into a barrel and you've got your Indian whiskey." (E. C. Abbott and Helena Huntington Smith, *We Pointed Them North* [New York, Farrar & Rinehart, 1939], 145.)

individual

The cowboy's privately owned horse.

inner circle

The shorter, or inside, circle on round-up, usually ridden by men whose horses had not yet become hardened to cow work.

INSECTS

See buffalo mange, cattle grubs, grubs, heel fly, no-see-ums, pants rats, seam squirrels, warbles, wolf.

in the brush

On the dodge. Early lawbreakers kept many a sheriff "ridin' the hocks off his hoss." Frequently they got close enough together to "swap lead and then have another hoss race."

in the gate

A term used in monte. After the shuffle and cut, the dealer holds the pack face downward, draws off the two bottom cards and places them face up on the table. This is called the *bottom layout*. Then from the top he draws two cards from the *top layout*. The pack is then turned face upward and the card exposed is the *gate*.

in the shade of the wagon
Said of one taking life easy.

iron
Short for a branding iron; also slang for a gun.

ironing him out
Taking the rough edges off a bucking horse.

ironing out the humps
Another expression for the above. This became the routine duty on roundup when fresh horses were saddled, especially in cool weather. On one particular roundup when the horses were unusually snuffy and riders were being thrown in all directions, one cowhand quietly observed that these riders were "fallin' off like wormy apples in a high wind." My observations of the cowboy are that no matter what the circumstances, he always has a comparison both witty and fitting.

iron-man
The man handling the branding irons at branding time.

iron-tender
The man who heats and tends to the branding irons.

ivories
Poker chips.

J

"The wilder the colt, the better the hoss"

jacal (hah-cahl')
A hut, a rude habitation, a hovel.

jack-knifing
A horse's clipping together of his front and hind legs, sometimes as a part of a "straight buck."

Jack-Mormon
A man who lives among the Mormons, follows their way of life, but never joins their church.

jackpot
An expression signifying either a general smash-up or a perplexing situation (Philip A. Rollins, *The Cowboy* [New York, Charles Scribner's Sons, 1936], 79).

jamboree
This word might mean anything from a dance or a drinking party to a gun fight or a stampede (Philip A. Rollins, *The Cowboy* [New York, Charles Scribner's Sons, 1936], 77).

jamoka
An occasional name for coffee made by combining Java and Mocha.

javalina (hav-ah-leen'ah)
A musk hog, native of the brush country, said to "look like a ball of hair with a butcher-knife run through it."

jawbone
Credit. A cowhand who lives on his credit until next payday is said to "live on his jawbone."

jaw cracker
A traveling dentist who goes from place to place over the range to relieve cowboys of their pain, teeth, and money.

jerked down
An expression used when a roped steer pulls the horse to the ground.

jerk line
"A single, continuous rein, starting from its fastening at the top of the brake handle, extended to and through the hand of the driver, who either was astride the wheel horse (the near one, if two) or was seated on the wagon's front. The line continued thence along the long file of horses' backs and to the left side

of the 'lead animal's' bit, without touching the bit of any intermediate brute. A single, steady pull on the line guided this lead animal to the left. Two or more short jerks turned it to the right." (Philip A. Rollins, *The Cowboy* [New York, Charles Scribner's Sons, 1936], 195.)

jerk-line string

A string of horses or mules harnessed in single file or in a series of spans, and following a well-trained leader controlled by a jerk-line (Philip A. Rollins, *The Cowboy* [New York, Charles Scribner's Sons, 1936], 195).

jerky

Dried beef. From the Mexican Indian word *charqui (char'kee)*. The Spanish and the Indians first dried buffalo meat by cutting it thin and drying it in the sun. When dry, it could be ground up like meal. When cooked in a soup, it swelled to considerable proportions and served as a nourishing food. Later the white man followed their example, and jerky became a staple food.

jewelry chest

An outside box on the front of the chuck wagon for storing hobbles, extra cartridges, and anything else that might be needed in a hurry in case of an emergency.

jigger

To overrun a horse.

jiggle

The ordinary gait of a cow horse, averaging about five miles per hour, to ride at this gait.

jinete (he-nay'tay)

Modern Spanish, meaning *a rider* or *a horseman*. Used in the cattle country in referring to a bronc buster, or a man who is an excellent rider.

jingler

Another name for the horse wrangler.

jingling

Rounding up the horse herd.

jingle-bob

An earmark, a deep slit that leaves the lower half of the ear flapping down, one

of the most hideous ever devised. This mark was made famous by John Chisum, a pioneer rancher of Lincoln County, New Mexico. Also the little pear-shaped pendants hanging loosely from the axle of a spur rowel, whose usefulness is restricted solely to making a music the cowboy loves to hear.

Jingle your spurs!

Get a move on, hurry up!

Job's comforter

The cowman's name for a boil.

John B.

Cowboy's hat, named thus after its maker, John B. Stetson. The cowman takes pride in the age of his Stetson. As one writer said, "A Stetson will take on weight with age and get to the point where you can smell it across the room, but you can't wear it out." The big Stetson is just as much a part of the cowboy as his hands and feet.

John Chinaman

What the cowboy calls boiled rice.

John Henry

What the cowboy calls his signature. He never signs a document, but puts his *John Henry* to it.

John Law

The frontier name for any law officer.

Johnny-come-lately

A tenderfoot, one new to the country.

Jones' place

The cowboy's reference to a line-camp; also a privy; sometimes used in reference to a honkytonk.

Judas steer

One used at slaughterhouses and so trained that he leads other cattle to slaughter. He is then returned to lead others.

jug handle

A mark of ownership made by cutting a long slash in the skin of the brisket, not cutting out at either end, a mark which, when healed, looks similar to the handle of a jug.

jughead

A horse which lacks intelligence and

has to be pulled around considerably before he is made to understand what is wanted of him.

juggling

A trick-roping term, being a body spin which repeatedly raises and lowers the noose from the ground to the limit of the operator's reach above his head.

jump

To come upon suddenly, as, "He jumped a brand burner at the edge of the range"; to take possession unlawfully, as, "to jump a claim."

juniper

The western equivalent of *hayseed*.

Junin' 'round

Restless.

junta (hoon'tah)

Spanish, meaning *a congress*, an as-
sembly, or *a council*, and used by the cowman in referring to a business meeting.

just a ball of hair

Said of a very thin cow or calf.

Justin's

Any cowman knows that this word is synonymous with good cowboy boots. From the day in 1879 when Joe Justin settled at Old Spanish Fort on the Texas side of Red River and made his first pair of boots, down through the years to the present modern factory in Fort Worth, Texas, run by his three sons, Justin's has set the style in cowboy boots. A few men have left their names to enrich permanently the vocabulary of the Westerner through the excellence and popularity of a necessary product. Among these are Colt, Stetson, Levi, and Justin. Even Easterners by now know what these names represent.

K

"Kickin' never gets you nowhere, 'less'n you're a mule"

kack

A slang name for a saddle.

kaffir-corner

A settler who raises kaffir corn, a farmer, any settler or nester.

Kansas City fish

Fried salt pork.

Kansas neck-blister

A bowie knife.

keeping cases

An expression used in faro. It means keeping a record of the cards as they are drawn from the faro box. The term soon became synonymous with the word *watch*. Therefore, to keep cases on anyone is to watch him.

keeping up the corners

In the old trail days this meant keeping the stronger cattle in the herd mov-
ing in such a way as not to impede the progress of any others, seeing that the rear of the column was no wider than the swing—that part between the leaders and the drags—or the cattle would become overheated, and seeing that the herd did not become spaced so that the marching column became too long.

keep your moccasins greased

This expression originated with the trappers and hunters and meant to step softly when stalking game. Later it was adopted by the cowman and used in the sense of *go easy*.

Kelly's

This name is known throughout the cattle country for hand-forged bits and spurs made by P. M. Kelly & Sons, of El Paso, Texas. As a school boy at Childress, Texas, the elder Kelly spent his spare time at ranch headquarters listening to the cowboys' criticisms of the bits and spurs then in vogue, and determined to make some which would be "just right."

With limited tools and the aid of a younger sister, he began making these riding tools by hand, selling them direct to the cowboys as fast as he could make them. From this start his business grew until his name became synonymous with good bits and spurs throughout cattle land.

keno

This word came from the gambling game, *keno*, and the cowman uses it to mean everything is all right. The conclusion of any act might evoke the exclamation, "Keno!"

kept his branding iron smooth

Said of a rustler when he worked overtime. A branding iron must be smooth and free from rust and scale to give satisfaction.

kept the double-doors swingin'

Said of an habitué of the saloons.

ketch dog

A dog trained and used to catch cattle by the nose and hold or throw them until they can be tied, or to worry a steer until a puncher gets there with his rope.

ketch hand

One whose duty it is to rope calves for branding.

Ketch my saddle!

The sure cry of a cowboy who has been thrown and whose mount is running away with his saddle. The horse belongs to the company, but the saddle is his own private and highly prized property.

ketch rope

What the cowboy calls his lariat to distinguish it from other ropes.

kettling

Synonymous with *bucking*.

kettle-bellied

Pot-gutted.

kick-back rider

One, who, in riding a bucking horse, spurs high behind. He often comes to

grief, because in spurring too high, he loses his knee grip.

kicked into a funeral procession

Said of one killed by a kicking horse.

KICKING

See kick like a bay steer, kicked into a funeral procession, let out.

kick like a bay steer

A common Texas saying meaning to kick vigorously or to complain bitterly. The cowhand rarely complains, for it is his philosophy that "kickin' never gets you nowhere, 'less'n you're a mule."

kick the frost out

To unlimber a horse.

kick the lid off

To start bucking, to start any violent action.

kidney pad

The contemptuous name the cowboy gave the little riding saddle used by an Easterner. Also called *kidney plaster*.

kidney shot

To shoot an animal in the region of the kidneys.

KILL

See bed him down, beefing, bit the dust, blow out his lamp, buck out, buck out in smoke, bushwhack, case of slow, credits, curled him up, dabble in gore, 'dobe wall, downed, dry gulch, hang up his hide, hired killer, land in a shallow grave, made wolf meat, man for breakfast, Mexicans don't count, Pecos, put windows in his skull, sawdust in his beard, slow elk, stand, strapped on his horse, toes down.

killer

A vicious horse; also a badman. Most of the professional gunmen were looked upon as killers because their guns were for hire.

killpecker guard

The period of herding from sundown until 8 P.M. is called this in some sections.

kip pile

Buffalo skinners sorted and graded

hides into different piles, the bulls in one pile, the cows in another, and the younger animals into a third known as the *kip pile*.

kissed the ground
Said of one thrown from a bucking horse.

knee grip
The clamping of a rider's knees against a horse when riding. This is an important asset in riding a bad horse, but he can not be ridden by knee grip alone. The feet should be braced forward, and out against the stirrups, to catch the rider's weight when the horse lands, thus enabling him to balance for the next jump.

kneeing
Splitting the hide on a wild steer about an inch and a half between the knee and ankle on one foreleg and cutting a small tendon or leader. When the steer is turned loose, he can walk, but his running days are over.

KNIVES
See Arkansas toothpick, Kansas neck-blister, skinning knife.

knobhead
A nickname for a mule.

knothead
A cowboy who never attains skill in his work; also an unintelligent horse.

KNOTS
See basket hitch, diamond hitch, Mormon tangle, squaw hitch.

KNOWLEDGE
See cow savvy, no medicine, quién sabe, savvy.

knows how to die standin' up
Said of one with courage, one unafraid in a fight.

kyack
Packsaddle. Kyacks might be described as hollow containers, one on each side of the horse, each of sufficient capacity to hold the equal of two five-gallon oil cans placed side by side.

L

"A loose hoss is always lookin' for new pastures"

laced his tree up
An expression sometimes used when the cowboy speaks of saddling. I remember Octillo Crane's telling me of his trying to ride a particularly vicious horse. He described the attempt in this manner: "I had trouble gettin' my wood on 'im, and when I did get my tree laced up, it didn't do me much good, 'cause I didn't get settled 'fore I goes sailin' off, flyin' low and usin' my face for a roughlock till I'd lost 'nough hide to make a pair o' leggin's."

ladinos (lah-dee'nos)
Outlaw cattle of the brush country. The Spanish word means *crafty* or *sagacious*. The term is often applied to any vicious animal.

lady broke
Said of a horse when he is thoroughly gentle.

lamb licker
The cowboy's contemptuous name for a sheepherder, taken from the ewe's habit of licking a new-born lamb.

lamp oil
A slang name for whiskey.

landed
Thrown from a horse.

landed fork end up
Thrown from a horse head first.

landed on his sombrero
Thrown from a horse head first.

land in a shallow grave

To be killed and buried without ceremony, to be killed out on the plains far from any settlement where graves can be dug properly. Many cowboys were buried thus when death resulted from stampedes, lightning, drowning, gun fights, and falling horses.

laneing

A term expressive of the action of an untrained helper. Through inexperience he will get on the side of the cattle opposite you to assist you in turning them. However, the two of you then form a lane which keeps the animals from turning. A man of experience comes up from behind and on the same side as the person he is assisting. (Duff Green to R.F.A.).

LARGE

See hefty, slew.

lariat

Originally a rope used in picketing animals, especially when made of horsehair. Sometimes a lariat is made of grass, and of course is often used for any purpose for which a rope is needed. The term is often used in the Southwest, but the word *rope* is used in the Northwest. The name is a contraction of the Spanish *la reata (lah-ray-ah'tah)*, the literal meaning of which may be expressed as *the tie back*. The rope may also be called a *reata* or a *riata. Lariat* may be used as a verb, as *to fasten* or *to catch* with a lariat, but *reata* is never used as a verb. Californians do not like the word *lariat* —they use either *reata* or *lass rope*.

larrup

Another name for molasses; also (as verb) to strike, to thrash.

larrupin' truck

"Great stuff."

lasher

A man who helps the driver of a string team by using the whip, handling the brakes, and helping with the swearing.

lash rope

A rope used to fasten packs on a pack-saddle.

lasso

A long line, usually made of hide, with a running noose. Mexicans introduced this name to the cow range, although the word is not of Spanish origin, but comes from the Portuguese *laco*, which has a meaning equivalent to *snare*. As in the case of *lariat*, it is used as a verb, meaning *to lasso*. The word is rarely used by cowmen, the term *rope* being preferred. Stockmen of the Pacific coast are the only ones using *lasso* to any extent.

lass rope

A slang name for rope.

last roundup

A reference to death.

last year's bronc

A horse in his second season of work.

latigo (lah'te-go)

Spanish, meaning *the end of every strap which must be passed through a buckle*. A long leather strap, used to fasten the saddle on, which is passed successively through the cinch ring and the rigging ring and tied much in the manner of a four-in-hand tie.

lawdog

A sheriff or deputy.

law wrangler

Frequently used title for a lawyer. The average cowman has little use for lawyers although he admires their learning. One cowhand referred to a certain attorney as "the smartest law-giver since Moses."

lay

A chance throw with a rope, the cowboy's bed, the name sometimes given a ranch or outfit.

lay 'em down

Said when a cowman dies; also when a player lays his cards on the table in a poker game.

lay for

To lie in wait for, to ambush.

layin' down his character

Said of one playing a deuce-spot in a card game. I heard one cowhand telling another of a game which he quit as a loser, and he finished by saying, "I tried all night to get somethin' higher than a two-spot." Another loser said that when he started the game he had " 'nough money to be called 'Mister,' but the trouble was I was jes' *called*—too many times."

layout

A frequently used name for a ranch, its employees, and equipment; also one's personal equipment.

layover

A voluntary stopping, during a drive, at ranches or in town.

lay the dust

To take a drink; also used in describing a light sprinkle of rain.

lay-up

A compulsory stopping of a drive.

lazy brand

One in which a letter or figure is lying on its side.

lead chucker

A slang name for a gun.

lead drive men

Men, chosen for their knowledge of the country, to make the circle drive on roundup. While other riders drop off at intervals to comb a given territory for cattle, the lead men ride on to complete the circle and drive in the cattle from the farthest edges.

lead man

Point rider of a trail herd. At the extreme forward tip of the moving column rode the two lead men, one on each side, called the point. This was the honored post of the cattle drive and the station of greatest responsibility, since it was these men who must determine the exact direction to be taken. See *point riders.*

lead plum

A bullet.

lead poisoned

Said of one who has been shot.

lead pusher

Another of the many names for a gun.

lead rope

A short rope used to lead a horse.

lead span

The lead team of a vehicle drawn by more than one team.

lead steer

A steer, who, by his aggressiveness and stamina, takes his place at the head of the trail herd and retains his leadership to the end of the trail. He is invaluable to the drover and, as an individual, is always honored with a name. There have been many stories written about famous lead steers; for example, those written by J. Frank Dobie, J. Evetts Haley, Jack Potter, and others; and these stories always move the heart of a real cowman. To him these steers are more than mere bovines.

leaky mouth

Said of one who talks too much. When two such men get together, Dick Blocker said they "jes' jabber at each other like a couple o' honkers on a new feed ground."

leaned against a bullet goin' past

An expression denoting that the one spoken of was shot.

lean forward and shove

To get out of the way in a hurry.

leather pounder

A slang name for the cowboy.

leather slapper

A gunman.

leather slapping

The act of drawing a gun and shooting.

leavin' Cheyenne

Going away. This expression is taken from the cowboy song "Goodbye, Old Paint, I'm Leavin' Cheyenne," a song usually used as a finale at a dance, much in the way that "Home Sweet Home" is used in other sections of the country.

leg bail

When a prisoner escapes from jail, he is said to take leg bail.

leggin' case

The punishment, imposed by a cowboy's kangaroo court, consisting of a lashing with a pair of leggin's or chaps.

leggin's

What the Southwest Texan calls chaps. He rarely uses the latter word.

leg jockey

The flat leather plate or flap overlying the stirrup leather where the stirrup leather issues from the side of the saddle. See *seat jockey.*

lent

A green hand.

leppy

Orphan calf.

let out

To kick. When a horse kicks, he is said to *let out.*

let the hammer down

To take the rough edges off a horse.

Levis (Lee-vies')

Overalls. This is perhaps the best-known first name of a man in the West. Only a "greener" would have to be told that Levis are overalls, called this from the name of Levi Strauss, of San Francisco, the pioneer overall manufacturer of the West. Since their introduction in 1850, practically all cowboys have worn them because they are stout and comfortable. They are not to be confused with the bib overalls that farmers wear. A cowhand would not be caught in a pair of these. Levis are made just like a pair of pants except that they have many copper rivets to reinforce seams and pockets. The cowboy wears them with turned-up cuffs, and when shoeing his horse, these cuffs serve as a handy repository for extra horseshoe nails.

lick

The cowboy's name for molasses.

lid

Hat.

light

To dismount.

light a shuck

To leave in a hurry, a quick departure. "In the early days, corn was carried as the principal food for man and beast. It was carried unshucked in the wagon beds. Selected shucks were placed at convenient places by all fires. On leaving one campfire to go to another, a man was usually blinded by the light of the fire he was just leaving. On turning his back to the fire, he found the surrounding woods pitch dark. To penetrate this blackness and give his eyes a chance to accustom themselves to it, so as not to fall over dead limbs, brush, and briars, the departing guest would light the tip of one of the whole corn shucks in the fire and lift it high above his head. The bright blaze would last for a matter of only a minute or so, just enough time to get well beyond the blinding light of the fire. Consequently, when a departing guest lit his shuck, he had to leave instantly or its light would be wasted. So, 'he lit a shuck and left'." (Frank Ryan, "On the Jefferson Road," *Texian Stomping Ground* [Austin, Texas, Folklore Publications, No. XVII, 1941], 9–10.)

light rider

One of those men who keep in balance upon and with the horse and can ride long distances without retightening the cinches or galling the horse's back, no matter how much their weight.

Like a steer, I can try.

This cowboy saying is applicable to many forms of conduct. It originated from the fact that the steer, like an old man, no matter how impotent, never loses his interest in the female; and when steers are brought together they will try to mount, or "ride," each other, no matter how fruitless their efforts. (J. Frank Dobie, *The Longhorns* [Boston, Little, Brown, 1941], 181.)

limb skinner

An appropriate name for a brush hand, but his limbs are the ones that get skinned.

line

A slang name for rope.

line-back

An animal with a stripe of a different

color from the rest of its body running down its back.

line breeding

The breeding of cattle of the same strain.

line-camp

An outpost cabin or dugout, upon a large ranch, to house line riders. See *boar's nest.*

line rider

A man who patrols a prescribed boundary to look after the interests of his employer. It is a hard, monotonous job, yet more interesting than fence riding, for he can ride a new route each day. While the fence rider looks primarily for breaks in the fence, the line rider looks for everything, including the condition of the watering places and the grazing lands. He pushes strays of his brand back on the range and drives off of it those which do not belong. The worse the weather the more he has to ride. Drifting cattle have to be thrown back into the brakes, holes have to be chopped in frozen watering places, and weak stock have to be tended.

It is a lonely job, and the line rider works long hours. He does his own cooking and has no one to talk to except his horses. He has no cheerful campfire to get up by on cold mornings, and he will smell no appetizing odors of fried meat and coffee until he builds a fire on the cold ashes of his little cookstove and cooks for himself. Sometimes two men are placed in camp, and although they spend the day riding in opposite directions, the job is not so lonely because they can keep each other company at night.

Perhaps the thing uppermost in the thoughts of this rider is the day when he can return to headquarters and hear a real cook yell, "Come an' get it." (J. Frank Dobie, *Vaquero of the Brush Country* [Dallas, Southwest Press, 1929], 149–50; John M. Hendrix, "Batchin' Camp," *Cattleman*, XX, No. 2 [July 2, 1934], 5; Philip A. Rollins, *The Cowboy* [New York, Charles Scribner's Sons, 1936], 206.)

lining his flue

Said of one eating.

lint-back

The cowboy's name for a cotton picker.

little feller

A cattleman with small holdings.

Little Mary

A nickname the old-time trail man frequently gave to the drivers of the calf wagon.

live dictionary

A school teacher, a talkative woman. One who, as Jug Jeter would say, "was shore in the lead when tongues was give out." Jug did not have much use for women, and he got his name because it was said that he "never went to town till his jug needed fillin'."

livin' lightnin'

Said of a bucking horse of ability.

lizard

A sled made of the fork of a tree supported by standards.

lizard scorcher

A camp stove.

lizzy

A slang name for the horn of the saddle.

llano (lyah'no)

Prairie, a flat, open plain without trees.

load

To deceive by tall tales, to lie.

load of hay on his skull

Said of a long-haired man.

LOAFING

See calf 'round, in the shade of the wagon, on the drift, pirooting, shadin', soakin'.

lobo

A gray wolf, sometimes called a *loafer.*

lobo stripe

The white, yellow, or brown stripe running down the back, from neck to tail, of a line-back animal, a characteristic of many Spanish cattle.

locate

To herd cattle on new range until they feel at home.

locked spurs

Spurs whose rowels have been fastened with a string or horsehair so that they will not move. When these spurs are held firmly in the cinch, it is next to impossible for a horse to unseat its rider, and their use is barred at all rodeos. When not locked, spurs do not assist the rider in staying on; on the contrary, they act in the manner of ball bearings to throw him.

lock horns

To engage in an argument or fight with another. Very commonly male animals of the plains, during fights, get their horns locked together, and, being unable to free themselves, remain in this state until they starve to death.

loco

In reference to stock, it means the result of feeding upon the toxic loco weed. In reference to humans, it means that the person called this is foolish, absurd, or crazy. The word is Spanish, meaning *mad, crazy,* or *stupid.*

loggerin'

Riding out of the chute at a rodeo with the hand, or hands, gripping the saddle horn.

loggin'

Tying a horse to a log. Since a log will move, this method of staking allows the horse more freedom and eliminates the danger of entanglements from more rigid staking.

lone ranger

A nickname for an unmarried man.

lone-wolfing

Living alone, avoiding companionship of others.

long-ear

To place a silk neckerchief on hard ground and listen by putting the ear upon it. Old plainsmen often followed this practice, and sounds otherwise inaudible are somehow magnified by this means. From this practice originated the saying, "Keep your ear to the ground," meaning to use caution, to go slowly, and listen frequently.

long-eared chuck wagon

A humorous name for the mules which pack the provisions when these animals have to be used instead of wagons in rough country.

long-haired partner

What the cowman sometimes calls his wife.

long-hairs

A slang name for the men of the early West who wore their hair long.

longhorn

A name given early cattle of Texas, because of the enormous spread of their horns; also the name for native men of Texas, the home of the longhorn cattle. The saga of the longhorn is interesting, and for a valuable and the only complete study of this historic bovine, I recommend *The Longhorns,* by an able recorder of the West, J. Frank Dobie (Boston, Little, Brown, 1941).

long horse

One which can travel great distances at high speed.

long-line skinner

A driver of two or more teams.

long rider

Another name for an outlaw. This name was given because he often had to ride long distances, or spend long hours in the saddle, to escape capture.

long rope

A slang name for a cattle thief.

long sweetenin'

Slang name for molasses.

long Tom

What the buffalo hunter frequently called his long rifle.

long trail

A reference to death.

long yearlin'

A calf eighteen months old or older.

lookin' at a mule's tail

Plowing. The cowhand despises any work which can not be done on horseback. The sentiment of the whole tribe was expressed by the one who said that he "wouldn't be caught on the blister end of *no* damned shovel."

lookin' down the neck of a bottle

Said of one drinking whiskey from a bottle.

lookin' for a dog to kick

Disgusted.

lookin' for someone

An expression meaning that one is seeking an enemy to down.

lookin' over his shoulder

Said of one on the dodge. One cowman expressed his philosophy to me with, "A man that looks over his shoulder at every piece o' straight road ain't leadin' a straight life." Looking over one's shoulder is breaking a strict code of range etiquette followed by honest men. When two riders meet on the trail, speak, and pass on, it is a violation of this code for either to look back. Such an act is interpreted as an expression of distrust, as though one feared a shot in the back.

lookin' through cottonwood leaves

Said of one hanged.

lookin' up a limb

Another expression meaning *hanged.*

Look out, cowboy!

When this cry goes up in a corral full of burned cattle, it is no disgrace to run.

look-see

When a cowman goes on an inspection tour or rides off to investigate anything, he refers to the act as going to take a look-see. The single word *look* is rarely used.

loose herd

To let cattle scatter somewhat, yet herd them.

lost his hair

Said of one scalped by Indians.

lost his hat and got off to look for it

Often said when one is thrown from a horse. An alibi which, of course, no one believes.

lost his horse

Said when a rider is thrown.

lost his topknot

Scalped.

low-necked clothes

The cowboy's very best garments, which he wears on special occasions. Tonto Sutton described a cowboy who attended a dance as "all spraddled out in his low-necked clothes," and, "He showed up public as a zebra, wearin' a b'iled shirt and smellin' of bear grease and lavender-flavored soap, lookin' as miserable as a razorback hog stroppin' hisself on a fencepost."

LOYAL

See he'll do to ride the river with, measured a full sixteen hands high, square, stand by.

lump oil

Coal oil or kerosene.

lunger

One suffering from tuberculosis who came west in search of health. Smoky Saddler described one with, "His lungs wasn't stronger than a hummin' bird's and he didn't have 'nough wind to blow out a lamp."

lynchin' bee

A hanging.

M

"A cow outfit's never better than its hosses"

Mac

A male parasite who makes his living pimping for some woman of the red-light districts of the cow towns.

machinery belting

Tough beef.

made a nine in his tail

Said of man or beast leaving in a hurry. When a cow runs from fright, she often lifts her tail in the shape of the figure nine, or at least in the shape of the figure the cowman uses in most "nine" brands; hence the saying.

made of the same leather

Said of men having the same dispositions, ideas, and tastes. According to one cowhand, they are "close 'nough to use the same toothpick."

made wolf meat

An expression of the early trappers, meaning to kill a man and leave him on the prairie for the wolves to eat; later adopted by the cowman.

mad scramble

A rodeo finale where fifteen or more Brahma bulls, steers, and mules, with a cowboy riding each animal, rush into the arena in all directions from the chutes.

maggots

Cowboy's name for sheep.

maguey (mah-gay' or McGay)

The century plant. The cowman uses the word to mean a four-strand rope of a scant three-eighths inch in diameter made from the fiber of this plant. It is a hard rope that throws easily and holds a wide loop. This is the rope used by trick ropers in making their fancy catches. In cow work it has its disadvantages, as it becomes very stiff in wet weather and breaks easily when tied hard and fast. It holds better when a dally is used.

mail-order catalog on foot

Said of a tenderfoot dressed in range clothes in an exaggerated manner.

mail-order cowboy

A tenderfoot, devoid of range experience, in custom-made cowboy regalia. The average mail-order cowboy "looks like he was raised on the Brooklyn Bridge."

make medicine

To hold a conference, to plan some action.

makin' a hand

A man is said to be making a hand—and this is a high compliment—when he can live up to the exacting code of the calling. This code calls for courage and loyalty, uncomplaining cheerfulness and laughter at dangers and hardships, lack of curiosity regarding another's past, and respect for womanhood. These, together with the embodiment of many other codes, constitute a religion that the cowboy lives up to if he makes a hand.

makin' far apart tracks

Running at speed on foot.

makin' hair bridles

Synonymous with being in the penitentiary. Most cowboys who were sent to prison spent their time making these bridles because the work seemed to bring them closer to a horse. Some of them have turned out masterpieces.

In typical cowboy language, Charlie Russell wrote a letter to a friend concerning a mutual acquaintance, saying: "Charley Cugar quit punchin' and went into the cow business for himself. His start was a couple o' cows and a work bull. Each cow had six to eight calves a year. People didn't say much till the bull got to havin' calves, and then they made it so disagreeable that Charley quit the business and is now makin' hoss-hair bridles. They say he hasn't changed much, but wears his hair very short and dresses awfully loud." (Charles M. Russell, *Good Medicine* [Garden City, Doubleday, Doran, 1930], 107.)

makin's

Cigarette material. The old-time cowboy never smoked any cigarettes other than the ones he rolled himself from his makin's. If he ran out of makin's when he was situated where he could not buy more, he asked another rider for them and they were never refused, unless the refusal was an intentional insult.

makin' shavetails

An expression used by cowboys of the Northwest for breaking horses. See *shavetails* and *tail pulling.*

makin' the town smoky

Said of one shooting up a town or raising hell generally.

maleta (mah-lay'tah)

A bag made of rawhide; also a satchel.

mal país (mahl pah-ees')

A Spanish term meaning *bad country.* The term is applied to the lava mesas of the Southwest.

manada (mah-nah'dah)

A Spanish feminine noun meaning *a herd of mares,* more especially brood mares. The verb *manar* means *to spring from, to issue.* (Don, "Vaquero Lingo," *Western Horseman,* II, No. 5 [September–October, 1937], 11.)

mañana (mahn-yahn'ah)

Spanish for *tomorrow;* sometime, perhaps never. The word is used freely by Americans along the Mexican border in association with a leisurely postponement. (Harold W. Bentley, *Dictionary of Spanish Terms in English* [New York, Columbia University Press, 1932], 161.)

man at the pot

If a man in camp, during meals, gets up to refill his cup with coffee and this is yelled at him, he is duty-bound by camp etiquette to go around with the pot and fill all the cups that are held out to him.

man for breakfast

Said of a killing. This saying originated in frontier days when there were so many killings at night in the tough cow towns and mining camps that when the good citizens awoke the next morning, they could see the body or bodies of the victims laid out before breakfast.

mangana (man-gah'nah)

A Spanish word meaning *lasso, a sleeve, net, or trap.* It is a throw which catches the animal by the forefeet and has come to mean *forefooting.* This throw is made by pointing the hand downward, dragging the loop forward and swinging it out so that it practically stands on edge. This throw stands a big loop in front of the animal, so that all he has to do is step into it. It is a loop which needs perfect timing to be successful, as it will cause an animal to stop rather than hit it, if it is stood too far ahead of him. The throw is reserved for horses and seldom used on cattle. (W. M. French, "Ropes and Roping," *Cattleman,* XXVI, No. 12 [May, 1940], 17–30.)

mangana de pie (man-gah'nah day pe-ay')

Pie means *foot,* hence this is a throw with the foot. Being a fancy throw, it is rarely used in actual work. It is made by putting a well-opened loop on the ground with the toe beneath the honda, and as the animal to be roped goes by, the loop is pitched straight forward with the foot.

maniac den

The cowboy's name for a sheep wagon or camp. The cowman feels that a sheepherder is more or less crazy or he would not be herding sheep, and for the disorderly arrangement of his camp, *den* is a fitting word.

Manila

A rope of Manila. Most of the ropes sold and used in the ranch country are made of Manila fiber, of three-strand construction, and laid extra hard for strength and smoothness.

man-killer

A vicious horse.

man-stopper

A slang name for a gun.

map of Mexico

The American cowboy's name for the intricate cattle brands of the Mexicans, which usually are large and give no clue to any name by which they can be called.

mark

The cutting of an animal's ears or other parts of the skin. Each kind of mark has a name and is registered along with the owner's brand. Used both as a noun and a verb.

marker

An animal with distinct coloration or other marks easily distinguished and remembered by the owner and his riders. Such an animal has frequently been the downfall of the rustler. The word also means a man who cuts the earmarks on cattle at branding time.

MARRIAGE

See draggin' her rope, dropped his rope on her, trap a squaw.

martingale

A strap from bridle to girth, passing between the horse's forelegs. It is intended to hold the horse's head down and thus keep him from rearing.

maverick

As a noun, it means an unbranded animal of unknown ownership; as a verb, it means to brand such an animal with one's own brand.

Many and varied stories are told concerning the origin of the use of this word (See J. Frank Dobie, *The Longhorns* [Boston, Little, Brown, 1941], 44-45). Some of the stories have even gone so far as to brand Mr. Maverick a thief, and nothing could be farther from the truth. He was a useful, prominent, and honorable citizen, a lawyer and one of the signers of the Texas Declaration of Independence. He never made any claims to being a cattleman. In fact, his ignorance regarding cattle was responsible for his leaving such a colorful addition to our language. Here is what is apparently the true story of the term.

The term is derived from the name of Samuel A. Maverick, who, as a lawyer, took over a bunch of cattle for a debt before the Civil War and placed them in charge of a Negro on the San Antonio River about fifty miles south of San Antonio, Texas. The Negro, being both ignorant of cattle and shiftless, failed to brand the increase of the herd and let them wander far and wide. In 1855 Maverick sold his entire outfit—brand, range, and all—to Toutant de Beauregard, a neighbor stockman. According to the terms of the deal, Beauregard, in addition to the number of cattle present and actually transferred in the trade, was to have all the others that he could find on Maverick's range, both branded and unbranded. Beauregard, being a thrifty man, instituted a systematic roundup, and whenever his riders found an unbranded animal, they claimed it to be a *Maverick*, put Beauregard's brand on it, and drove it in. These riders took in so much territory, at a time when the prairies were full of unbranded cattle, that the news began to spread. From these circumstances the term *maverick* was applied to unbranded range cattle. The term spread over the entire cattle country and gained such common usage that it found its way into the dictionary. (*Prose and Poetry of the Cattle Industry* [Denver, 1905]; George M. Maverick [son of Samuel A. Maverick], *St. Louis Republic*, November 16, 1889.)

The term is also now used in speaking of a human who does not mix with others, or one who holds himself aloof from a crowd.

maverick brand

An unrecorded brand. A thief can easily hold an animal on the range with one of these unrecorded brands until he is able to drive it off. In case suspicion is aroused, there are no records to connect him with the theft.

mavericker

A man who rode the ranges in the early days to hunt and brand mavericks. In the beginning this practice of roping and branding any calf which was not at the time following its mother was not considered stealing, but legitimate thriftiness. Calves of this kind were considered anyone's cattle. Many ranchers, who would not condone theft in any form, sent their cowboys out "to do a little mavericking" at so much per head.

When the cowboy saw how easy it was to build up a herd for his boss, he began wondering why it would not be just as legitimate and a lot more profitable to himself to maverick on his own hook. Not until then did ranch owners decide it was stealing and caused laws to be passed against it. After this *mavericker* was but another name for a cow thief.

maverick factory
Said of the rustler's making mavericks by killing the mother with her tell-tale brand.

mavericking
The act of hunting down and branding unbranded calves. It became a synonym for *stealing*.

mealy nose
A cow or steer of the longhorn type with lines and dots of a color lighter than the rest of its body around the eyes, face, and nose. Such an animal is said to be *mealy nosed*.

MEAN
See cultus, raised on sour milk, snake blood, snake eyes, snaky, tough lay, wool in his teeth.

measured a full sixteen hands high
The appraisement of a man's worth, and a high compliment to his ability and honesty.

meat in the pot
Slang name for a rifle, because this weapon is used by the hunter to secure meat for the camp.

mecate (may-cah'tay)
Americanized to the familiar *McCarty*, meaning a hair, or maguey, rope used as saddle reins with a hackamore, or as a tie or lead rope. Because a hair rope for this purpose has long been traditional, there has developed a tendency to call all hair ropes *mecates*. A hair rope is never used as a reata. It kinks too easily and is too light to throw.

MEDDLER
See eyeballer, feedin' off his range, hornin' in, Paul Pry, wedgers in.

medicine tongue
Fluent talk, wordiness.

medicine wolf
Slang name for a coyote.

MEETING
See junta, make medicine, powwow.

MEN
(other than stockmen) *See* Arizona tenor, arriero, badlander, badman, batch, blacksmithing, blue-belly, bone picker, breed, buckboard driver, bucknun, buffalo skinner, buffalo soldier, bullwhacker, can't whistle, capper, chuck-eater, claim jumper, coffee cooler, converter, desert rat, ditch rider, duffer, fence cutter, forty-niner, four-up driver, freak, free ranger, great seizer, grissel-heel, gunman, hair pounder, hard-winter bunch, headlight to a snow storm, hill rat, hombre, home-sucker, hoof-shaper, Jack Mormon, jaw cracker, John Law, lasher, lawdog, law wrangler, load of hay on his skull, long hairs, long-line skinner, long rider, lunger, mac, messenger, mover, mulero, mustanger, mustangler, pearl diver, phildoodle, pocket hunter, posse, raised on prunes and proverbs, redcoats, remittance man, river sniper, rolls his own hoop, roustabout, saddler, sagebrusher, sagebrush philosopher, sage rat, sand cutter, savage, sin-buster, skinner, sky-pilot, sloper, snow bird, squatter, squawman, startoter, stiff man, stinker, swamper, swivel dude, tiger, tumbleweed, two-gun man, two-up driver, vigilantes, wagon herder, wisdom bringer, wolfer, wood monkey, wood sheller, yack.

MENTALLY WEAK
See couldn't drive nails in a snow bank, feather-headed, haywire, His thinker is puny., needs a wet nurse, off his mental reservation, ought to be bored for the hollow horn, ought to be playing with a string of spools.

merry-go-round
A trick-roping term. The rope is spun with an independent noose around and clear of the body, the roper using first one hand and then the other.

98

merry-go-round in high water

The milling of cattle in a stream. Although it is highly desirable to get stampeding cattle to mill on land, when they do so in water the result is anything but desirable. When they get to swimming around in an ever-tightening circle in water, they become hopelessly massed, and the loss from drowning is enormous unless the herders are fortunate in breaking up this mass in its early stages. To stop them is difficult and a dangerous task, as the rider can not enter the center of the mass to break it up, and pushing from the outside causes it to become tighter.

mesa (may'sah)

A flat-topped hill, an elevated plateau, a mountain shaped like a table.

mesquital (meth-kee'tahl)

A region covered with mesquite, clump of mesquite shrubs. From the Spanish *mezquital.*

mesquite (meth-kee'tay or ma-skeet')

Spanish *mezquite,* probably of Mexican-Indian origin. A tree or shrub found in the Southwest, especially in the flat country. The wood is exceedingly hard and durable underground. The plant is covered with thorns, and its fruit is a pulpy bean full of grape-sugar upon which cattle feed when they can get nothing better.

messenger

A man, who, in the days of the stagecoach, rode beside the driver to defend the company's or shipper's property with a sawed-off shotgun; also called a *shotgun messenger.*

mess house

The cook shack.

mess wagon

Another name for the chuck wagon.

mesteño (mes-tay'nyo)

A horse, a mustang. From the Spanish which really means *an animal running wild on the range.*

met his shadow on the ground

Said of one thrown from a bucking horse.

MEXICAN

See chili, chili-eater, greaser, neversweat, oiler, pelados, pepper-gut, scab herder, shuck, spic, sun-grinner.

Mexican buckskin

What the northern cowboy sometimes called a longhorn driven up the trail from Texas.

Mexican iron

A slang name for rawhide, called this because it was used extensively by the Mexicans and wore like iron.

Mexicans don't count

A boast of the gunman of the Southwest who felt it beneath his dignity to "count coup" on the Mexicans and Indians he killed. Some gunmen kept a careful record of the white men they killed by filing notches on their guns for their victims.

Mexican standoff

Getting away alive from any serious difficulty. The Mexican has never had the reputation, among the cowboys, for being a sticker in a fight. They claim that, if he does not win quickly in a gun battle or if he finds much opposition, he leaves in a hurry.

Mexican strawberries

A slang name for dried beans.

mid-air dance

A hanging.

milk pitcher

A cow giving milk.

miller

One who tends the windmills on a ranch.

milling

The marching of cattle in a compact circle. This formation is resorted to in stopping stampedes. As the cattle mill in a circle, they wind themselves up into a narrowing mass which becomes tighter and tighter until finally it is so tight they can no longer move. When the same action takes place with horses, it is spoken of as *rounding-up*, the term *milling* being reserved strictly for cattle.

MILLING

See merry-go-round in high water, milling.

mill rider

One whose duty it is to keep the windmills on the ranch in repair.

minin' for lead

Probing for a bullet in a wounded person.

misty beyond

A cowboy's reference to death, something he does not fully understand.

mixed cattle

Cattle of various grades, ages, and sexes.

mixed herd

A herd of mixed sexes.

mix the medicine

Ability to cope with any situation.

moan

Sometimes used as a bucking term. As a rider mounts a bronc, another cowboy may give such useless warnings as "Look out, he's goin' to moan with you!"

moccasin mail

During trapper days, when one party preceded another, the leading party left messages of warning or reassurance by tying in a tree a moccasin in which the message was placed. Later, when cowmen on the trail left similar messages in the sand or in trees, they still spoke of them by this name.

moccasin telegraph

The grapevine system of information on the plains (W. S. Campbell [Stanley Vestal] to R.F.A.).

mochila (mo-chee'lah)

Spanish, meaning *knapsack*. A large piece of leather covering the saddle and put on after the saddle is cinched on the horse. It has a hole cut for the horn to go through and a narrow slit to let the cantle slip through. The contraption is

virtually obsolete now, but was frequently used in the early days, especially in California. The term was originally used in Pony Express days with reference to the mail pouches built into the skirts of the saddle.

mocho (mo'cho)

From the Spanish *desmochar (desmo-char')*, to decapitate or cut off; also *cropped, dishonored*. An animal which has lost part of its ear or tail is called a *mocho*; also a gotched or droop-horned animal.

mockey

A wild mare.

MONEY

See blow in, bonanza, cowboy change, dinero, down to his last chip, dust, fightin' wages, get-away money, gold colic, grass-bellied with spot cash, grass money, hard money, out of the money, savin' money for the bartender, short bit, time, wallow in velvet.

monkey nose

A slang name for a tapadero, which takes this name from its shape—a short, turned-up front.

monkey style

A riding term. In riding monkey style, the rider seizes the horn of the saddle with one or both hands, pushes himself sideways out of the saddle, and standing in one stirrup, with the knee on the outside rigid, and his other leg, resting midway between hip and knee, across the seat of the saddle. His flexed knee-joint and both hip-joints absorb the shock. (Philip A. Rollins, *The Cowboy* [New York, Charles Scribner's Sons, 1936], 312.)

Monkey-Ward cowboy

One wearing a mail-order outfit, and having little or no range experience.

Montgomery Ward woman sent west on approval

A homely woman. The cowman has his own unique expressions for this lack of beauty. Roarin' Edens spoke of a woman he considered shy of beauty by saying, "She had a face built for a hackamore." Dutch Roeder spoke of a certain lady whose beauty he did not admire with the statement that "she ain't nothin' for a drinkin' man to look at." Another puncher, speaking of a woman of considerable heftiness, said that she "only needed four more pounds o' lard to git into a sideshow," while Rowdy Bibbs spoke of another as being "uglier'n a Mexican sheep."

montura (mon-too'rah)

Spanish, meaning *horse intended for the saddle;* also *saddle, trappings,* and *accoutrements* of horses. The American occasionally uses it to mean his saddle.

moon-eyed

Said of a horse with white, glassy eyes.

moonlight 'em

To night ride for cattle.

moonlight roping

Brush cattle lie out in the brush in daytime and come out to little clearings to feed at night. On moonlight nights the cowman takes advantage of this habit, and his work is called moonlight roping.

moonshinin'

Working on roundup in a country so rough that packs have to be used in place of chuck wagons; also a night drive and a dry camp.

more guts than you could hang on a fence

Said of one with unusual courage.

more lip than a muley cow

Said of one who talks too much.

More straw!

The call of the branders for more calves to be brought to the branding fire.

more wrinkles on his horns

Said of one who has become older and wiser. This saying came from the fact that the wild cattle of the brush and brakes were horn-wrinkled from old age reached through the freedom bought by wisdom.

Mormon blanket

A quilt made from scraps of faded overalls and jumpers.

Mormon brakes

A tree tied behind a wagon to retard its speed downhill. This device was first used by Mormon pioneers in crossing the San Bernado Mountains in 1850.

Mormon dog

A tin can filled with rocks, used in place of dogs in some sections of the Northwest to scare cattle from their hiding place in the rough country.

Mormon tangle

A squaw hitch, a packer's knot.

moros

A horse of bluish color.

morral (mor-rahl')

Spanish for a food bag for horses. This fiber bag is carried on the saddle horn when the rider is going on a trip and is riding a grain-fed horse. The word is widely used in the cattle country, and the bag is also called a *nose bag.*

mossy-horn

A Texas longhorn steer, six or more years old, whose horns have become wrinkled and scaly; also called a *moss horn.* The term sometimes is slangily applied to old cowmen.

Mother-Hubbard loop

An extra-large loop.

Mother-Hubbard saddle

An early-day saddle, the first improvement upon the Mexican saddle, which consisted of little more than a tree and stirrup leathers. The Mother-Hubbard had a housing like the mochila, an almost square piece of leather with a hole for the horn and a slit for the cantle, the whole being detachable. Later this was made a permanent part of the saddle, and was designed to give more comfort to both horse and rider.

mother up

Said when female stock claim their young.

motte

A clump of trees.

mount

The number of horses assigned to a rider for his personal use during his stay at the ranch (as noun); to climb astride a horse (as verb). The number of horses assigned a rider depends largely upon the size of the ranch and the kind of country to be worked. Seven to ten head is an average mount, and in this number is included one or two broncs which the cowboy rides on circle to get them gradually used to cow work. The word *mount* is usually used in sections which employ the term *remuda* in speaking of the band of saddle horses. In the northern, or *cavvy*, country personal horses are called the *string*.

mountain boomer

One of cattle of the hilly country; also a species of large mountain lizard.

mountain oyster

A testicle of a bull. Some find it a choice delicacy when roasted or fried.

MOUNTING

See changing mounts, cheeking, flying mount, fork, hairpin, Indian side of a horse, light, mount, off side, pony express mount, settin' on his arm, step across, take a run.

mouthy

One inclined to talk a great deal. Such a person is not usually held in high repute by the cowman. "The bigger the mouth the better it looks when shut" is cowman philosophy.

mover

One habitually moving from one range to another in a covered wagon, usually a squatter. Very commonly squatters, as one cowboy said, "had 'nough offspring to start a public school." Another cowman of my acquaintance once referred to such an outfit with, "By the number of descendants he's got he musta been a Bishop in Utah."

moving camp

When a roundup camp is to be moved, the wagon boss gives instructions which no one but a cowhand familiar with the country could understand. The nighthawk drives up the remuda early. Saddle horses are caught and saddled, and the rest of the horses are left to graze near by. The rope corral is coiled and put into the wagon, beds are rolled and piled into it, too. Every cowhand finds something to do, or he is not a cowboy. Some harness the cook's teams while others help him pack and stow his pots and utensils.

When everything is ready, the cook crawls upon his wagon seat and is handed the lines by a thoughtful cowhand, who, before he realizes the lines are out of his hands, sees the cook herding his half raw broncs across the rough, roadless country. The mess wagon is rattling and swaying behind that running team until he wonders how the outfit holds together. By the time the cowboys reach the new camp at noon, the cook will have camp set up and a hot meal waiting for them.

movin' sheep

When cowboys ran sheep over a cliff or off the range during a war between sheep and cattle factions.

mozo (mo'tho)

Spanish, meaning *a young man, an assistant*. Americans usually use the word in speaking of the assistant of a pack train.

muck-a-muck

Cayuse Indian jargon for food. Sometimes used by cowboys of the Northwest.

mug

To bulldog a calf.

mujer (moo-herr')

A girl or young lady. The cowboy uses this word for color and variety when speaking of his girl.

mulada (moo-lah'dah)

A drove or herd of mules. Occasionally used by Americans as a convenience, since it is shorter than *mule herd*, or *herd of mules*.

mule-ears

Boots made with pull-on straps at the top; also a slang name for tapaderos, taking this name from their shape.

mule-hipped horse

One with hips that slope too much.

mulero (moo-lay'ro)

A mule driver; also called *a mule skinner*—mules are always skinned, never driven.

MULES

See Arizona nightingale, burro, desert canary, hard-tail, hatajo, head-and-tail string, knobhead, long-eared chuck wagon, mulata, pack mule, prospector's compass, Rocky Mountain canary.

mule's breakfast

A straw bed.

muley

A hornless cow. Being handicapped in defending herself from other cattle, she beds down at night on the outside edge of the herd away from the horned stuff. Coming thus under the cowboy's personal observation as he circles the herd, she is either "cussed" or called something endearing by him. The cowhand does not like to drive muley cattle because they jam together, suffer from the heat, and lose more weight than horned cattle. Then, too, they cause him to use the greatest patience. (J. Evetts Haley, *XIT Ranch* [Chicago, Lakeside Press, 1929], 192.)

muley saddle

One without a horn.

music roots

A Westerner's name for sweet potatoes.

mustang

A wild horse, restricted to the unmixed variety (as noun). From the Spanish *mesteño*, which comes from *mesta*, meaning a group of horse raisers. The suffix *eno* means *belonging to*, and so the horses that escaped from the early *mestas* and ran wild were *mesteños*, or mustangs. To catch mustangs (as verb).

mustanger

(Spanish, *mesteñero*) A man engaged in catching mustangs for a livelihood.

mustangler

A herder of mustangs.

mustard the cattle

To stir them up and get them heated, or excited.

mutton puncher

Cowboy's humorous term to describe a sheepherder.

N

"You can judge a man by the hoss he rides"

narrow at the equator

Hungry. I heard one puncher say that his "stomach was so shrunk it wouldn't chamber a liver-pill," and another that his "tapeworm was hollerin' for fodder."

navvy

A Navajo Indian pony, which is held to be about the poorest specimen of horseflesh on earth.

necking

This word, in range lingo, has a very different meaning from that which is used today in metropolitan circles. On the range, an unruly cow or one with roving disposition will often be *necked* or tied to a more tractable animal. This practice was especially resorted to in the days of the longhorn. After the two animals had worn themselves out trying to go in different directions at the same time, the wilder one was enough subdued to move along in company of its fellows. A good neck animal is valued highly by its owner.

neck meat or nothin'

The cowboy's equivalent to *whole hog or nothing* (William MacLeod Raine to R.F.A.).

neck oil

Slang name for whiskey.

neck-reiner

A horse trained to turn at the slightest pressure of the reins on his neck.

necktie social

A lynching, a hanging.

needle-gun

A rifle used on the frontier and called this because of its long firing pin which detonated the powder by plunging through the paper cartridge to strike the primer at the base of the bullet.

needs a wet-nurse

Said of an irresponsible or ignorant person.

Nellie

An old skinny cow or steer.

nester

A squatter who settles on state or government land. This term is applied with contempt by the cattleman of the Southwest to the early homesteaders who began tilling the soil in the range country. Viewed from some ridge, the early nester's home, as he cleared his little patch of brush and stacked it in a circular form to protect his first feed patch from range cattle, looked like a gigantic bird's nest. The cowboy, ever quick to catch resemblances, mentioned it to the next man he met, and the name spread and stuck to every man that settled on the plains to till the soil. (John M. Hendrix, "Feedin'," *West Texas Today* [March, 1936], 6.)

nesting

Homesteading.

never-sweat

A slang name for the Mexican.

new ground

An occasional name for a tenderfoot.

nice kitty

Occasional nickname for a skunk.

nickel-plated

The cowboy's term for the best in anything, from the nickel-plated decorations upon his person and riding gear to a well-dressed woman.

nicking

Another term the mustanger used in speaking of *creasing* a horse. See *creasing*.

nigger brand

A galled sore on a horse's back caused by careless riding (as noun); to ride so as to cause such sores (as verb).

nigger-catcher

A small, slotted leather flap on one or both sides of the saddle, usually at the base of the fork or cantle, if a two-cinched saddle. Its purpose is to hold the long, free end of the latigo through the slit when cinched up.

nigger-heeled

Said of a horse whose front toes turn out with the heels in.

nigger horse

One of black color.

nigger-in-a-blanket

A cowboy dessert, usually made of raisins in dough.

night drive

The trailing of cattle at night.

night guard

The watching of the cattle herd at night. Each man in camp, except the cook and the wrangler, must serve his turn. Usually there were two men to each guard for the average herd. Upon reaching the bed-ground, they rode in opposite directions as they circled the herd. This answered the double purpose of keeping the men separated and having a man looking each way so that no animal could slip away unnoticed in the dark. Two punchers riding side by side and talking are bound to neglect their job. If things went smoothly, they kept this riding up until they were relieved.

This was truly a job for a man "with fur on his brisket" on stormy nights when it was so dark "he couldn't find his nose with both hands." He had no stars to comfort him and could not even strike a match. If the cattle were extremely nervous, he had to be equally extremely cautious. As one cowhand put it, "You had to ride a mile to spit." On pleasant nights the work was not so hard, but even then the cowboy must stay in the saddle all the time, and the hours seemed long and lonesome.

When working with the roundup or with a trail herd, the cowhand did not get much sleep, and what he did get was interrupted by his having to take his turn at night guard. But after he was on the job a while, he rarely needed to be wakened. Sleeping with his ear to the ground, he could hear the rider coming off herd when he was still a great distance away, and by the time he reached camp, the new guard was ready to take his place.

night-hawk

A person who herds saddle horses at night—one of those fellows who is said to have "swapped his bed for a lantern." Though his duties, keeping the saddle horses from straying too far away, are identical with those of the day wrangler, colloquial usage causes the day man to *wrangle* horses, and the night-hawk to *herd* them. (Philip A. Rollins, *The Cowboy* [New York, Charles Scribner's Sons, 1936], 220.)

Some outfits use only one wrangler and have no night-hawk. The job is a lonely one, and it is hard for the night-hawk to keep from dozing in the saddle, because the sleep he gets in the daytime at a noisy camp makes him long for a softer job. If the horses are quiet, and he stands in with the cook, he may sneak in and get a cup of coffee from the pot which is kept on the coals for the night herders when they change shifts.

If the night is dark, he is apt to lose a few horses and will be late bringing up the remuda at daylight. Then he catches it from the boss, for no matter how good his excuse, it has no room with the man in charge.

night herd

To take charge of cattle on the bed-ground.

night herder

A cowhand whose immediate duty it is to herd cattle at night.

night horse

A horse picketed so that he can be in-stantly caught for night use. A good night horse is of a special type, and in the days of the open range was one of the most essential horses. He is selected for his sure-footedness, good eyesight, and sense of direction. He must not be high-strung, but must be gentle, unexcitable, and intelligent. He is never used except for night work, and during stampedes much depends on him. He holds his rider's life in his ability to see, run, dodge, and keep his footing. He will see an animal straying from the herd and turn it back without guidance, and he can find his way back to camp on the darkest night. Every cowman loves his night horse and prizes him beyond price.

night mare

An humorous name for the night horse, though it is never a mare.

no beans in the wheel

An expression meaning that there are no cartridges in the cylinder of a gun.

no breakfast forever

Said of one caught in a prairie fire.

no medicine

No information upon a subject.

norther

A driving gale from the north that hurtles over the Southwest, and, coming into collision with preceding warm, moist breezes from the Gulf of Mexico, causes a sudden and extreme drop in temperature. What is called a blizzard in the rest of the West is called a *norther* in Texas and the Southwest. As one cowhand at Amarillo, Texas, said, "They jes' pour off the North Pole with nothin' to stop 'em but a bob-wire fence and it's full o' knot-holes."

nose-bag

A morral; also slang name for an eating-house.

no-see-ums

What the Indian called the buffalo gnats because they are so small, and the cowboy adopted the name.

nose paint

Slang name for whiskey. One cowhand spoke of another at a bar "paintin' his nose with cow-swallers o' that stuff that cures snake bites."

notch in his tail

Said of a horse which has killed a man.

no time

If a contestant in a calf-roping or bulldogging contest fails within the allotted time, he is given *no time*. These sad words have wrecked many a contestant's hopes for a chance at final money.

nubbin'

Another slang name for the saddle horn.

nursey

The name, given in ridicule, to the driver of the old-time calf wagon used on trail drives. What the driver answered when called this was salty, but unprintable.

nutcrackers

A slang name for teeth.

O

"Another man's life don't make no soft pillow at night"

ocean wave

Trick roping, which consists in filiping a noose backward and forward in an undulating movement.

off herd

Not at the time on duty with the herd.

off his feed

Said of one who looks or feels bad.

off his mental reservation

Said of a weak-minded person.

OFFICERS

See great seizer, John Law, lawdog, posse, redcoats, star-toter.

off side

The right side, because the horseman mounts from the left side.

off the reservation

This refers to Indians who had left their reservations for no good purpose; also to anyone speaking or acting out of turn (W. S. Campbell [Stanley Vestal] to R.F.A.).

oiler

A slang name for a Mexican.

oily bronc

A bad horse.

Oklahoma rain

A dust storm.

old cedar

A slang name for a gun; a gun with a cedar stock.

old man

The boss or owner of the outfit.

Old man him!

Throwing a looped rope over the neck or back of a wild bronc in a corner or crowded enclosure, moving him over and passing the free end of the rope through the loop, thus roping him anywhere one sees fit, for greater control and security.

old reliable

The cowman's pet name for his Sharps rifle, called this because it could always be depended upon.

old-timer

One who had lived in the country a long time. Most old-timers had had to fight many battles before the country became settled, and it could be said of many: "His scars was a regular war map." It was said of all good old-time Texans that they were "raised to vote the Democratic ticket, to love good whiskey, and hate Mexicans."

OLD-TIMER

See alkalied, don't travel like a colt no more, entitled to a warm corner, forty-niner, grissel-heel, old-timer.

old woman

Affectionate name for the cook, but said behind his back.

on circle

A roundup term. Cowboys on circle leave camp in a group but are turned off separately or in smaller groups by the ranch foreman to gather the cattle and drive them to a designated roundup ground. This ground is changed each day until the range has been covered.

one-eared bridle

One composed of a single broad strap with a slit in it which fits over one ear to keep it in place.

one-eyed scribe

Slang name for a six-gun.

one foot in the stirrup

An expression meaning, according to context, to do something half-heartedly, or to be ready for an emergency.

one-horse outfit

A small outfit or ranch.

one-man horse

A horse broken in such a way that he would let no one ride him except the man who had broken him.

on the Black Hills

An early expression which meant the driving of a man from his chosen range and attempting to push him so far north that his final destination would be the Bad Lands of the Dakotas, a place compared by the southern cowman with hell (C. L. Douglas, *Cattle Kings of Texas* [Dallas, Cecil Baugh Co., 1939], 40).

on the cuidado

Dodging the law; literally, *on the lookout.*

on the dodge

Another phrase for hiding from the law. A man on the dodge is usually, as Dewlap Burdick said, "one o' them fellers that keeps his hoss wonderin' at the hurry they're in, and he don't leave 'nough tracks to trip an ant."

ON THE DODGE

See among the willows, belly through the brush, fixin' for high ridin', gone to Texas, hankerin' to sniff Gulf breeze, head for the settin' sun, in the brush, lookin' over his shoulder, on the cuidado, on the dodge, on the lookout, on the scout, pull for the Rio Grande, ridin' the high-lines, running wild, summer name, stampede to the wild bunch, travels the lonesome places, two jumps ahead of the sheriff, whippin' a tired pony out of Texas.

on the drift

Looking for a job, aimlessly riding through the country.

on the hoof

Live cattle; also used in referring to cattle traveling by trail under their own power as against going by rail.

on their heads

Cattle, when grazing, are said to be standing on their heads.

on the lift

Said of an animal which is down and can not get up without help.

on the lookout

Dodging the law.

on the peck

Fighting mad. Jim Houston, in telling a yarn about being charged, while afoot in a corral, by a cow on the peck, said: "There wasn't no love-light in that cow's eyes as she makes for me. I fogs it across the corral like I'm goin' to a dance and she's scratchin' the grease off my pants at ever' jump. Seein' I can't make the fence in time, Brazos Gowdy jumps down and throws his hat in the old gal's face. Seein' a cowboy come apart in pieces like that makes her hesitate till I climbs the fence without losin' anything more'n some confidence, a lot o' wind, and a little dignity. Y'u can take it from me that a cow with a fresh-branded calf might be a mother, but she shore ain't no lady."

on the prod
Another phrase for *on the peck*. See *on the peck*.

on the scout
Synonymous with *on the dodge*.

on the warpath
Fighting mad. As one cowman said, "mad as a bear with two cubs and a sore tail."

on tick
On credit.

open a snap
To start a crooked gambling layout.

open brand
One not boxed with framing lines.

open-faced cattle
White-faced Herefords.

open heifer
One not spayed.

open range
Range not fenced.

open-range branding
The branding of calves or cattle on the open range away from corrals. This is done by the larger outfits, or in two other instances. First, it is sometimes done by rightful owners when they come across a calf that has been overlooked in the regular branding. To avoid a long drive back to headquarters, the cowboy will rope the calf, tie it down, build a fire, and brand it where he finds it. Second, it is frequently done by the rustler, especially if he is where he is not apt to be seen by some range rider.

It is more difficult to drive one or two head of cattle than a large herd, and a good cowman avoids driving his stock as much as possible, hence his recourse to branding on the open range. In the early days all branding was done in the open, but later it was looked upon with suspicion unless done in the presence of a regular roundup crew. (Editorial, "Branding in the Open," *Cattleman*, XIX, No. 10 [March, 1939], 45.)

open reins
Reins not tied together, each independent of the other. Most cowhands prefer open reins because if the horse falls or the rider is thrown, the reins will fall to the ground and the horse will step on them, giving the rider a chance to catch the horse.

open roundup
A roundup where the final bunching of cattle is not within a corral, but in the open.

open-shop pants
Slang name for chaps.

open stirrups
Stirrups without tapaderos, or toe-fenders.

open-toed holster
One with an open end, usually swung with a rivet.

open winter
A mild winter with no blizzards and storms.

OPPORTUNITY
See while the gate's still open.

op'ra
The riding of a wild horse, branding.

op'ra house
The top rail of the corral fence where one can watch the riding of a bucking horse. It is also a time-honored conference place for all true range men where they talk over things in true range style —using laconic phrases that state their meaning without frills or mental reservations and silences that carry their thoughts forward to the next utterance.

Oregon puddin' foot
A type of horse in the development of which a riding horse has been crossed with a draft horse, such as a Percheron or Clydesdale. This type was developed to some extent in Oregon for mountain work. Also called Oregon bigfoot.

orejano (o-ray-hah'no)
From the Spanish *oreja*, ear, literally *an eared animal*. The word really means *long-eared*, that is, not earmarked. An unbranded and unmarked animal, the term being used principally in California, Oregon, and Nevada.

otie

Short for coyote.

ought to be bored for the hollow horn

In the early days if an animal became ill, the sickness was pronounced a case of *hollow horn,* and as a cure a small hole was bored in the horn. From this practice the above saying was applied to persons who seemed to be feeble-minded. (J. Frank Dobie, *The Longhorns* [Boston, Little, Brown, 1941], 211.) One cowhand spoke of a feeble-minded person with, "The Lord poured in his brains with a teaspoon and somebody joggled His arm."

ought to be playin' with a string of spools

Said of one young or foolish; also of an ignorant or crazy person.

outer circle

The longer, outside circle on roundup, reaching to the outside limits of the territory to be "worked." As more territory is covered, the tougher horses are used.

outfit

This word has various meanings. It means, according to the context, all the people engaged in any one enterprise or living in any one establishment, a party of people traveling together, or the physical belongings of any person or group of persons. (Philip A. Rollins, *The Cowboy* [Charles Scribner's Sons, 1936], 201.)

outfox

The Westerner's word when he means *outsmart* or *outguess.*

outlaw

A horse which is particularly vicious and untamable, a wild cow or steer, a man who has committed deeds that have placed him on the wrong side of the law. He is a man who follows the western philosophy of "the best health resorts are the places unknown." Some of the early outlaws lived a life, as Charlie Russell said in *Trails Plowed Under,* "that'd make some o' them scary yellerbacked novels look like a primer."

OUTLAWS

See badman, bandido, black book, cabron, cash in his six-shooter, cat-eyed, gone to Texas, high-line rider, hired killer, hold-up man, hole up, killer, ladinos, long rider, outlaw, ridin' the owlhoot trail, road agent, short-trigger man, wanted, wild bunch.

out of the money

Said of a rodeo riding contestant who loses, either by being thrown, drawing an inferior horse, or breaking some rule.

outrider

One whose duty it is to ride about the range and keep a sharp lookout for anything that might happen to the detriment of his employer. While his duties are similar to the line rider's, unlike the line rider, who patrols a prescribed boundary, the outrider is commissioned to ride anywhere.

outriding

The outrider's activities.

outside man

A man who represents his brand at outside ranches during a general roundup. He is usually at the top of the cowboy profession and is a riding encyclopedia on brands and earmarks. His work is done in following the roundups of other ranges and turning back strays of his brand. His eye is so well trained that he can discover cattle belonging to his outfit in a vast, milling herd through a dust fog that an ordinary man could not see through. See *rep.*

over-bit

An earmark made by doubling the ear in and cutting a small piece, perhaps an inch, out of the upper part of the ear, an inch in length, and, perhaps one-third of an inch in depth.

over-hack

An earmark made by simply cutting down about an inch on the upper side of the ear.

over-half-crop

An earmark made by splitting the ear from the top, midway, about halfway back to the head and cutting off the upper half.

overhand toss

A roping term. A favorite method of catching horses in a corral. The only difference between it and the hooley-ann is that the hooley-ann turns over as the whirl is started, and the overhand toss turns over as it leaves the hand. The loop is fairly small, and, while held at shoulder height, the bottom part of it is kept swinging back and forth. When the throw is made, the loop is swung backward around the head and released toward the target. The loop is turned over as it is swung upward before it is let go, so that at the final moment the back of the hand is facing the left, thumb down. In this way, when the loop comes down, the honda is on the right instead of on the left. (W. M. French, "Ropes and Roping," *Cattleman*, XXVI, No. 12 [May, 1940], 17–30.)

overhead loop

A throw made by starting the whirl across the front of the thrower to the left, with two or three whirls around the head for momentum, then casting at the target by whirling the loop out in front as it comes across the right shoulder (W. M. French, "Ropes and Roping," *Cattleman*, XXVI, No. 12 [May, 1940], 17–30).

overo

This is a word given us by Argentina and used among breeders because no better English word has been found. It is used to distinguish color characteristics in the pinto horse, where the white spots on the body always begin at the belly and extend upward. The dark spots are usually smaller and more plentiful. See *tobiano*. (George M. Glendenning, "Overos and Tobianos," *Western Horseman*, VII, No. 1 [January–February, 1942], 12.)

over-round

An earmark made by cutting a half-circle from the top of the ear.

over-slope

An earmark made by cutting the ear about two-thirds of the way back from the tip, straight to the center of the ear at its upper side.

over-split

A simple split of the ear downward on the upper side.

over the willows

When the trail boss rode back to the place where the herd was being held up after he had viewed the turbulent river ahead and announced that it was "over the willows," he meant that it was at flood stage and there would be several hundred yards of swimming water.

owlhead

A horse that can not be trained to work or to be ridden.

ox-bow

The old style, large wooden stirrups.

ox-yokes

Another slang name for the stirrups mentioned above.

P

"A change of pasture sometimes makes the calf fatter"

pack

A bundle or bale (as noun); to carry (as verb). A cowman never carries anything, but packs it, as "packs a gun," "packs his saddle," and so on.

pack covers

Canvas sheets to roll packs in.

packs his gun loose

This expression means that the one spoken of is always ready for a gun fight.

pack mule
A mule used to carry packs of freight.

pack rat
A western rodent which always leaves something in exchange when he carries anything off (commonly called a *trade rat*), a petty thief; the term is also sometimes used to mean guides and packers.

packsaddle
A saddle used for carrying freight, camp equipment, and other materials.

packs a long rope
Said of a rustler.

pack train
A group of animals carrying packs of freight. One of the West's principal means of transportation in early days, especially in rough country.

padding out his belly
Said of one who eats at every opportunity.

paddle
The gait of a horse, in which he wings out with his front feet.

pail fed
Said of a calf raised on skimmed milk.

paint
A horse with irregular patterns of white with colored areas. It is a favorite with fiction writers, but fails to meet with much favor as a cow horse. Not being good for close, quick work, it does not develop into a cutting horse and is inclined to get the habit of fighting the bits.

Paint horses are very showy, and for this reason the cowboy does not object to having one in his string to use as his gallin' horse, but when it comes to real cow work, he prefers a solid-colored horse (John M. Hendrix, "Paints as Cow Horses," *Cattleman*, XXI, No. 6 [November, 1934], 13). An adage of the cow country is, "Color don't count if the colt don't trot."

painted cat
A name frequently given a woman of the frontier dance hall and bawdy house.

painter
The West's name for a panther, or mountain lion.

paint for war
To prepare to do battle, to lose one's temper.

paintin' his nose
Said of one getting drunk.

paint the tonsils
To drink whiskey. I once heard a cowhand speak of another's drinking by saying: "He's takin' the first layer off his tonsils."

paisano (pay-e-sah'no)
A road runner, a chaparral bird. The word is originally from *pais*, meaning *country*, and was applied to a fellow countryman or peasant.

palomilla (pah-lo-meel'lyah)
A milk-white or cream-colored horse with a white mane and tail.

palomino (pah-lo-mee'nah)
A dun-colored or golden horse with a white, silver, or ivory mane and tail.

pancake
The cowboy's contemptuous name for the small English riding saddle.

pants rats
What the cowboy calls body lice. When one of the hands of a certain Montana ranch came home after spending a week in an Indian camp, the boys decided that his clothes needed delousing. They made him strip and throw his clothes to them to be put into a pot of boiling water. When he quit throwing garments through the door, one of the boys yelled to find out if that was all, and the naked cowboy yelled back, "I can't go no deeper without a skinnin' knife."

Charlie Russell tells an amusing story about these insects. "It's one spring roundup, back in the early '80s," he wrote. "We're out on circle, and me and Pete's ridin' together. Mine's a center-fire saddle, and I drop back to straighten the blanket and set it. I ain't but a few minutes behind him, but the next I see Pete is on the bank of this creek, which didn't have no name then. He's off his hoss and has stripped his shirt off. With one boulder on the ground and another about the same size in his hand, he's poundin' the seams of his shirt. He's so busy he don't hear me when I ride up, and he's cussin' and swearin' to himself. I hear him mutter, 'I'm damned if this don't get some of the big ones!'

"Well, from this day on, this stream is known as Louse Creek." (Charles M. Russell, *Trails Plowed Under* [Garden City, Doubleday, Doran, 1935], 77.)

paper-backed

Physical weakness. Ben Langford spoke of one being "so weak he couldn't lick his upper lip," and I heard a cowhand of the Three T refer to another as being "so puny he couldn't pull my hat off."

parada (pah-rah'dah)

Synonymous with *main herd* and used principally in California, Oregon, and Nevada; sometimes used in referring to a herd of broken horses.

parada grounds

The location selected to work a herd of cattle; from *parar*, meaning *to stop, to detain*.

parflêche (par'flesh)

A Canadian-French word meaning the prepared hide of an animal, as of a buffalo dried on a frame after the hair has been removed. The cowboy uses this word in speaking of his poke, or warbag, and has changed it to *parflesh*. The word is sometimes used in the Northwest, but rarely in the Southwest.

parker

Bed comfort.

parlor gun

What the cowman calls a derringer or small gun. By this name he expresses his contempt for anything but a "man-sized gun."

parlor house

A house of the red-light district, one of the better houses which has a parlor. Cheaper and parlorless houses are *cribs*.

parrot-bill

A pistol with a semiround butt.

paesear (pah-say-ar')

Spanish, meaning *to walk slowly, to wander*. Commonly used in the Southwest as meaning to go some place leisurely, or to go on an inspection tour.

PARTNERSHIP

See cahoots, compadre, made of the same leather, throw in.

paso (pah'so)

A pass, a ford; a double-step, six feet.

pass in his chips

To die.

pass the buck

This common saying originated in the West in the late 1860's. In poker, during its early days, it was customary for the players to cut for deal, and the winner of the opening pot continued to deal until he lost, when the privilege then went to his conqueror. With the introduction of draw poker, it became the custom to pass the deal to the left after each hand.

On the western frontier this practice led to the custom of using a *buck*. It could be any object, but was usually a knife, and since most western men in those days carried knives with buckhorn handles, this name was adopted. The buck was placed in front of the dealer to mark the deal and was passed along at the conclusion of each pot. In some sections a player who did not wish to deal was permitted to ante and pass the buck. Thus the term became a slang expression for letting someone else perform a task originally imposed upon you, or letting someone else take the blame for an act. (Herbert Asbury, *Sucker's Progress* [New York, Dodd, Mead & Co., 1938], 28.)

pasture count

Counting cattle on the range or in a pasture without throwing them together for that purpose. The counters ride through the pasture counting each bunch of grazing cattle and drifting it back so that it does not get mixed with the uncounted cattle ahead. This method of counting is usually done at the request, and in the presence, of a representative of the bank that holds the papers against the herd.

Pastures

See democrat pasture, grazing permit, pony pasture, put to grass, rustle the pasture, shipping trap, starve-out, Texas gate.

Paul Pry

A meddler.

paunched

Shot in the stomach. One cowhand spoke of another's being paunched with, "He got a pill in his stomach he couldn't digest."

peacemaker

This 1873 model Colt became the most famous revolver in the world and was the favorite of many famous gunmen. It was originally chambered for the .45 caliber, center-fire, black-powder cartridge, but almost immediately after its introduction was chambered for the .44 Winchester (.44–.40) center-fire cartridge, and was used as a companion arm to the equally famous Winchester model 1873 rifle.

peal (pay-ahl')

A sock, foot, or stocking (as noun); also a worthless person; to rope an animal by the hind foot (as verb). This throw is commonly used in "stretching out" a cow or steer—never a horse—that has been roped by the head or neck. When adroitly cast, the loop turns so as to form a figure eight, and one hind foot is caught in one half of the figure and the other in the other half. (J. Frank Dobie, *Vaquero of the Brush Country* [Dallas, Southwest Press, 1929], 263.)

pearl diver

A slang name for a dishwasher in a restaurant.

pecker-neck

A saddle horse, untrained for cow work.

Pecos (Pay'cos)

After the Pecos River. To shoot a man and roll his body into the river.

Pecos Bill

A liar, a mythical character of the West.

Pecos swap

A trade made without consent or knowledge of the other interested party, to steal.

peddler of loads

A teller of tall tales. It did not take much persuading to start a cowman on a "campaign against truth," and he "could color up a story redder than a Navajo blanket."

peeler

One who skins, sometimes called *stripper;* also short for *bronc peeler.*

peeling

Skinning the hide off cattle, riding a rough horse.

peewees

Boots with short tops, today the most popular style of boot found upon the range.

Carl B. Livingston, of Santa Fé, New Mexico, tells the following story of the origin of the short-top boot: "A group of the best ropers and riders of the plains went on a roping expedition to South America in 1905. Among these were some of the champions of the world. . . . The American cowboy by far excelled the *gaucho* of the Pampas in roping. They took in a great deal of money at their roping exhibitions, but always, unfortunately, there was some law of which they had violated, and would have to pay out immediately all they had taken in.

"The papers in the states were full of the exploits of the North Americans, as they were called. Among the events exhibited was the American cowboy's method of throwing a yearling, plunging at the end of a lariat. The orthodox American cowboy method was to grab the yearling by an ear with one hand and by the flank with the other hand, while the yearling was bouncing in the air, catch him on the bounce, and then bust him on the ground. These yearlings were wild and strong and the boys did not always throw them on the first bounce. Sometimes the bawling yearlings, in pitching, would run a hoof down a cowboy's high-top bootleg, thus the legs of the boots became ripped and torn. The boys, about whom the papers had made over so much, were at least returning home a great success in their adventures, but sadly low in finances.

"Heroes could not come home with ragged boots. They simply whacked off the tops, and laced the edges together with string. When the crowd came stomping into Old Sol's Lone Wolf Saloon, in Carlsbad, they were shockingly asked by their comrades who had stayed at home, 'Where'd you git such funny boots?' The adventurers reared back their shoulders, indignantly stuck out their chests, and replied simply, 'Them's the style!' And so they have become the customary height of boot from that day to this, for these boys who had roped all over North and South America, were princes of the cowboy profession, and set the styles." (Carl B. Livingston, "Development of the Cattle Industry in New Mexico," *Cattleman*, XXIV, No. 12 [May, 1938], 21–31.)

pegging
Ramming one horn of a downed steer into the ground to hold him down. This is not allowed in contests.

peg pony
A saddle horse which, when galloping in one direction, can stop short in his tracks, change his direction, and instantly bound off on a new course. He is highly valued by the cowman, especially for cutting work. Also called a *peg horse* or *pegger*.

pelados (pay-lah'dos)
From the Spanish *pelar*, meaning *to remove the hair or skin, to cut or pull out the hair, to strip one of his possessions*. The border American uses this word as a name for the Mexican, by whom it is greatly resented. (Harold W. Bentley, *Dictionary of Spanish Terms in English* [Columbia University Press, 1932], 178.)

pelter
A slang name for the saddle.

pepper-and-salt rope
A hair rope made with alternating strands of black and white horsehair.

pepper-gut
Slang name for the Mexican.

PERSONAL EQUIPMENT
See boughten bag, bring-'em-close glasses, coffin, concha, ditty, dofunnies, go-easter, maleta, Mormon blanket, parflêche, plunder, poke, poncha, quirt, quisto, teguas, thirty years' gathering, tucker bag, war-bag, wipes, yannigan bag.

PERSUADE
See rib up.

persuader
Slang name for a six-gun; also a spur.

pestle-tail
A wild horse with brush or burr tail.

petalta (pay-tal'tah)
A herd of cattle rounded up for cutting out.

petate (pay-tah'tay)
A square piece of matting made of palm to place over packs to protect them from rain.

petmakers
Slang name for spurs.

phildoodle
A drugstore cowboy. One who imitates the cowboy in dress and speech.

picked brand
Accomplished by picking out tufts of hair in the lines desired by the aid of a jackknife. It is seldom done except by dishonest men until they can get the animal out of the country, as it is only a temporary marking.

picket
To stake a horse.

picket pin
A wooden stake, driven into the ground, to which an animal is picketed. When staking night horses is the practice, stake pins are carried as part of the chuck-wagon equipment. If the horseman has no picket pin, he digs a hole in the ground, ties a knot in the end of his rope and buries it, then tamps the dirt closely around it. It is surprising how well it will hold.

picket rope
A rope used for picketing horses. The

cowboy will not use his lariat for staking if he can help it. He has to tie an extra knot to make a slip noose to keep from choking the horse, and this causes a kink that makes the rope unfit for any other use.

Pick him up!

A cry given by the judges at rodeos to pick up a rider after his time is up or the horse has bucked himself out. It means to catch the animal so that the rider can dismount and the saddle can be removed. Also the expressions *take him up* or *cage him up* are used.

pickin' daisies

Said of a thrown rider.

picking a sleeper

Frequently on the range an animal is found whose brand is difficult to decipher, or it is hard to tell whether the animal has ever been branded or not. This occurs especially in winter when the animal's hair is long and rough. When an animal of this sort is found, it is caught and held down while men pluck the hair around the brand. Frequently a brand will be discernible to the touch, but has not been burned deep enough to give lasting legibility. Again, some rustler may have hair branded the animal and not been able to return to pick it up until the hair had grown out again. The operation of picking such a brand is known as *picking a sleeper*. (Editorial, "Picking a Sleeper," *Cattleman*, XIX, No. 10 [March, 1933], 35.)

pick up his hind feet

To rope an animal by the hind feet.

pick up his toes

To rope an animal by the front feet.

pick-up man

A horseman who stands ready to take up the horse ridden by a rodeo contestant when the ride is over.

piebald

Spotted, painted, the color of a horse, horses with patches of white and black colors.

pie-biter

A horse which secretly forages the camp kitchen to indulge his acquired tastes.

pie-box

A slang name for the chuck wagon, perhaps in wishful thinking.

pie wagon

A trailer used behind the chuck wagon.

pig

Nickname for the saddle horn.

piggin' string

A short rope used for hog-tying. See *hoggin' rope.*

pig's vest with buttons

Salt pork, or sowbelly.

piker

In faro, one who makes small bets all over the "layout." From this, the term developed into meaning a cheap sport and a man without courage.

piket (pee-kay')

A slang name for a skunk.

piled

Thrown from a horse. After making a very hard ride, one cowhand of the TU Ranch said, "After that ride all I needed to make me a cripple was a handful o' lead pencils."

pile-driver

A horse which humps its back and comes down with all four legs as stiff as ramrods when it bucks.

pile it on

To throw a rope upon.

pilgrim

One new to the country. The word was first applied to the imported hot-blooded cattle, but later was more commonly used as reference to a tenderfoot.

pilot

A man whose duty it is to guide the roundup wagons over the roadless plains and brakes to the next camping place. He has to be well acquainted with the country and to use good judgment concerning the location of the next camp with regard to water and suitable surroundings for working cattle.

pill roller
Nickname for a doctor.

pimple
The cowboy's contemptuous name for the little eastern riding saddles.

piñon
Dwarf pine.

pins crape on the kid
Said when a rustler kills the mother cow to steal her calf.

pinto
From the Spanish *pintar (peen'tah)*, meaning *spot* or *mark* by which a thing is known. A piebald or spotted horse.

pinto chaps
Hair chaps, the hair made spotted by sewing in pieces of another color.

pinwheel
When a horse leaps forward in an upward jump, and turns, feet in air, and lands on his back. A horse that will do this is very rare. Used as a gun term, it means that the gun is held in virtual firing position except that the forefinger is not in the trigger guard. The gun is fliped into the air so that it revolves and the butt drops naturally into the palm of the hand. The movement is started by throwing the butt down with a jerk of the wrist, with the muzzle up.

pioneer bucker
A horse which bucks in circles and figure eights, called this because he is always seeking new territory.

pirooting
Meandering, "foolin' 'round."

pistol
A young rider, inexperienced hand. The cowboy never calls his gun a pistol.

pistol whip
To whip one with the barrel of a six-gun. Sug Morgan, speaking of such an incident, said, "I let 'im feel my gun where the hair was thinnest and put a knot on his head that'd sweat a rat to run around." Some writers of westerns have their heroes grasping the guns by the barrels and clubbing with the butts.

No one but a greener would pull this stunt. What do they think the villain would be doing all the time it takes the hero to get hold of the barrel?

pitching
The Texans' name for bucking.

pitchin' fence-cornered
Said when a horse leaves the ground while headed in one direction and lands in another at approximately a forty-five degree angle.

pitted
When cattle are caught in a corner or draw during a snowstorm.

plain trail
Clearly visible sign in trailing.

plant
To bury. A beautiful sentiment was expressed at many early-day cowboy burials. The dead man's horse, fully saddled, was led beside the grave. There the horse was silently unsaddled from the off, or wrong, side—a solemn announcement that none of the mourners were the dead man's equal in equestrian skill.

play a lone hand
To do or live alone.

playin' a hand with his eyes shut
Said of one taking a chance.

playin' cat's cradle with his neck
Said of one hanged.

pliersman
A name given in derision by the rustler to the loyal cowboy who works for a fenced ranch.

plow-boying
Riding with a rein in each hand and pulling the horse's head around with one rein while the other is pulled against the neck.

plow chaser
A slang name for the farmer.

plow-handle
Slang name for a six-gun, taking this name from the shape of the stock found on the Colt single action army revolver

116

made in one piece of walnut or other hardwood and polished smooth. This gun was designed so that it recoiled freely in the hand, thus making a smooth stock preferable, for the gun was muzzle heavy and its almost perfect balance allowed it to slip back to shooting position after the recoil.

PLOWING
See lookin' at a mule's tail, turnin' the grass upside down.

plug
A broken-down horse (as noun); to shoot one with a gun (as verb).

plumb cultus
An expression meaning as bad as they make them, cussedness. *Cultus* comes from a Chinook Indian word, meaning *worthless*.

plunder
Personal belongings of odds and ends.

pocket hunter
A prospector, one who searches for pockets of gold or silver.

poco (po'ko)
Little, scanty, a small amount. Often used by southwestern cowboys in connection with such words as *tiempo (time)* and *malo (bad)*.

poddy
An occasional name for an orphan calf, usually big-bellied and undernourished.

point rider
One of the men who ride at the head of a column of cattle on the trail and act as pilots. They usually work in pairs, and when they desire to change the course of the herd, they will ride abreast the foremost cattle, one on each side of the column. Then they will quietly veer in the desired direction, and the leading cattle will swerve away from the horseman approaching them and toward the one going away from them. This is the honored post of the drive, and also the most dangerous and responsible. These men were the first to swim rivers and the first to meet attacks by Indians. See *lead men*.

poke
Sack in which the cowboy carries his "plunder." The term is rarely used except in the Northwest; in other sections the sacks are called *war-sacks* or *war-bags*.

pole team
The horses nearest the vehicle when two or more teams are used.

poncho
A covering made by cutting a hole for the head through the middle of a blanket, and used by Mexicans and cowboys as a protection against the weather.

pony beeves
Young cattle about two years old, the right age for fattening for market.

pony express mount
A running mount made by leaping into the saddle without touching the feet to the stirrups.

pony pasture
A small pasture used for saddle horses.

pooch
The name of a dish made of tomatoes, sugar, and bread.

pool camp
The roundup camp of several ranches which have thrown in together.

pool roundup
When cattlemen over a wide range of territory pool their resources and men for a general rounding up of cattle.

POOR
See bed-slat ribs, bone-yard, buzzard-bait, crow bait, get rid of his leaf lard, had a bilious look, just a ball of hair, rusties, shad bellied, slab-sided.

poor doe
Lean, tough venison of any kind.

port
The raised portion of a bit.

posse
A band of men organized to run down lawbreakers. One reformed outlaw told of a posse keeping on his trail until he "got saddle sores."

possum-belly

A rawhide hanging beneath the wagon bed for carrying fuel. See *cuña*.

postage stamp

A ridiculous name for the little riding saddle used by Easterners.

post hay

Referring to the act of tying a horse to a post and then not bringing feed to the animal.

pot

Cowboy's name for a derby hat.

pot-bellied

Bloated; also called *pot-gutted*.

pothole

A bog hole.

pothole rider

A bog rider. See *bog rider*.

pothook

A hook used for holding pots over the fire.

pothooks

A slang name for the cook.

potluck

As used by the cowman and other frontiersmen, this means food contributed by a guest. To bring potluck is to bring food with one.

pot-rack outfit

A ranch crew which uses no tents on roundup when it is the custom of the country to do so.

potros (po'tros)

Young horses, up to the time when they change their milk teeth, or about four and one-half years of age; colts, fillies.

pot rustler

Another slang name for the cook.

pounding 'em on the back

A term used with reference to the duty of riding drag.

poverty cattle

Feeders.

powder burnin' contest

A gun battle. After participating in such a fight, Carey Nelms said, "After that powder burnin' contest my gun was emptier'n a banker's heart." He did not get hit, but one bullet came so close it "raised a blister."

Powder River! Let 'er buck!

A shout of encouragement, a password, a cry of derision. This is a very familiar cry throughout the cattle country of the Northwest. During World War I, in the Argonne, it was the battle cry of the Ninety-first Division, and it might be said that it has been heard around the world.

While in Cheyenne, Wyoming, I met Agnes Wright Spring, a member of the editorial staff of the *Wyoming Stockman-Farmer*, who gave me a story of the origin of this famous phrase, originally told by E. J. Farlow, a former cowman mayor of Lander. According to Mr. Farlow, the saying originated after a roundup in the fall of 1893, when a herd of cattle was being driven to Caspar:

"The night we camped on the divide between the head of Poison Creek, near where the town of Hiland now stands, and the headwaters of 'Dry Powder' River, I told the boys we would water the herd in Powder River at about 10 o'clock the next morning.

"None of them had ever seen Powder River and they were all excited. In the morning when they were catching horses for the day, I called out to them to get their swimming horses as we were going to cross Powder River several times before night. Missouri Bill Shultz, who had already roped his horse, turned him loose, muttering that 'this damn buckskin couldn't even wade a river.'

"About 10 o'clock the lead of the herd reached the river and it was almost dry, the water standing in holes and barely running from one hole to the other. The herd followed down stream for a distance of about two miles before they were watered, and we crossed it many times.

"When Missouri Bill saw it he looked at it very seriously for some time and then said, 'So this is Powder River,' and that night in camp he told us he had heard of Powder River and now he had seen Powder River, and he kept referring to Powder River nearly every day until we reached Caspar which we did in twenty-eight days trailing.

"In the evening before we were going to load for shipping, and the cattle were all bedded down near the stockyards, the boys all adjourned to the saloon for a social drink, and Missouri Bill said 'Boys, come and have a drink on me. I've crossed Powder River.' They had the drinks, then a few more and were getting pretty sociable.

"When Missouri Bill again ordered he said to the boys, 'Have another drink on me, I've swum Powder River,' this time with a distinct emphasis on the words *Powder River.* 'Yes, sir, by God, Powder River,' with a little stronger emphasis. When the drinks were all set up he said, 'Well, here's to Powder River, let 'er buck!'

"Soon he grew louder and was heard to say 'Powder River is comin' up—eeyeeep!—Yes sir, Powder River is risin',' and soon after with a yip and a yell, he pulls out his old six-gun and throwed a few shots through the ceiling and yelled, 'Powder River is up, come an' have 'nother drink.' Bang! Bang! 'Yeow, I'm a wolf and it's my night to howl.' Powder River is out of 'er banks. I'm wild and wooly and full o' fleas, and never been curried below the knees.'

"Bill was loaded for bear, and that is the first time I ever heard the slogan, and from there it went around the world."

Many a cowboy, exuberant with whiskey, brought to light his own version, such as: "Powder River, let 'er buck—she's a mile wide—an inch deep—full o' dust and flat fish—swimmin' holes for grasshoppers—cross 'er anywhere—yeouuhh—yippee—she rolls up hill from Texas."

powders
Orders from the boss.

powwow
From the Indian, meaning a conjuration performed for the cure of diseases, attended with noise and confusion, and often with dancing; any meeting, as for a conference, attended by confusion. The cowman uses the word to refer to a "get together" for a conference.

prairie coal
Dried cow chips used for fuel.

prairie dog court
Kangaroo court.

prairie feathers
What the cowboy calls beds stuffed with hay.

prairie lawyer
A name frequently given to a coyote because it makes so much chatter.

prairie pancakes
Dried cow chips.

prairie schooner
The wagon of the early days, the canvas cover of which suggested a schooner under full sail.

prairie strawberries
A slang name for beans.

prairie wool
A slang name for grass.

PRANKS
See cut a big gut, cut a shine, horseplay, prairie dog court, rim firing a horse.

prayer book
What the cowboy calls his book of cigaret papers.

prayin' cow
A cow rises from the ground rear end first. By the time her hindquarters are in a standing position, her knees are on the ground in a praying attitude. It is when she is in this position that the name *prayin' cow* is suggested to the cowboy.

presidente (pray-se-den'tay)
An occasional name for the big boss of the ranch. From the Spanish, meaning *a local government official.*

PRISON
See hoosgow, makin' hair bridles, skookum house, tiger.

private cuss words
An individual creation of the profanity

for which the public accords a sort of copyright to the inventor. The words may not even be profane, but the public soon learns that the user only releases them when he's "madder'n a drunk squaw," and they can be so effective as to "take the frost out of a zero mornin'."

prod pole
A pole about six feet long, with a steel spike on the end and with a heavy handle. It is used to prod cattle into stockcars. Near the business end and extending out a short distance at right angles from the pole is driven a flat-headed screw. This screw is twisted into the matted end of a steer's tail when he is down and refuses to get up, and this method usually gets a "rise" out of him.

PROFICIENT
See salty, salty dog, top.

pronto
Quickly, soon, hurry. It is no longer restricted to the part of the country under Spanish influence, but is commonly used throughout the United States.

PROSPECTOR
See coffee cooler, desert rat, grisselheel, pocket hunter, prospector's compass, river sniper, sage rat.

prospector's compass
A burro's tail.

prowl
To go back over a territory after a roundup in search of cattle which may have been missed.

puddin' foot
A big-footed or awkward horse.

pueblo (poo-ay'blo)
Town.

puller
A horse which is always leaning on the bit and wanting to go.

pull for the Rio Grande
To hit for that line which has, for so many men on both sides, meant life or death (J. Frank Dobie, *Vaquero of the Brush Country* [Dallas, Southwest Press, 1929], 125); used in the sense of *on the dodge*.

pulling bog
Pulling cattle from bog holes.

pull in his horns
Said of one who backs down from a fight.

pull leather
To grab the saddle horn during the riding of an unruly horse.

pull stakes
To leave, to move, bag and baggage.

pull the trip
Cowboy parlance for, after roping a cow, dropping the rope under the animal's right hip bone and around its buttocks for the busting. See *steer busting*.

pump-handle
A bucking term used when the horse bucks with a see-saw effect, landing alternately on his front and hind feet. He is an easy horse to ride, and as one cowboy said, "A baby couldn't fall off him." A man who draws such a horse at a riding contest feels himself to be cheated, and the sarcastic remarks from the sidelines do not improve his temper.

pumpkin roller
The name given to a grumbler or agitator. Such persons are not tolerated in a cow camp. They are also called *freaks*, because the cowboy, being such an uncomplaining and loyal soul by nature, feels that such people do not belong to the calling. Also a name for a green hand.

pumpkin-seed saddle
A slang name for a small saddle.

pumpkin skin
What cowmen in some localities call a palomino horse.

puncher
A man who works cattle; short for *cowpuncher*.

punch the breeze
To go in a hurry.

puncture lady
This means a woman who prefers to sit on the sidelines at a dance and gossip

rather than dance. She usually makes a good job of puncturing someone's reputation.

punk
An inexperienced hand.

pup's nest
A prairie dog's hole.

pure
A thoroughbred, one who is loyal.

push on the reins
A colloquialism for urging one's mount to full speed.

pussy-back
Said of mild bucking with arched back; same as *cat-back*.

put a kid on a horse
In the ranch country when any errands are to be run or any messages to be sent, it is common practice to put a kid on a horse to do the job.

put a spoke in his wheel
To hinder or stop anyone from carrying out some action or intention.

Put 'em east and west, boy!
This expression is generally shouted by a judge to a cowboy in a riding contest when he is spur buttoning, and means for him to spur the horse's shoulders with toes pointed outward.

put his saddle in the wagon
This expression signifies that the one spoken of is fired and is no longer riding for the ranch.

put leather on his horse
Said when a cowboy saddles his horse.

put on tallow
To fatten, to gain flesh.

put the loop on
To lasso.

put the saddle on him
When referring to a man, this expression means that one tried to bluff, or "ride," another.

puttin' the leggin's
Whipping one with leggin's, chapping.

putto
A wooden stake, which is driven into the ground and to which one end of the picket-rope is attached; the word is derived from the French *poteau*, meaning *post* (Philip A. Rollins, *The Cowboy* [New York, Charles Scribner's Sons, 1936], 140).

put to bed with a pick and shovel
Said of a burial.

put to grass
To turn stock out on a range or into a pasture.

put windows in his skull
To shoot one through the head.

Q

"Any hoss's tail kin ketch cockleburs"

Quaker
What the cowman calls quaking aspen.

QUALITY
See from who laid the chunk, top.

QUANTITY
See caboodle, neck meat or nothin', whole shebang.

QUARRELING
See whittle whanging.

quarter horse
See *short horse*.

quick-draw artist
An expert in the art of drawing a gun rapidly.

QUICKNESS

See first rattle out of the box, pronto.

quién sabe (ke-en′ sah′bay)

The cowman pronounces it *kin′savvy*. Spanish for *Who knows? I don't know.* Commonly used by all ranchmen, especially when they admit that they have no information upon a subject.

quirly

The cowboy's name for his cigarette.

quirt

A flexible, woven-leather whip made with a short stock about a foot long and carrying a lash of three or four heavy, loose thongs. Its stock is usually filled with lead to strike down a rearing horse which threatens to fall backward, and it can also be effective as a blackjack. A loop extending from the head provides means of attachment to either the rider's wrist or the saddle horn. The word is derived from the Mexican *cuarta*, meaning *whip;* this, in turn, is from the Spanish *cuerda*, meaning *cord*. (Philip A. Rollins, *The Cowboy* [New York, Charles Scribner's Sons, 1936], 137.)

quisto

A slang name for a quirt.

R

"Montana for bronc riders and hoss-thieves,
Texas for ropers and rustlers"

race

A crooked blaze on a horse's forehead.

rack

A word the cowboy frequently uses to mean *to ride*, the gait of a horse.

raftering

Lying under a blanket or tarp with the knees stuck up. This is done by some cowboys sleeping in the open during a rain, thus making a watershed.

rafter brand

One having semi cone-shaped lines above the letter or figure, similar to the roof of a house.

RAIN

See fence lifter, goose drownder, gully-washer.

rainbowin'

When a horse bucks with bowed back and shaking head.

raise

To see someone or something in the distance, as, "He raised a posse comin' over the hill."

raised on prunes and proverbs

Said of a fastidious and religiously inclined person.

raised on sour milk

Said of a crank or a disagreeable person.

raking

Synonymous with *scratching*. It generally applies when the rider gives his legs a free swing, rolling the rowels of his spurs along the horse's sides from shoulder to rump, and is one of the highest accomplishments aspired to by bronc riders.

ram pasture

An occasional name for the bunkhouse.

ran a butcher shop and got his cattle mixed

Said of a rustler who had been caught.

ranahan

A top hand, a cowboy who is efficient.

ranch

Either an entire ranching establishment including buildings, lands, and live-stock, or else the principal building, which usually is the owner's dwelling, or else the owner's dwelling together with other structures adjacent to it, or else the collective persons who operate the establishment. From the Spanish *rancho*, meaning *farm*, particularly one devoted to the breeding and raising of livestock. Used both as a verb and as a noun.

rancher
A man who operates a ranch. A title restricted to members of the proprietor class.

RANCHER
See cattleman, corrida, cow crowd, cow folks, cowman, dogieman, white-collar rancher.

ranchero (ran-chay'ro)
Spanish for *rancher*, though a *ranchero* is more commonly a Mexican, while a *rancher* may be either Mexican or American.

RANCHES
See cap-and-ball layout, cocklebur outfit, dude ranch, dugout, floating outfit, good lay, greasy-sack outfit, hacienda, haywire outfit, homestead, lay, layout, line-camp, one-horse outfit, op'ra house, outfit, ranch, shirttail outfit, sign camp, silk, siwash outfit, three-up outfit, tough lay, water rights. *See also entries under* houses.

ranchman
Anyone connected with the running of a ranch; a word including employees as well as employers.

range
Open country where cattle graze.

RANGE
See between hay and grass, bog holes, elbow room, free grass, green up, home range, hundred-and-sixty, open range, pothole, pup's nest, range, range count, range delivery, range riding, range rights, water hole, water rights.

range boss
A man who works mostly with company-owned outfits. His work is to se-cure and protect the company's range, run its business, keep the men and wagons at work, and see that the cattle are bred up. He sees that fences are kept in repair, that the water supply functions, and does everything within his ability to better the interests of his employers. He has to be a leader of men and know horses, cattle, and the range to be successful. (John M. Hendrix, "Bosses," *Cattleman*, XXIII, No. 10 [March, 1937], 65–75.)

range branded
Said of cattle branded upon the range away from corrals.

range bum
A professional chuck-line rider.

range count
Counting each grazing bunch of cattle where it is found on the range and drifting it back so that it does not mix with the uncounted cattle. See *pasture count*.

range delivery
This means that the buyer, after examining the seller's ranch records and considering his reputation for truthfulness, pays for what the seller claims to own, then rides out and tries to find it. (Philip A. Rollins, *The Cowboy* [New York, Charles Scribner's Sons, 1936], 225.)

range horse
A horse born and bred on the range. With the exception of being branded, range horses are never handled until old enough to break.

range pirate
In the open-range days this term meant a man who turned stock loose on the range without owning open water and range in proportion to the cattle turned loose.

range riding
See *outriding*.

range rights
The right to the use of a certain range in consequence of priority of occupation and continuous possession.

range word
When a cowman gives his *range word*, it can be safely taken as law and gospel.

When trying to protect a friend or telling a "windy" to a tenderfoot, he can lie bigger and better than anyone else. To him, as one cowman said, "Ananias was jes' an ambitious amateur." But when he prefaces his remarks with "speakin' for the ranch" or "I'm givin' my range word for it," you can expect to hear the truth.

ranny
A top hand. Short for *ranahan.*

rattle his hocks
To travel at speed.

rat-tailed horse
One having a tail with little hair.

rawhide
The hide of a cow or steer (as noun). It was one of the most useful products of the pioneer cattleman. From it he made ropes, hobbles, clotheslines, bed-springs, seats for chairs, overcoats, trousers, brogans, and shirts. It patched saddles and shoes; strips of it bound loose wagon tires or lashed together pieces of broken wagon tongue, as well as substituting for nails and many other things. To tease (as verb).

rawhide
A weak cow.

RAWHIDE
See Mexican iron, rawhide, robe hide.

rawhider
This name was attached to a class of the early-day movers who traveled from one section of the West to another. Their outstanding characteristic was always having their wagons full of cowhides, which they cut into strips, and they used the whangs for every known purpose. The term was sometimes used with reference to the operator of a small cattle ranch; also it was a name the northern cowboy called the Texan.

rawhide lumber
Unfinished slabs with the bark left on, usually cottonwood.

rawhidin'
The act of gathering cattle alone on the range with an individual camp outfit, teasing.

raw one
The cowboy often uses this term in speaking of a green bronc.

reach
To make a motion as if to draw a gun; also used for the actual drawing of a gun. When a man goes after his gun, he does so with a single, serious purpose. There is no such thing as bluff. Every action is toward shooting as speedily and as accurately as possible, and making his first shot the last of the fight.

reachin' for the apple
Catching hold of the saddle horn during a ride.

readin' sign
The act of interpreting the markings in following a trail. One cowhand spoke of a good tracker as being able to "follow a wood tick on solid rock in the dark o' the moon"; another referred to one that "had a nose so keen he could track a bear through runnin' water"; and on one occasion Pima Norton spoke of a friend that "could track bees in a blizzard."

read the Scriptures
To lay down the law, to give orders.

rearback
When a bucking horse stands upon its hind legs, loses its balance, and falls backward.

rear cinch
The hind one, if two.

rear girth
The Texan's name for the rear cinch.

rear jockey
The leather on top of the skirt of the saddle, fitting closely around the cantle.

reata (ray-ah'tah)
From *reatar,* to retie; Spanish, meaning *a rope which ties one animal to another.* A rope, particularly one made of braided leather or rawhide.

RECOVER
See get his hog back.

redcoats
The name by which cowboys of the

Northwest call the mounted police of Canada.

red disturbance

A slang name for whiskey. Some of it, in the words of John West, "would make a muley cow grow horns."

red-eye

Another slang name for whiskey.

red-eyed

Angry.

red-ink

Still another name for whiskey.

reefing

Spurring, scratching.

regular

What the old-time trail driver called a drive that went "as fine as split silk" to the Wichita Mountains, and "hell broke loose" from there to the end of the drive.

relief

The change of guard for the herd.

remittance man

Usually socially outcast members of the nobility of England who came west to relieve their families of further embarrassment. They were called this because they depended for existence upon the remittance of money from their families overseas.

remuda (ray-moo'dah)

From the Spanish *remudar*, meaning *to exchange, re-exchange. Remuda de caballos* means *relay of horses.* The cowman uses the word to mean the extra mounts of each cowboy herded together and not at the time under saddle; also called *remontha*, this latter word a corruption of the Spanish *remonta*. The word is pronounced *remootha* in the Southwest, but most Texas cowmen merely say *hosses.* The remuda is to the Southwest what the cavvy is to the Northwest, though the northwestern cowboy usually called these horses the *saddle band.*

A horse usually goes into the remuda when he is four years old. By the time he is six, he is fairly trained for cow work, but doesn't reach his full period of usefulness until he is about ten years old. Each year the remuda is culled of horses too old for the best work. A good and faithful cow horse is pensioned for a life of ease and grass; otherwise, the horse is sold for farm work.

A good cowman knows that his outfit is no better than its horses, and he watches them closely. Every day he checks the horses and counts them out to the wrangler. Each cowboy is responsible for the condition of his string, and the man who abuses his horses doesn't last long with the outfit. No horse is overworked, no horse overlooked. Each man realizes that the horse is his motive power and that his work is handicapped unless these horses are in top condition.

A rule of all remudas is that all horses must be geldings. Mares are never a part of the remuda, because they are bunch-quitters and failures as saddle horses. As Charlie Russell said, "Lady hosses are like their human sisters. They get notions of goin' home, and no gentleman cayuse would think of lettin' a lady go alone." Stallions, on the other hand, fight and otherwise disturb a peaceful remuda.

When the work is over in the fall, the remuda is turned out to run the range, rest, and heal their scars. A small portion of the horses are kept up to be grain fed and used by the men who remain to do what winter riding there is to be done. The average remuda holds from ninety to one hundred horses, a number necessary to mount a cow outfit of eight to ten men.

remudera (ray-moo-day'rah)

The Mexican name for a bell mare.

remudero (ray-moo-day'ro)

The Mexican name for a wrangler.

renegade rider

A cowboy employed to visit ranches, sometimes as far as fifty or more miles away, and pick up any stock branded with his employer's brand found anywhere, taking it with him to the next ranch or range. He takes his gather to the home ranch as often as he can, changes horses, and goes again.

rep

A cowboy who represents his brand at outside ranches (as noun); to represent (as verb). Also called *outside man* or *stray man*. This cowboy's task developed from the efforts of ranch owners to recover their stray cattle. It became a regular part of the open-range system to have one man of each ranch work with the roundup to look out for and carry along cattle in his employer's brand until he could return them to their home range, branding their calves in the roundup. He assisted in the work of the roundup, but his first duty was to look after the cattle of his brand.

As a rule, the top hand of an outfit is given this enviable position and he is considered a notch higher than the common puncher and gets more pay. He has to know brands, and the job is a responsible one. He likes the work because he can travel around, mingle with old friends, and make new ones in other outfits.

When he reaches the outside limit of the drift from his company's range, he cuts from the day herd the cattle of his brand, takes his mount from the remuda, packs a horse with his bedroll and "drags it for home," driving his gather before him.

REP

See outside man, rep, rep's cut, stray man.

rep's cut

During the roundup the rep of an outside ranch looked through the gathered cattle and designated which were of his brand. Then these were cut into a bunch called the *rep's cut*.

RESTLESS

See homeless as a poker chip, Junin' 'round.

ribbons

What the West calls the lines of a harnessed team.

rib up

To persuade.

rib wrenches

A slang name for spurs.

ride herd on

To take care of.

ride herd on a woman

Said of one courting a woman.

ride like a deputy sheriff

To ride recklessly, in a hurry.

ride over that trail again

A request to explain more simply and more fully.

RIDERS

See afoot, Bill-show cowboy, bog rider, bootblack cowpuncher, bronc breaker, bronc buster, bronc fighter, bronc peeler, bronc scratcher, bronc snapper, bronc squeezer, bronc stomper, bronc twister, brush buster, brush hand, brush popper, brush roper, brush thumpers, brush whacker, buckaroo, bull-bat, buster, caballero, chuck-line rider, choppers, circle rider, contract buster, couldn't ride nothin' wilder'n a wheel chair, cowboys, drag rider, fence rider, flank rider, flash rider, glory rider, greasy-sack rider, grub-line rider, hand, hillbilly cowboy, jinete, kick-back rider, leather pounder, light rider, line rider, long rider, miller, mill rider, outrider, outside man, peeler, point rider, posse, pothole rider, puncher, renegade rider, rep, rough-string rider, saddle slicker, saddle stiff, saddle tramp, saddle warmer, salty rider, scissor-bill, shadow rider, swing rider, tail rider, three-up screw, twister, vaquero, windmiller, windmill monkey.

ridge runner

A wild horse which keeps to ridges and high points to watch for danger and warn the herd.

ridin' bog

Riding over boggy areas in the spring to extricate animals mired in bog holes. Usually cattle are in poor condition and likely to bog down at this season.

ridin' circle

The act, during the roundup, of searching out and driving before one all the cattle found over a wide range of territory to a designated holding spot.

ridin' 'em down

A trail expression signifying the gradual urging of the point and drag cattle closer together to put them on the bedground.

ridin' fence

The duty of keeping the fences in repair. See *fence rider*.

ridin' for the brand

The cowboy never *worked* for a ranch; the word *work* was suggestive of the day laborer. He *rode* for a certain outfit. *Ridin' for the brand* has a deep significance on the range. It means that the cowboy is loyal, tireless in looking after the interests of the brand, and willing to fight for it, even laying down his life for it, as long as he is riding for it.

RIDING

See bake, beefsteak, bicycling, bite the dust, breaking brush, business riding, cantle-boarding, cheeking, choke the horn, choke rope, claw leather, close seat, coasting on the spurs, comb, couldn't find his saddle-seat with a forked stick, curry him out, curry the kinks out, cut 'er loose, daylightin', fanning, fannin' on her fat, gimlet, Give 'im air!, grabbin' the apple, grabbin' the nubbin', grabbin' the post, hoppin' dog holes, huggin' rawhide, hunting leather, ironing him out, ironing out the humps, jiggle, jingling, knee grip, monkey style, nigger brand, peeling, plow-boying, pulling bog, pull leather, put a kid on a horse, rack, reachin' for the apple, ride like a deputy sheriff, ridin' bog, ridin' circle, ridin' fence, ridin' for the brand, ridin' it out, ridin' line, ridin' on his spurs, ridin' safe, ridin' sign, ridin' slick, ridin' straight up, ridin' the ditch, ridin' the grub-line, ridin' the rough string, ridin' the shows, safety first, savin' saddle leather, scratching gravel, seeing daylight, set afoot, set the hair, settin' close to the plaster, settin' deep in his tree, settin' the buck, shakin' hands with grandma, sloppy riding, soundin' the horn, spiked his horse's tail, spur buttoning, squeeze the biscuit, squeezin' Lizzie, stay in one's tree, Stay with him!, stickin' like a postage stamp, taking leather, three-legged riding, three saddles, thumbing, tied to the ground, tightlegging, top off, touchin' leather.

riding aprons

See *armitas*.

ridin' herd on a woman

Courting.

ridin' into his dust

Following someone or following another's lead.

ridin' it out

Staying with a bad horse until he is conquered.

ridin' line

Patrolling a prescribed boundary to look after the interests of an employer. See *line riding*.

ridin' on his spurs

Said when a rider hooks his spurs in the cinch, keeping them there during the ride.

ridin' out of town with nothin' but a head

Said of one the morning after a big drunk. As one cowhand remarked, he "had a headache that's built for a hoss," and another declared he "had a taste in my mouth like I'd had supper with a kiyote."

ridin' safe

Sitting close to the saddle, legs tightly clenched against the horse's sides, the spurs set firmly in the cinch.

ridin' sign

The act of riding the range to follow animals which have strayed too far and turn them back, or to pull cattle from bog holes, turn them away from loco patches, and do anything else in the interest of an employer.

ridin' slick

To ride without locked spurs or hobbled stirrups, and without a saddle roll.

ridin' straight up

The rider sits straight up in the saddle, holding the reins in one hand, with the other hand in the air.

ridin' the bag-line

Synonymous with *ridin' the grub-line*.

ridin' the bed wagon
Laying off on account of sickness or accident.

ridin' the ditch
Looking after the water supply of an irrigation system.

ridin' the grub-line
The jobless cowboy's going from ranch to ranch and accepting meals without paying for them. Also called *ridin' the chuck-line* and *ridin' the bag-line*.

ridin' the high-lines
On the scout. Said of an outlaw. Many badmen were forced to ride trails "that'd make a mountain goat nervous."

ridin' the owlhoot trail
Said of an outlaw because he does much of his riding at night.

ridin' the rough string
Said of one whose job it is to break horses, and such a job "ain't like attendin' a knittin' bee."

ridin' the shows
Competing for prize money at rodeos. Said of a professional buster who follows rodeos.

ridin' under a cottonwood limb
Said of a hanging; also of one committing an act for which he deserves to be hanged.

ridin' with an extra cinch-ring
Said of a rustler or one suspected of stealing.

rig
Short name for saddle.

rigging
The middle leathers attached to the tree of the saddle connecting with and supporting the cinch by latigos through the rigging ring.

rigging ring
The iron ring attached to the saddle for fastening the cinch; also called *tree ring* or *saddle ring*.

right-hand man
Foreman.

rildy
A comfort or blanket.

riled
Angry, stirred up.

rim fire
A saddle with one cinch, which is placed far to the front; also called *Spanish rig* and *rimmy*.

rim firing a horse
Putting a burr under the saddle blanket to make the horse pitch. One of the many pranks of cowboys.

rim rockin' sheep
Running sheep over a cliff to destruction. This was often done during the wars between the cattle and the sheep factions.

rincón (rin-cone')
In Spanish the word means *a corner* or *secluded spot*. The Southwesterner uses it to mean a nook, secluded place, or a bend in a river. (Harold W. Bentley, *Dictionary of Spanish Terms in English* [New York, Columbia University Press, 1932], 197.)

ring bit
A bit with a metal circle slipped over the lower jaw of the horse. This cruel Spanish bit is not looked upon with favor by American cowmen. It can be extremely severe unless handled carefully, and is hardly a bit for a man who loses his temper.

ringey
Angry, riled.

RIVERS
See big swimming, boggy crossing, crossing, dugways, he'll do to ride the river with, over the willows, rincón, startin' the swim, swimming the herd, swimming water, watering the herd.

river sniper
A gold panner.

road agent
A robber, more commonly a robber of stagecoaches.

road agent's spin
A gun spin made just the reverse of the single roll; sometimes called the *Curly Bill spin*.

road brand

A special brand of any design for trail herds as a sign of ownership en route. This brand helped the herders keep from mingling their herd with outside cattle and spiriting off their home range these animals of disinterested ownership. (Philip A. Rollins, *The Cowboy* [New York, Charles Scribner's Sons, 1936], 240.)

This type of brand originated in Texas during the trail days when a law was passed that all cattle being driven beyond the northern limits of the state were to be branded by the drover with "a large and plain mark, composed of any mark or device he may choose, which mark shall be branded on the left side of the stock behind the shoulder." With the passing of trail driving, this brand was no longer used.

road house

A corral in an out-of-the-way place used by rustlers for the temporary holding of stolen stock.

road runner

See *chaparral bird.*

roan

A horse which shows a more or less uniform mixture of white and colored hairs over the entire body. If the ground color is sorrel, the color resulting is strawberry roan; if bay, it is red-roan; and if mahogany bay or black, it is blue- or black-roan.

Rob

See stood up.

robe hide

When buffalo robes were popular, they were made from buffalo killed in winter when their hides were heavy. They brought much better prices than those from animals killed in other seasons.

rockin' chair horse

One with an easy gait.

rocking brand

One resting upon and connected with a quarter-circle.

Rocky Mountain canary

Another name for a burro.

rod

The boss.

roddin' the spread

Bossing the outfit.

rodeo (ro-day'o)

Derived from the Spanish *rodear (ro-day-ar')*, meaning *to encompass, the act of encircling*, and, in colloquial Mexican, signifying the rounding-up of cattle. In later days it referred strictly to cowboy contests. Recently the word has been used in two different senses and has two different pronunciations, as well as a different meaning from the original Spanish. The cowboy contest is commonly called *ro'de-o*, while the roundup is called *ro-day'o*, and in the latter sense the word is rapidly becoming obsolete.

Some rules of rodeo riding are: Only one rein is allowed, and it must be free from knots or tape and must not be wrapped around the hand. While making a ride, the rider must not change hands on the rein, and his rein hand must be held above the horse's neck. The rider must leave the chute with both feet in the stirrups and both spurs against the horse's shoulders. He must scratch ahead for the first five jumps, then behind. He has to stay on the horse and ride clean for ten seconds. If he loses a stirrup or touches leather with either hand, hits the horse with his hat, or looks cross-eyed at the judges, he is disqualified.

Fanning a horse with the hat used to be considered spectacular, but modern rodeos forbid quirting, fanning, or even touching the animal with the hand.

Rodeo Terms

See bite 'em lip, blow a stirrup, blow the plug, boggin' 'em in, bulldog, bulldogger, bull riding, bull riggin', calf roping, carnival hand, choke rope, chute crazy, close-to-the-ground bucker, Committee saddle, crying room, cut 'er loose, final horses, flank riggin', get-away money, head and heel, hit the daylight, Hook 'em cow!, hot shot, kick-back rider, locked spurs, loggerin', Look out, cowboy!, mad scramble, no time, out of the money, Pick him up!, pick-up man, Powder River! Let 'er buck!, Put 'em east and west, boy!, ridin' the shows, rodeo, runaway bucker, scratcher cinch, show bucker, snubber, snub horse, spur buttoning, sulker, sunfishing, time judge, twisting down, whistle judge, wild cow milking.

roll

A corkscrew, wavelike motion of a rope, which, traveling along its end, lands on the object roped with a jar (Philip A. Rollins, *The Cowboy* [New York, Charles Scribner's Sons, 1936], 240). Many ropers use the roll to release their nooses from the roped animals when they desire to recover their ropes from grown cattle which have been heeled. See also *saddle roll.*

Roll your bed!

A command meaning that you are fired.

rolling a calf

A method of throwing a calf for branding. This is a spectacular stunt requiring considerable strength and skill. It is somewhat dangerous and a very tiring method of getting a calf down. It is accomplished by reaching over the back of the calf, catching it with one hand and at the same time jambing your leg in front of the calf. The cowboy does not resort to this method unless he wants to show off or there happens to be a girl visiting the wagon for the day. (Editorial, *Cattleman*, XXII, No. 1 [June, 1935], 5–7.)

roll the cotton

To roll one's bed and move camp, to take a trip.

rolls his gun

Said when one starts shooting.

rolls his own hoop

Said of one attending to his own business.

roll his tail

Another slang expression for leaving on the run.

rolls it

Roping slang.

roll out

A loop which is made by jerking the noose forward over the hand and wrist and releasing it so that it will roll out on edge, leaning somewhat to the right. It is usually only effective when thrown at animals passing in front of the roper toward his right. It can be used to forefoot horses, but is better as a heel loop for cattle, a rather small loop being rolled under the belly of an animal and in position to catch both hind feet. (W. M. French, "Ropes and Roping," *Cattleman*, XXVI, No. 12 [May, 1940], 17–30.) It also means to start with a wagon, or get up in the morning.

roll-overs

A trick-roping term. These spins are started either vertically or horizontally, and the noose is made to roll over the shoulders or one or both arms.

roll your wheels

This term was used in the early days by freighters, bullwhackers, and mule skinners. It meant *start your team,* but by the time the cowman seized it for his own, it meant *get goin'* in any sense.

romal

A flexible whip made on the bridle reins when they are fastened together. In Spanish the word is spelled *ramal* and pronounced *r-r-rah-mahl'.* *El ramal* means literally *a branch road, a division,* or *a ramification.* Thus, attached as it is by the loop to the bridle reins, the romal becomes but a ramification of the rein, a handy addition that may be used as a quirt and dropped from the hand without fear of its getting lost.

roostered

Drunk.

rooter

The cowboy's name for a hog.

rope

The most important tool of the cowman, made of many different materials and serving many purposes. It catches his horse, throws his cattle, drags his wood to camp, pulls cattle from bog holes, and helps pull his wagons across rivers and rough places. It ties his bed up, helps in fighting prairie fires, secures his packs, stakes his horses, serves as a corral, is useful as a cow-whip, and is a weapon for killing snakes. It also serves as a guide in snow storms when tied from his bunkhouse door to the stable or the wood pile, and it was frequently used to mete out frontier justice. Without it the cowboy would be practically useless. It is said that he does everything with a rope except eat with it. There are truly many men who can do anything with a rope except throw it straight up and climb it.

rope-and-ring man

A rustler, given this name because he uses a rope and a cinch ring to run his illegal brands. I once heard a reformed rustler admit that he "quit rustlin' cows for the good of my gullet."

rope corral

A temporary corral at the cow camp, made by three or four cowhands holding ropes between them to form an obtuse U, and used to pen saddle horses until they can be caught for saddling.

The corral is formed by using a heavy rope called a cable, held about three feet off the ground, either by men or, sometimes, by forked sticks. This seemingly makes a frail prison for a bunch of horses, but early in his life the range horse learns to respect the rope. He remembers the burns and falls he received when he was first thrown and branded. If a horse has not learned his lesson and breaks out of the corral a time or two, the top roper of the outfit is given the nod to "pick up his toes" the next time he breaks out. It may break the horse's neck, but the boss would rather have him dead than have him spoiling the other horses. Frequently the rope cable is shaken vigorously to remind the horses that it is a rope.

As soon as the desired horses are caught, the rope is dropped and the remaining horses are allowed to go back to grazing. This is done quietly, and all rushing or jamming is carefully avoided. Having performed its duty, the cable is coiled up and placed in the wagon to be ready for the next saddling.

rope croup

A hanging.

rope horse

A horse especially fitted for and trained in the work of roping. A man can learn to ride and do ordinary cow work in a short time, but to become a proficient roper requires years of practice; yet no matter how expert a roper may become, he will have small success without a good rope horse.

The rope horse must have strength and intelligence, both well trained. Roping requires the most skill and is the hardest and the most dangerous of all cow work. When the roped animal is "tied onto," the slightest pull on the reins causes the well-trained horse to sit back, hind feet well under him, forefeet braced well out in front to receive the shock. The slightest pressure on the side of the neck with the reins causes him to whirl instantly to face the catch.

A good rope horse never allows a cow to get a side run on him, nor does he allow an inch of slack to let the rope wind him up. Experience has taught him the consequences of such blunders. The instant the roped animal falls, the horse will pull against the rope, dragging the dead weight along the ground.

When running an animal to be roped, the educated rope horse knows when the cowboy takes down his rope and what is expected of him. He runs like the wind to the left side of the cow but never past her. There he sticks until his rider casts his rope; then he "does his stuff." If the roper misses, he knows that too. At a roundup where a large crew is working, the top ropers and the top roping horses stand out above the rest. Any successful contest roper gives his horse most of the credit. As the late Will Rogers once said, "Contest ropin' is just like a marriage. It's a partnership affair between the roper and his mount."

rope meat

The victim of a hanging.

ROPERS

See brush roper, dally man, ketch hand, rope tosser, small loop man, smooth roper, tie-hard, tie-man, tie-down man, tying fast.

ROPES

See cabestro, cable, catgut, choke rope, clothesline, coil, doll-babies, fling-line, hair rope, hemp, hoggin' rope, honda, hot rope, ketch rope, lariat, lash rope, lasso, lass rope, lead rope, line, maguey, Manila, mecate, pepper-and-salt rope, picket rope, piggin' string, reata, rope, rope corral, running W, seago, skin string, sling rope, stake rope, string, tie rope, Tom Horn, twine, twitch, W, whale line.

rope shy

Said of a horse that jumps away from the rope when its rider is roping.

rope tosser

A roper, who, instead of swinging the rope around his head before throwing, spreads it out behind and to one side of him, and with a quick, graceful throw, or toss, launches it with unerring aim over the head of the animal at which he throws. This method is used almost entirely in catching calves out of a herd, as it is done so quietly and easily that the animal is snared before it has a chance to dodge or move.

roping out

Said when cowhands rope their mounts in a corral, catching them for saddling.

ROPING TERMS

See bedded, belly rope, Blocker loop, body spin, building a loop, butterfly, calf on the ground, calf on the string, calf roping, California twist, coffee grinding, community loop, complex spin, cotton-patch loop, dab, dally, diamond hitch, dog fall, fair ground, figure eight, forefooting, goin' down the rope, goin' over the withers, head and heel, head catch, heel, high-low, hog-tie, Hooley-ann, hop-skip, hornswoggling, hungry loop, jerked down, juggling, lay, mangana, mangana de pie, merry-go-round, moonlight ropin', Mother-Hubbard loop, ocean wave, Old man him!, overhead loop, overhead toss, peal, pick up his hind feet, pick up his toes, pile it on, pull the trip, roll, roll out, roll-overs, rolls it, roping out, run on the rope, settin' spin, shakin' out, sing, skipping, smear, snail, snare, snubbing, spread, stack it on, star gazing, steer busting, steer roping, stretchin' out, Texas tie, tying down, underhand pitch, washerwoman loop, waste a loop, wedding ring, whirling.

rosadero (ro-sah-day'ro)

A vertical, wide leather shield sewed to the back of the stirrup leather.

rotten loggin'

Term used when romantic couples sit on a log by moonlight to court. A practice seldom followed on the range.

rough break

To rope, choke down, blindfold, and saddle a green bronc, then mount, strip off the blindfold, dig in with the spurs, slam the horse with the quirt, and proceed to fight it out. Many ranches follow this method of breaking horses, and three such rides by the buster are considered sufficient before turning the horse over to the cowboy.

rough steer

One of poor breeding and scrawny development.

rough string

A string composed of wild and semi-wild horses which fight every time they are saddled. Every ranch that raises its own horses has some which have never felt the saddle.

rough-string rider

A professional bronc buster. Of necessity all cowboys are good riders, but the men who handle the rough strings have to be bronc busters, and they draw down a few extra dollars per month for this perilous work. However, it is not so much the money that most of them care about as it is the honor. It is a sign of ability to say that you ride the first rough string for a large outfit. As one cowhand said, "The rider of the rough string maybe ain't strong on brains, but he ain't short on guts."

Each man has his own way of breaking a horse, but all good busters strive to break so that the horse's spirit remains unbroken, for a spiritless horse is worthless. The buster strives to break quickly, as it means time and money to the boss. He is more interested in staying on the horse than in the manner of his performance. His very calling demands that he stay on, as a matter of pride and because horses become outlaws when they can throw their riders.

round pan

The large pan, or tub, which receives the dirty dishes after a meal at a cow camp. For a cowhand to fail to throw his dishes into this pan is a breach of range etiquette, and he will certainly be called names by the cook that would "burn the grass to cinders for yards around."

round-pen

An occasional name for the corral.

roundup

The gathering of cattle, the cattleman's harvest. The roundup was the most important function in cattle land. There were two a year, the spring roundup for the branding of the calf crop, and the fall roundup for the gathering of beeves for shipment and the branding of late calves and those overlooked in the spring.

Unlike most customs of the cattle country, the roundup is neither Spanish-Mexican nor Western-American in origin. It originated in the mountain country of Kentucky, Tennessee, the Carolinas, and the Virginias. The people of those states let their cattle run loose and annually held roundups to gather them, but they performed the function in a haphazard sort of way. (*Prose and Poetry of the Cattle Industry* [Denver, 1905].) The western cowman perfected the system and brought it to the attention of the public as an important and colorful phase of the cattle industry.

It is true that the early western attempts were crude and called *cow hunts*, or *cow drives;* but as the industry grew and spread over the West, it became the perfect system that we know today. When fences came, the vogue passed as an unnecessary pageant, but in the open-range days the roundup sometimes covered thousands of miles. Stockmen found it necessary for their mutual protection to take some co-operative action; therefore, the roundup system was adopted and perfected. It might vary in detail in different sections, but, in the main, roundups were essentially the same throughout the cattle country.

Each ranchman of the district being worked furnished men and bore his share of the general expense, this share proportioned according to the number of cattle owned. Each ranch furnished a sufficient number of horses for its riders, but only the larger outfits sent chuck wagons. Each district was worked successively by ranges until each was cleaned up in regular rotation. At the end of the drive every owner knew by the carefully kept tally the increase of his herd and the number of older cattle he owned that had been gathered in by this raking of the range.

The open roundup system lasted only a comparatively few years, but during its existence it was the event every cowman looked forward to with interest and eagerness. Not only was it his harvest time, but it served as a reunion with old friends and a means of cultivating new acquaintances.

roundup captain

The man chosen to act as boss of a roundup. He was boss over all and his word was law, no matter if he did not own a hoof. The owners of the cattle were as much under his orders as any common puncher or horse wrangler. He knew all the brands of the country and had to be a diplomat to keep peace between warring factions. He had to know men and cattle and select the right man for the right job, as well as the proper roundup grounds. Certain men knew certain ranges better than others; accordingly he sent them out to scour these ranges for cattle. He selected from among the cowboys he knew to have good judgment as many lieutenants as he needed. These he put in charge of small units to run the cattle out of the brakes, arroyos, and other parts of the range. One cowboy's description of a roundup boss was, "He's the feller that never seems to need sleep and it makes 'im mad to see somebody that does."

ROUNDUP TERMS

See beddin' out, beef cut, beef roundup, blackballed outfit, book count, books won't freeze, brush roundup, bunch ground, calf roundup, choppers, combings, covered his dog, cow camp, cow hunt, cut, cut-backs, cut of cows with calves, cutter, cutting out, fall roundup, gather, general work, greasy-sack ride, handbill roundup, holding spot, inner circle, laneing, lead drive men, moonlight 'em, moonshinin', moving camp, on circle, open roundup, outer circle, parada grounds, petalta, pilot, pool camp, pool roundup, pot-rack outfit, powders, prowl, rawhidin', rep's cut, rodeo, roundup, roundup captain, running cattle, scattering the riders, shipped her, shove down, shotgun wagon, sleepin' out, smoking out the cattle, spring roundup, tellin' off the riders, throwing over, wagon boss, wasted 'er, work, working ahead of the roundup, working the herd.

roustabout
A man of all work around a cow camp.

rowel
The wheel of a spur.

run a brand
To give or use a brand, to burn a brand on an animal with a running iron.

runaway bucker
A type of bucking horse. This type of bucker will, when the chute gate is opened, leave at a fast run instead of bucking. After traveling about fifty yards he will "break in two" and start bucking. Generally his first leap will be high and mighty, and if the rider is caught unprepared, he does not have much chance of collecting prize money. When a horse is running his best, then leaps four or five feet into the air and comes down stiff-legged, he lights heavy. The fast forward motion stops so abruptly that the horse appears to shove himself backwards as he hits the ground. This trick has caused many riders to meet their Waterloo. (Bruce Clinton, "Buckin' Horses," *Western Horseman*, III, No. 3 [May–June, 1938], 10.)

run down his mainspring
Said of a runaway horse which is allowed to run until he quits of his own accord.

run like a Nueces steer
A common Texas expression. It originated from the fact that the wild cattle of the Nueces River country were exceptionally speedy for cattle and endowed with an utter disregard for obstacles in their path.

RUNNING
See burn the breeze, curled his tail, draggin' his navel in the sand, drag it, dust, fixin' for high ridin', flag his kite, fogging, goin' like the heel flies are after him, heating his axles, hell-for-leather, high-tail, hit the breeze, hit the trail, humped his tail at the shore end, jigger, lean forward and shove, made a nine in his tail, makin' far apart tracks, run down his mainspring, run like a Nueces steer, runnin' meat, stampede, take to the tall timbers, take to the tules.

running brand
A brand with flowing curves at its ends.

running cattle
Working cattle, a rounding-up.

running iron
A branding iron made in the form of a straight poker or a rod curved at the end and used much in the free style of writing upon a blackboard with chalk. In the seventies Texas passed a law forbidding the use of this iron in branding. This was a blow aimed at the brand blotter, whose innocent single iron would tell no tales if he were caught riding across the range. The law made an object of suspicion the man found with the single running iron, and he was sometimes obliged to explain to a very urgent jury.

running mount
Mounting a horse on the run without the use of the stirrups.

running W
A rope running from the hobbles to a ring in the cinch, forming the letter *W*. Used as a rule on horses that are likely to run away.

running wild
Said of one dodging the law. Also means *on a tear* or *whooping it up*.

runnin' mate
Used by the cowboy to refer to his pal or his wife.

runnin' meat
Said of a buffalo hunt.

runnin' the outfit

Said of the duties of the boss.

run on the rope

Said of an animal, especially a horse, when he starts away after being roped and is snubbed up violently. It is a part of the education of the range horse.

run over

A cattle guard built on a highway. It is made of green poles and sometimes covered with rawhide.

rusties

Culled, wild, or lean cattle.

rustle

To wrangle or herd horses, to steal cattle.

rustler

This word was first used as a synonym for *hustle*, becoming an established term for any person who was active, pushing, and hustling in any enterprise; it was used as a name for the wrangler; and, as verb, meant to herd horses. Later the word became almost exclusively applied to a cattle thief, starting from the days of the maverick when cowboys were paid by their employers to "get out and rustle a few mavericks." These same cowboys soon became interested in putting their own brands upon motherless calves to get a start in the cattle business, and this practice was looked upon as thievery. Thus the word connoted a thief. Texans, however, prefer the blunter term *cow thief*.

Winter is open season on the rustler, as then he is busiest. Dodging range riders, he rides through the grazing cattle, picking up big calves that had been missed during the summer and fall branding.

RUSTLERS AND RUSTLING

See blot, botch, brand artist, brand blotter, burnin' rawhide, careless with his brandin' iron, Cattle Kate, decoy herd, didn't keep his twine on the tree, droop-eyed, hair brand, hide with a stovepipe hole, His calves don't suck the right cows., His cows have twins., hot foot, kept his brandin' iron smooth, long rope, mavericker, maverick factory, mavericking, packs a long rope, picked brand, pins crape on the kid, ran a butchershop and got his cattle mixed, ridin' with an extra cinch ring, road house, rope-and-ring man, rustler, rustling, sleeperin', slow brand, sticky rope, swing a wide loop, tongue splitter, too handy with the rope, waddy, wave 'round, working ahead of the roundup, working brands.

rustle the pasture

To bring in the saddle horses.

rustling

Stealing cattle.

rust the boiler

To drink alkaline water.

S

"If the saddle creaks, it's not paid for"

sabinas (sah-bee'nas)

A Spanish word used to describe cattle of red and white peppered and splotched coloring.

sabino (sah-bee'no)

Usually used in referring to a horse with a peculiar shade of light reddish, almost pinkish, roan-colored body and pure white belly.

sachet kitten

Cowboy's name for a skunk.

sack

To flip a blanket at a horse to get him used to it.

sacked his saddle

Said when a cowman dies. The saying arose from the cowman's custom, when returning home by train from a trail trip, of placing his saddle in a grain sack to be checked. When he died, this figure of speech was used to convey the thought that he was now on the return journey to his eternal home.

sacking

A saddle blanket (as noun); filiping a blanket or cloth about a horse (as verb).

sacking out

Tying the hind leg of a horse up and waving a saddle blanket about him to gentle him for saddling.

S. A. Cowboy

A dude wrangler, short for *Show About Cowboy*.

SAD

See daunsy, tear squeezer.

saddle

A seat for a man on horseback. The stock saddle is built to fulfill the cowboy's requirements in cattle work, and the slight variations in shape cause special names to be given to these saddles according to the shape of their trees. Many changes and improvements have been made in saddles through the years.

saddle a dead horse on him

To burden one with an unwelcome obligation.

SADDLES

See ación, alforja, anquera, aparejo, apple, apple-horn, Association saddle, back jockey, bag pannier, basto, beartrap, billet, biscuit, box pannier, bronc saddle, bronc tree, bucking rim, bucking roll, buck strap, bulldogs, California rig, California skirts, cantinesses, cantle, cantle drop, center-fire, Cheyenne roll, chicken saddle, cinch, cinch ring, Committee saddle, contest saddle, corus, crossbuck, dinner plate, dish, dog-house stirrups, double barreled, drop stirrup, eagle-bill, empty saddle, fenders, fiveeighths rig, flank girth, flank riggin', fork, form-fitter, front jockey, fullrigged, full-seat, full-stamp, fuste, geld-ing smacker, girth, gullet, half-rigged saddle, handle, hobbled stirrups, hog skin, horn, horn string, hull, kack, Ketch my saddle!, kidney pad, kyack, latigo, leg jockey, lizzy, mochila, monkey nose, montura, Mother-Hubbard saddle, muley saddle, nigger-catcher, nubbin', open stirrups, ox-bows, ox-yokes, pack covers, packsaddle, pancakes, pelter, petate, pig, pimple, postage stamp, pumpkin-seed saddle, rear cinch, rear girth, rear jockey, rig, rigging, rigging ring, rim fire, rosadero, saddle, saddle blanket, saddle ring, saddle roll, saddle strings, salea, seat, seat jockey, seven-eighths rig, side jockey, single-barreled, single-fire, single-rigged, skeleton rig, skirt, slick fork, slick saddle, soak, stirrups, stirrup leathers, strainer, strings, sudadero, swellfork, tack-berry buckle, tapadero, tarrabee, teeth in the saddle, terrapin, Texas skirt, three-quarter rig, three-quarter seat, trap, tree, trunk strap, visa, whang strings, wood, xerga.

saddlebag doctor

The doctor of the early frontier who carried his medicine and implements in saddlebags as he rode over the range calling upon his patients.

saddle band

This term is commonly used in the Northwest for the remuda or cavvy of saddle horses.

saddle blanket

The blanket placed upon the horse's back beneath the saddle; also a slang name for griddlecakes. One good blanket is all that is necessary for a horse. Too much padding under the saddle makes him sweat unduly, and an overheated back becomes tender. After the saddle is thrown on and before it is cinched up, a couple of fingers should be inserted under the blanket where it comes over the withers to work up a little slack.

saddle-blanket gambler

A term applied to a cowboy addicted to gambling around the campfire on a saddle blanket, a small-time gambler. Charlie Russell used to say *(Trails Plowed Under)*, "You can tell a saddleblanket gambler's luck by the rig he's ridin'." Rowdy McCloud, a friend of mine with a weakness for cards, told me of his "settin' up all night tryin' to find somethin' better than some very young clubs," in a game where the dealer "seemed to know both sides of the cards the way luck set on his shirt-tail." His opponents, said Rowdy, "kept showin' me hands that looked as big as a log house and after that session I could count my coin without takin' it from my pocket."

saddle gun

A rifle or Winchester carried in the saddle scabbard. See *saddle scabbard*.

saddler

A man who makes saddles, an easy-gaited horse.

saddle ring

A metal ring fastened to the tree of the saddle from which the latigo straps hang.

saddle roll

A roll of blankets tied across the saddle just behind the fork to help wedge the rider in the saddle.

saddle scabbard

A heavy saddle-leather case in which to carry a rifle or Winchester when riding. The gun fits in as far as the hammer, leaving the stock exposed. The favorite way of carrying the gun is to loop the front strap at the very end of the scabbard over the saddle horn, while the other end, or barrel section, is merely slipped through a loop formed by a second strap from the back rigging ring on the saddle. To take off both rifle and scabbard, all that is necessary is to slip the front strap off the horn and slide the whole thing out of the back loop. The height of the scabbard must be adjusted to come at the bend of the knee. Most riders carry the gun on the left side, butt to the front. This arrangement allows them to have the gun on the same side when they get off to shoot.

saddle slicker

A slang name for the cowboy.

saddle stiff

Another slang name for the cowboy.

saddle strings

Little rawhide strings which hold the saddle leathers together. The ends are tied and left hanging, allowing packages to be tied on as well as serving as a decoration.

saddle tramp

A professional chuck-line rider.

saddle warmer

A man employed in riding horseback, a cowboy.

SADDLING

See blinder, cinch up, laced his tree up, put leather on his horse, slappin' his tree on, teeth in the saddle.

safety first

Holding the saddle horn when riding a bucking horse.

sag

A slope.

sagebrusher

A resident of a remote place, a tourist.

sagebrush philosopher

A loquacious Westerner.

sage hen

A nickname for a woman.

sage-henning

Being forced to stay overnight in the desert without blankets.

sage rat

A resident of the arid land, a prospector.

saint

The rustler's contemptuous name for a loyal cowboy.

salado (sah-lah'do)

Americanized to *salowed* and said of a wind-broken horse.

salea

A raw and softened sheepskin placed on a pack animal's back for padding beneath a packsaddle.

salivate

To liquidate, to shoot full of holes.

Sallie

A nickname for the cook.

SALOON

See bar-dog, deadfall, gaboon, sober side of the bar, water hole, wearin' callouses on his elbow, whiskey mill.

salty

When this word is used in speaking of a man, it means he is a good hand, of a horse, it means he is a hard bucker. The word is also used in the sense of showing fight and aggression. I heard one cowhand speak of another's being "salty as Lot's wife"; and another spoke of one's being "salty as Utah."

salty bronc

A mean horse.

salty dog

This name applies to anyone especially good or a master in his line of endeavor.

salty rider

One with guts.

sanchos (sahn'chos)

The Mexican name for dogies, scrubby calves.

sand

Courage. Skeets Moore characterized a friend with, "His craw was plumb full o' sand and fightin' tallow"; and a cowhand in Wyoming spoke of another's having " 'nough sand for a lake front."

sand cutter

A native of Kansas.

sand eel

An occasional name for a snake. Spade Kruger used to tell of a section of the country where "y'u have to parade 'round on stilts to keep from gettin' bit." Cactus Price concluded another tale by saying, "That's the biggest snake I ever seen without the aid o' likker."

savage

Cowboy's name for a hitchhiking tourist.

savin' money for the bartender

Riding a freight train to save fare.

savin' saddle leather

Standing up in the stirrups and riding so that the rider's seat does not touch the seat of the saddle. Tenderfoot riders sometimes ride this way to ease their saddle sores.

savvy

From *quien sabe*. Knowledge, understanding. A man with plenty of savvy is said to be as "smart as a bunkhouse rat," as "wise as a tree full of owls," or as "full of information as a mail-order catalog." Used as a query it means *Do you understand?*

saw-bones

A doctor. Most of the frontier doctors were "right there with a parin' knife when it comes to minin' for lead."

sawdust in his beard

Said of one shot down in a saloon.

scab herder

Cowboy's name for a sheepherder, especially a Mexican.

scalawag

A worthless cut-back, generally wild and old; also applied to humans, but not with reference to their age.

scalawag bunch

A group of horses which are mean and hard to handle, the rough string.

scamper juice

Slang name for whiskey.

SCARE

See booger, spook.

scatter-gun

Cowboy's name for a shotgun. Every Westerner has a deep respect for the scatter-gun, especially if it is loaded with buckshot. In western parlance, "Buckshot means buryin' ever' time"; "buckshot leaves a mean and oozy corpse"; and "absorb a load o' buckshot and they'll have to pick y'u up with a blotter."

scattering the riders

When the roundup captain gives directions to the men starting on circle to drive cattle in from the surrounding country, designating which section each man or group of men shall cover. When the riders stop to receive these orders, they dismount to reset their saddles and air their horse's backs a little before re-cinching for the hard ride ahead. The men are sent in pairs. A man unfamiliar with the country will be paired with one who knows that particular range; one riding an unreliable horse will be accompanied by one riding a more trustworthy one.

scissor-bill

One who does not do his work well.

scorcher

Slang name for the branding iron.

scotch hobble

A hobble made with a large loop that will not slip, placed around the horse's neck and arranged so that a bowline knot lies back on one shoulder. The long end of the rope is then placed around a hind leg just below the ankle joint and the end is run back into the neck loop and tied, just short enough so that the foot, when the animal is standing, will be three or four inches off the ground. To keep the horse from kicking out of the rope, it is usually necessary to take an extra turn about the ankle or twist the rope back on itself. A half-hitch on the ankle will stay on, but as the cowboy says, "You'll play hell gittin' it off."

scratch

To spur a horse backward and forward while riding.

scratcher cinch

A strap or cinch which fastens far back around the horse's flank; used in rodeos to make the horse buck. See *flank rigging*.

scratching

The act of keeping the feet moving in a kicking motion when riding a bucking horse, one of the acts necessary to win at a real bucking contest; using the spurs in a raking motion along the horse's sides.

Stan Adler, in *Hoofs and Horns*, told this amusing little story: "Every year some of them platinum haided leedle gals from Hollywood movie studios come to the Old Pueblo to take in the rodeo an' they shore get bronc ideas about what it's all about. Like the time the bareback rider come out on one of them big Brahma bulls an' rode him right purty and slick.

"'Dang, he's a-scratching' that critter a-plenty,' says one of them old waddies in the stands.

"'Ain't that plumb kind of him?' pipes up one of them leedle blond movie gals. 'The way that old cow is wrigglin' she must be itchin' somethin' scandalous.'"

scratching gravel

Climbing a steep bank on horseback.

screwing down

The act of sinking the spurs into the cinch while riding a bucking horse and failing to move the feet in a kicking motion as provided by rodeo rules.

scrub

An animal that does not grade high in breeding and flesh.

seago

From *la soga*. A rope. Applied more particularly to a loosely twisted hemp rope which is used for lassoing purposes.

sea lions

A name given the early-day long-horned cattle "that came right out of the Gulf" of Mexico. They could swim like ducks and were as wild. (J. Frank Dobie, *Vaquero of the Brush Country* [Dallas, Southwest Press, 1929], 20.)

seam squirrels

The cowboy's name for body lice. When one cowhand I knew spoke of another "a-settin' on the side of his bunk readin' his shirt by lamplight," we knew what he was talking about.

sea plum

The cowboy's name for an oyster.

seat

That part of the saddle upon which the rider sits, said to be the easiest to find, but the hardest to keep.

seat jockey

The flat leather plate overlying the stirrup leather when the latter issues from the seat of the saddle. Same as *leg jockey*.

SEE

See look-see, raise.

seeing daylight

A term applied when a rider leaves his seat with each jump of the horse, so that spectators can see between rider and saddle.

segundo (say-goon'do)

Spanish, meaning *second, immediately following the first*. The assistant trail boss, or second in command.

sendero (sen-day'ro)

Spanish for *footpath*. A trail, path, or clearing. Commonly used in the Southwest.

send up a smoke

A colloquialism for giving a warning or making a signal. Founded upon Indian smoke signals, a method of distant communication.

seraglios

A herd of wild mares with stallion.

set afoot

Said when, from any cause, a cowman loses his horse and has to walk back.

set back

To pull back.

set brand

A brand made with an iron, the design of which has been made in one piece.

set down

Being fired from a job without having a horse to ride away. In the early days, if a man thus fired had no private horse, this manner of firing often ended in gun smoke. Most ranchers recognized the seriousness of "settin' a man afoot" and lent him a company horse to ride to town. There he could leave the horse at a livery stable or turn him loose to find his way back to the home range.

set fast

Saddlesore.

set his gun goin'

To start shooting.

set the hair

To ride a horse long enough to take the meanness out of him.

settin' close to the plaster

Keeping a close and firm seat in the saddle.

settin' deep in his tree

An expression signifying that the one spoken of is a good, dependable, and trustworthy hand.

settin' on his arm

Said when a tenderfoot tries to mount a horse with one hand on the horn and the other on the cantle of the saddle. Never attempt to mount a horse in this manner. Not only does it brand you a novice, but it is the most awkward and ungraceful way to climb aboard a horse. If the horse starts off as soon as you swing off the ground—and most western horses do—you will land behind the saddle and not in it, and that may mean you will get bucked off.

settin' spin

A trick-roping term. It means jumping in and out of a spinning noose from a sitting position.

settin' the bag

Courting; also called *settin' 'er*. Bud Taylor used to say, "That naked little runt with the Injun's shootin' iron can shore booger up a good peeler."

settin' the buck

Riding a bucking horse successfully.

seven-eighths rig

A saddle with the cinch placed between the Spanish, or rim fire, and the three-quarter rig.

seven over-bit

An earmark made by cutting the ear straight down near the tip for about an inch on the top side, then from near the upper base of the ear, making the cut slope to meet the straight-down first cut.

seven under-bit

An earmark made like the seven over-bit except it is made on the lower side of the ear.

shack

Slang name for the bunkhouse.

shad bellied

Lean flanked.

shadin'

Often when a cowboy is riding the range, if he finds a shady spot, he will dismount and loosen his cinches to give his horse's back some air. If the horse is reliable, he takes the bits from its mouth to allow it a few mouthfuls of grass. Perhaps he takes this opportunity to remove his own boots and straighten the wrinkles in his socks, to smoke a cigarette or two and dream of the future. (John M. Hendrix, Editorial, *Cattleman*, XXI, No. 12 [May, 1935], 5.)

shadow rider

A cowboy who spends much of his time admiring his own shadow as he rides the range. This is a substitute for looking at himself in mirrors, for they are usually scarce on the range. Cloudy days have no silver linings for this type of cowboy. Speaking of a fancy cowboy whom the other riders called Pretty Shadow, Charlie Russell said, "When the sun hit him with all his silver on, he blazes up like some big piece of jewelry. You could see him for miles when he's ridin' the high country." (Charles M. Russell, *Trails Plowed Under* [Garden City, Doubleday Doran, 1935], 5.)

shakedown

The cowboy's name for his bed.

shakin' a hoof

Dancing. At many cowboy dances there were some religious fellows who could not stand temptation and were soon "dancin' themselves right out o' the church." There were others, too, scattered through the crowd, who were "cussin'" the blisters on their feet and the new boots that made 'em, but they wasn't missin' a dance, even if their feet was on fire."

shakin' hands with grandma

Synonymous with *pulling leather*.

shakin' hands with St. Peter

The cowboy's reference to death.

shakin' out

Opening the noose of a rope with a few quick jerks toward the front, as the right hand grasps the rope at the honda.

This is done in preparation for making a cast.

shank

That part of the spur to which the rowel is fastened.

shank of the afternoon

Late afternoon, near the close of day.

shape up

To put into an orderly condition.

sharp

An earmark made by cutting an over-slope and an under-slope upon the same ear, giving it a sharp or pointed appearance. One of the sayings of the West is, "When you see a man grubbin' and sharpin' the ears of his cows, you can bet he's a thief."

sharpen his hoe

To thrash one.

sharpen his horns

Said of one who works himself into a fit of anger or a fighting mood.

Sharps

A heavy caliber, single-shot, lever-action rifle commonly used on the frontier, and a favorite until the "repeater" took its place. Very early models were made with the percussion cap. All were breechloaders.

sharpshooter

A buyer of cattle, who is neither a feeder nor a commission man, but who buys up small bunches of cattle for a profit.

shavetail

In the northern cattle country it is the custom to "pull" the tails of broken horses. Then, when they are turned loose to run the range and mix with the unbroken horses, the riders who want to gather them for the next season's work can tell them from the wild ones at a distance. These horses are called shavetails to distinguish them from the broom tails, or long bushy-tailed horses. When a rider of Montana or Wyoming says he is "making shavetails," a fellow cowhand knows that he is breaking horses, for when a buster gives a horse his last ride, he pulls his tail as a sign that he is broken. (Bud Cowan, *Range Rider* [Garden City, Doubleday Doran, 1930], 224.)

SHEEP

See baa-a-ah, cooking mutton, hoofed locust, maggots, maniac den, movin' sheep, rim rockin' sheep, sheeped out, underwears, wagon herder, walkin' sheep, woolies.

sheep-dipper

The rustler's contemptuous name for a loyal cowboy.

sheeped out

Said when a cowman is forced to move on account of the influx of sheep. Steve Gates told of one range being "so ag'in' sheep I wouldn't ride through it with a wool shirt on."

sheepherder

One who herds or tends sheep. The cowman never called him a shepherd. Since Christ was a shepherd, that word sounded too pastoral and honored, and the cowman had anything but Christlike feelings toward the sheepman. As one cowboy said, "There ain't nothin' dumber than sheep except the man who herds 'em."

SHEEP MEN

See lamb licker, mutton puncher, scab herder, sheep herder, sheep puncher, snoozer, wagon herder.

sheep puncher

The cowboy's occasional name for a sheepherder.

sheet

A canvas used as a wagon sheet.

sheffi

A nickname for the cook.

shepherd's Bible

Common name for a mail-order catalog. There is a story of one cowboy who fell for a picture of a girl in one. Thinking that everything he saw pictured was for sale, he sat down and ordered her for a wife, fluffy dress and all, "if she wasn't already took." Then he bragged of how "it won't cost nothin' to have her

delivered 'cause the company sends ever'thing *postpaid*."

she stuff

A term used to designate cattle of the feminine gender.

shindig

A cowboy dance. A cowboy dance usually lasts all night. When it breaks up at daylight, the ladies retire to "freshen up their spit curls and chalk their noses," and "sort out the weaners that's beginnin' to stir off the bed-ground" in the next room. The old bowlegs on the dance floor pass the last bottle around, saving a big drink for the fiddler to get him to play a final tune. Then they throw a stag dance "that's apt to be kinda rough and end up in a wrastlin' match." Like a horse with plenty of bottom, these old saddle slickers just won't tire down. But finally, having no more wet goods to bribe the fiddler with, they call the dance a success and limp to the kitchen for a final cup of coffee, their feet feeling "like they'd wintered on a hard pasture."

shipper her

A common expression used when a puncher runs off after a cow and comes back without her. When he admits his defeat, the foreman does not hold it against him. He knows the puncher did his best. Punchers are that kind of men. The other kind don't last long.

SHIPPING

See prod pole, shipping close, shipping point, shipping trap.

shipping close

Shipping every head of cattle fit for market that could be gathered from the range.

shipping point

A railroad station from which cattle are shipped to market.

shipping trap

A small pasture located near a shipping chute and used to hold cattle before being shipped.

shirttail outfit

A small ranch which employs only one or two men.

shoe

A horseshoe with calked heel is called a *shoe* to distinguish it from a slipper or a boot.

shook a rope at him

An expression meaning that the one referred to had been warned of his misconduct and that his fate would rest upon his future behavior.

shootin' 'em out

Getting cattle out of a corral and on the range.

SHOOTING

See ambush, build a smoke under his hoofs, burn powder, carvin' scollops on his gun, case of slow, come a-smokin', corpse and cartridge occasion, crease, 'dobe wall, dry gulch, fanning, flip-cock, fort up, fumble, gunnin' for someone, gun slinging, gut shot, hip shooting, hot lead, I'll shoot through the water barrel and drown you, kidney shot, lead poisoned, leaned against a bullet goin' past, leather slapping, makin' the town smoky, paunched, Pecos, plug, powder burnin' contest, put windows in his skull, rolls his gun, set his gun goin', singed, slip shooting, smoke one out, smoke up, smoking out the cattle, throw gravel in his boots, throw lead, treeing the marshal, trigger is delicate, trigger itch, unravel some cartridges.

shootin' iron

A slang name for a gun.

shoots his back

Said when a horse bucks.

shore had tallow

Plenty fat; as one cowboy said, "beef plumb to the hocks."

short bit

A dime, ten cents.

shorten his stake rope

To place one at a disadvantage, to cramp one's style.

shorthorn

One not native to the cattle country, a tenderfoot, a breed of cattle with short horns, such as the Hereford.

short horse

An old name for the quarter-of-a-mile race horse, now commonly called *quarter horse.*

short-trigger man

A badman, a gunman.

short yearling

A calf which lacks a little of being a year old.

shotgun cavvy

A band of saddle horses made up of the mounts of many different ranches on the same roundup.

shotgun chaps

So called because sewing the outside seam together all the way down the leg made them look like the twin barrels of a shotgun, with a choke at the muzzle. This style proved more comfortable on the windy northern ranges than the batwings.

shotgun wagon

When a few ranchers got together and sent out a roundup wagon independent of the larger outfits, it was called a shotgun wagon.

shoulder draw

A draw made from a shoulder holster under the arm pit. It is essentially a cross draw.

shove down

This term is used in certain mountain ranges when, during the fall months, cattle are rounded up from the higher country and shoved down into the valleys or lower country to winter.

shove in the steel

To spur a horse.

show bucker

A horse that bucks hard, straight away, with nose between front legs, though not difficult to ride. In rodeos he looks good from the grandstand, but is never used in the semifinals.

show up on the skyline

To come into view, to appear.

shuck

A cigarette made with corn husk for

wrapping, a slang name for a Mexican; as a verb, it means to discard, as, "He shucked his chaps."

sí (see)

Spanish for *yes, without a doubt indeed.* Used commonly in colloquial parlance in the Southwest.

SICK

See airin' the paunch, case of worms, epizootic, Job's comforters, ridin' the bed wagon, salado, Spanish fever, splitting the tail, Texas fever, week on the bed wagon.

side jockey

The leather side extensions of the seat of the saddle.

sideline

To tie together with hobbles the front and the hind foot on the same side of an animal to prevent it from traveling at speed.

sidewinder

A rattlesnake, usually found in the desert, which strikes by swinging its head and part of its body to the left and the right; also used in speaking of humans of little principle.

sign

Tracks and other evidence of their passing left by animals or men.

sign camp

A building or dugout where the cowboy sleeps and cooks his meals while line riding.

sign language

The cowman adopted this from the Indian. It is quite often a convenient method of communication. The trail boss who had ridden ahead to look for water need not ride all the way back to the herd to give directions. On the horizon he could give these directions with his hat or his hands. The wagon boss of a roundup could likewise give signs which saved him much riding.

silk

A slang name for barbed wire.

silver thaw

Rain which freezes as it hits.

sin-buster

A preacher. Old man Hobbs used to say, "A heap o' folks would do more prayin' if they could find a soft spot for their knees."

sing

Said of the hissing sound made by a rope when thrown.

singed

Said when one receives a flesh wound from a bullet.

singin' to 'em

Standing night guard. This is the time when the cowboy does most of his singing, and night herding came to be spoken of almost entirely as *singin' to 'em.*

One day while I was discussing cowboy songs with a group of punchers, one of them offered the following disillusioning comment: "A heap o' folks make the mistake of thinkin' a puncher sings his cows to sleep. He's not tryin' to amuse nobody but himself. In the first place, he don't have any motherly love for them bovines. All he's tryin' to do is keep 'em from jumpin' the bed-ground and runnin' off a lot o' tallow. In the second place, these brutes don't have no ear for music, which is maybe a good thing because the average puncher's voice and the songs he sings ain't soothin'. Mostly he has a voice like a burro with a bad cold, and the noise he calls singin'd drive all the coyotes out o' the country."

Another offered the opinion, "Mostly the songs he sings are mighty shy on melody and a heap strong on noise, but a man don't have to be a born vocalist to sing when he's alone in the dark if he's got a clear conscience and ain't hidin' out."

Another advised that at the change of guard, the new man had to sing as he approached the herd so that he "wouldn't bulge up on 'em unawares 'cause the confidence a steer's got in the dark's mighty frail, and once spooked they'll leave a bed-ground quicker'n y'u can spit and holler howdy."

singin' with his tail up

Said of a happy and carefree person.

single-barreled

A name given a one-cinch saddle.

single fire
Another name for the one-cinch saddle.

single-rigged
Still another title for the saddle mentioned above.

single roll
Spinning a gun forward on the trigger finger, cocking and releasing the hammer as it comes under the web or lower part of the thumb.

sinkers
Slang name for biscuits.

SITUATIONS
See bogged to the saddle skirts, hair in the butter, jackpot, jamboree.

siwash
Meaning an Indian and used in the sense of not being up to the white man's standard.

siwash outfit
Contemptuous name for an unenterprising ranch.

six-gun
The common name for the pistol used in the West.

skeleton rig
An early-day saddle consisting of nothing but a tree, the rigging for the cinch, and the straps reaching to the wide ox-bow stirrups; a saddle without skirts or fenders.

skewbald
A horse with patterns of white on any basic color except black.

skid grease
Slang name for butter.

skillet of snakes
The cowboy's name for the intricate Mexican brands.

skim-milk cowboy
A tenderfoot duded up in range regalia, but without range experience.

skimmy
A calf raised on skim milk.

skinner
One employed in skinning buffalo in the early days, one employed in skinning cattle after a wholesale die-up; also a teamster or freighter who used mules; an ox-team driver was called a *bull-whacker*. In range English, one did not drive a jerk-line string, but instead *skinned* it.

skinning knife
A long knife used in skinning the hide from buffalo or cattle.

skins his gun
Said of one drawing a gun from a holster.

skin string
Slang name for a rawhide rope.

skipping
A trick-roping term. The trick is to jump into and out of a vertical noose and keep it spinning.

skirt
The broad leathers of a saddle which go next to the horse.

skookum
An Indian term, meaning *good, great*.

skookum house
A jail on an Indian reservation.

skull cracker
Cowboy's name for the Indian's tomahawk.

skunk boat
A heavy canvas shaped like a narrow scow with sides about a foot high, which, when propped up at each corner with a small stick, forms a barrier about the sleeper's bed, over which he believes no skunk can make his way to bite the one thus protected (Will C. Barnes, "The Hydrophobia Skunk," *Cattleman*, XVII, No. 12 [May, 1931], 17–19).

SKUNK
See nice kitty, piket, sachet kitten, wood pussy.

sky-pilot
The West's name for a preacher.

slab-sided
Flat-ribbed, poor.

slappin' a brand on
Putting a brand on an animal.

slappin' his tree on
Slang phrase for saddling a horse.

slattin' his sails
Said of a bucking horse.

sleeper
A calf which has been earmarked by a cattle thief who intends to come back later and steal the animal (as noun). The earmark is used by the cattleman as a quick means of identification. Thus, during roundup, when the ranch hands came upon such an animal, they were likely to take it for granted that it had been branded when it was earmarked and leave it to roam, so that the thief might return later and put his own brand upon it or drive it away. To so mark such an animal (as verb). See *sleepering*.

sleeper brands
Cattle with unrecorded and unknown brands on that particular range.

sleepering
The rustler's taking an unbranded calf, earmarking it with the mother's earmark, and turning it loose unbranded. Since the earmark is that of the outfit to which it belongs, it attracts no undue attention. If the calf passes the notice of the riders of that ranch, the rustler will return when the calf is about six months old, wean it away from its mother, and slap his own brand upon it. Then he will change the earmark to go with his brand, and the new mark is one which usually destroys other earmarks.

SLEEPING
See covered his back with his belly, raftering, sage-henning, sleeping out.

sleepin' out
A term often used in speaking of the roundup season, for at this time the cowboy does his sleeping in the open.

sleeve-gun
A derringer such as a gambler carried up his sleeve.

slew
A large amount.

slick
A name for an unbranded animal, particularly a horse.

slick-ear
An animal which has not been earmarked or branded.

slick fork
A saddle with little bulge or roll at the fork.

slick-heeled
Without spurs.

slick saddle
A saddle without a saddle roll.

slick up
To dress up in one's best. When a group of boys at a ranch started slickin' up for a shindig, it was, as Dave Hall once said, "shore hard on the soap supply and stock water." An old-time trail driver gave me this description of a cowboy cleaning up after a trail drive: "The first thing he does when he hits the town at the end of the trail is to rattle his hocks for a barbership where he can take a civilized soakin' in hot water with a big woolly towel and plenty of sweet smellin' soap. After he comes out of that dippin' vat, he buys ever'thing the barber's got. When he comes out from under them operations, he's so clean and brown he looks like he's been scrubbed with saddle soap and his own folks wouldn't know 'im either by sight or smell."

At the ranch his everyday cleanliness consists mostly of "hoofin' it to a wash basin in the mornin' to snort in it a couple o' times to get the sleep from his eyes, after which he paws over a towel, which, judgin' from its complexion, has been plumb pop'lar."

sliding the groove
Vernacular for following a trail so clearly blazoned it can not be lost.

sling rope
A long rope used to lash panniers on a packsaddle.

slip gun
A pistol so altered that it can be fired by slipping the thumb off the hammer. Generally the hammer spur is lowered,

SMOOTHIN' OUT THE HUMPS

the trigger removed or tied down, and the barrel cut short so that the weapon may be carried in the pants pocket. (Foster-Harris to R.F.A.)

slipped his hobbles
Said of a horse which has escaped his hobbles; also said of a person who has fallen from grace.

slipper
A horseshoe, smooth and without calks.

slip shooting
Accomplished by thumbing the hammer with a wiping motion. It is slower than fanning, but the shots are placed more accurately. Even then accuracy is limited to close range.

slope
To go.

sloper
One who lives on the Pacific coast.

sloppy riding
Sitting loosely in the saddle, allowing the body to flop about in response to the pitching of the horse.

slow brand
An unrecorded brand, employed in one form of cattle stealing. It is unlawful for anyone to mutilate a brand, and the law also requires that every brand must be recorded in the county of its origin. A rustler who blots out one brand and puts another in its place of course hesitates to record this new brand. He simply uses it, trusting that he can get the cattle out of the country before discovery. An unrecorded brand such as this is said to be a slow brand. (J. Frank Dobie, *Vaquero of the Brush Country* [Dallas, Southwest Press, 1929], 121.)

slow elk
To kill for food an animal belonging to someone else (as verb); beef butchered without the owner's knowledge (as noun). Some cowmen followed the philosophy that "One's own beef don't taste as good as the other feller's because fat, tender yearling's what you kill when they're other folk's stuff." See *big antelope*.

SMALL
See *fryin' size, half-pint size*.

small loop man
One who uses a small loop in roping. Cowboys of the brush country come under this classification.

smear
A roping term, as, "He smeared a rope on it."

smoke one out
Shooting to make one come out of hiding, to make one surrender, to make one divulge a secret.

smokes his pipe
Said of a horse with his lip torn where the bridle bit rests.

smoke signal
This term is taken from the Indian custom of communication, and the cowboy uses the phrase in referring to any kind of sign or signal of warning.

smoke the peace pipe
To forgive and become friends after a quarrel. Taken from the Indians' custom of smoking the pipe of peace at counsels.

smoke up
To shoot at someone. One cowboy picked up his hat which had been shot off his head. Having no enemies, he supposed it had been done by some rough joker. As he looked at the top of the crown shot away, he said, "That's a helluva joke. How'd he know how much o' my head was in that hat?"

smoke wagon
Slang name for a gun; also called *smoke pole*.

smoking out the cattle
Shooting to scare cattle from their hiding place in a rough or brushy country when riding circle on roundup.

smooth
Said of an unshod horse.

smoothin' out the humps
Taking the rough edges off a horse. Some horses are inclined to pitch when saddled regardless of their years in serv-

147

ice, especially in the spring when the grass is green and they are putting on flesh and feeling good. If there is anything that will cause horses to pitch, it is grass fat. After a winter of idleness the cowboy has to do some tall riding before he succeeds in smoothing the humps out of these horses. Also, usually there are one or two last year's broncs in his string that are starting their careers as cow horses and they are apt to pitch for some time. (Editorial, "Changing Mounts," *Cattleman*, XIX, No. 10 [March, 1933], 50.)

smooth mouth
An aged horse.

smooth roper
A man expert in the use of the rope. One who goes about his task without flourish.

snaffle bit
Similar to the bar bit except that it is made in two pieces and connected with two interlocking eyes at the middle.

snail
To drag with a rope.

snake
A reptile, a low-principled man (as noun); to drag with a rope (as verb).

snake blood
Mean. One cowhand was heard to say of another, "He's got snake blood and's so tough he has to sneak up on the dipper to get a drink o' water."

snake eyes
Said of a mean horse.

snake-head whiskey
Strong and cheap whiskey of which it was said the maker put snake heads in the barrel to give it potency. One cowhand used to say he "wondered how they kept such stuff corked."

snake poison
Whiskey; also called *snake water*.

SNAKES
See sand eel, sidewinder, snake, snake's alarm clock.

snake's alarm clock
A rattlesnake's rattles.

snaky
Mean, treacherous.

snare
To catch with a rope.

snappin' broncs
Breaking wild horses.

snappin' turtle
A narrow branding chute.

snatch team
A strong team used to supplement another on a hard pull.

SNEAKING
See chaparral fox, coyotin' 'round, Indian up.

snip
When the white color of a horse's forehead jumps to the nose as company for the star or star-strip, it is called a snip.

snoozer
A contemptuous name for the sheepman, for in the cowman's opinion he does nothing but sleep.

snorter
An excitable horse.

snortin' post
Hitching post or rack.

snorty
Said of a high-spirited horse; also of a man easy to anger.

snow bird
A soldier on the frontier who enlisted for the winter and deserted in the spring (W. S. Campbell [Stanley Vestal] to R.F.A.).

snubbed
Dehorned.

snubbed stock
Dehorned cattle.

snubber
A man who snubs a bad horse while the rider mounts. He performs this function mostly at rodeos. On the range the cowboy is mostly "on his own" and has no help.

snubbing

The act of tying a horse's head to some fixed object, dehorning cattle.

snubbing post

A vertical, round timber about five feet high, firmly set in the earth at the center of the corral and stout enough to stand the strains to which it is subjected.

snub horse

A horse used in rodeos to snub a bucker to.

snuffy

A little wild, spirited.

soak

Often the cowboy lets his horse soak for a few minutes after saddling it to allow it to get over the notion of pitching.

soakin'

The cowboy's term for loafing.

sober side of the bar

Obviously the bartender's side.

sobre paso (so'bray pay'so)

A gait of a horse, a slow Spanish trot.

sock

When a horse has white on his feet that extends only to his fetlocks, he is said to have socks.

sod-buster

A nickname for a farmer, one who plows.

soddy

A nester, because the early ones usually lived in sod houses.

sod-pawin' mood

Angry. Taken from the example of the bull pawing up the ground when angry.

soft

A term applied to a horse which tires easily.

soft grub

Hotel food, fancy victuals.

sold his saddle

The last word for a man disgraced; also used to refer to a person utterly broke. This cow-country phrase has many other interpretations. If a man has betrayed his trust or has done something else to earn the contempt of his fellows, he's sold his saddle. If he has lost his business and become destitute, he's sold his saddle, but with a note of pity rather than scorn. If his mind is deranged, he's sold his saddle, with a still different inflection. The words imply the ultimate in the abandonment of fate.

Even the children of the rangeland had their conception of this phrase. Philip A. Rollins, in his excellent book, *The Cowboy*, tells this fitting story: "Years ago in a little school at Gardiner, Montana, a small, tow-headed youth, when asked by the teacher as to who Benedict Arnold was and what he had done, replied: 'He was one of our generals and he sold his saddle.' " (*The Cowboy* [New York, Charles Scribner's Sons, 1936], 133–34.)

Somebody stole his rudder.

I heard this remark made about a drunken man weaving his way up the sidewalk. To watch some drunken cowboys try to walk in high heels under a load of liquor you would think, as one cowboy said, "walkin' was a lost art." Any drunken cowboy walking in high-heeled boots under this condition looks as if "his legs was a burden."

Some deck is shy a joker.

Said of an outlandishly dressed person, usually a tenderfoot.

SONGS

See hymns, singin' to 'em.

son-of-a-bitch-in-a-sack

Dried fruit rolled in dough, sewed in a sack, and steamed. It takes plenty of patience and "cussin' " to make it for it has to be hung in a big hot-water bucket over a pot rack to steam. After seeing one of them made, you will agree that the cook has given it a fitting name.

son-of-a-bitch stew

A favorite dish of the cowboy, made of the brains, sweetbreads, and choice pieces of a freshly killed calf. If the cowhand wishes to be polite he calls it *son-of-a-gun*, but if no delicate ears are present, he calls it by its true fighting name.

When a calf is killed, the tongue, liver, heart, lights, kidneys, sweetbreads, and brain are carried to the cook; and he knows what is expected of him. He chops all these ingredients up into small bits with his butcher knife and prepares to stew them slowly in an iron kettle. There are as many different ways to make this dish as there are cooks. Some may throw in some potatoes, a can of tomatoes, or anything else that is handy. If the eater can tell what's in it, it is not a first-class stew. As the cowboy says, "You throw ever'thing in the pot but the hair, horns, and holler." The longer it is cooked the better it is.

Sonora reds

A nickname given by the northern cowboy to the red Mexican cattle which came up the trail.

Sooners

Men who went out on the range and branded cattle before the date set by the official roundup association. These set dates gave every man an equal opportunity as well as avoiding working the cattle more than once, but there were always some dishonest men who worked only to their own selfish advantage. By working ahead of the regular roundup, these men could pick up many mavericks, calves whose mothers had been killed by wolves or had died from natural causes, and those missed in the last branding.

sop

Cowboy's name for gravy.

sop and 'taters

A slang name for the cook; also a horse that paces.

sorrel

A horse of the chestnut type, but lighter, with a yellowish and reddish golden color.

soundin' the horn

Taking hold of the saddle horn when a horse starts bucking.

sourdough

A bachelor; also a title of the cook.

sourdough bullet

A slang name for a biscuit, not called this within hearing of the cook.

sourdough keg

A small wooden keg, usually holding about five gallons, in which the cook kept his sourdough. When getting ready for the coming roundup, the cook put three or four quarts of flour into this keg and added a dash of salt and just enough water to make a medium-thick batter. The keg was then placed in the sun to let the heat ferment the contents for several days. Sometimes a little vinegar or molasses was added to hasten the fermentation.

The first batch of batter was merely to season the keg. After the fermentation was well started, it was poured out, and enough new batter mixed up to fill the keg. Each day it was put into the sun to hasten fermentation and each night it was wrapped in blankets to keep the batter warm and working. Some cooks even slept with their kegs.

After several days of this treatment, the dough was ready to use. From then to the end of the season the keg was never cleaned out. Every time the cook took out enough dough for a meal, he put back enough of the flour, salt, and water to replace it. In this way he always had plenty of dough working.

When making up his bread, he simply added enough flour and water to this batter to make a medium-stiff dough. Every wagon cook thought his sourdough the best ever, and he took great pride in his product. An outfit that let anything happen to its sourdough keg was in a bad shape, and most cooks would just about defend their kegs with their lives. (Will C. Barnes in the *Dallas Morning News*, October 18, 1931.)

sourdoughs

Either the plural of *sourdough* or biscuits.

sow bosom

Salt pork.

spade bit

A bit with a piece shaped like a broad

screwdriver on the mouth bar, three or four inches in length, and bent backward at the top (Philip A. Rollins, *The Cowboy* [New York, Charles Scribner's Sons, 1936], 148–49). A good rider never forgets that it is a spade, and that it can do damage, and he handles his reins lightly.

Spanish fever

A splenic fever caused by ticks and spread by the immune, but tick-infested, cattle of the southern country to cattle of more northern latitudes. The prevalence of this fever was greatly responsible for stopping the old trail drives.

Spanish supper

The tightening of the belt a notch or two as a substitute for food.

spic

A common name for the Mexican.

spiked his horse's tail

Said when a rider, going at full speed, pulls his horse to such a sudden stop that he literally sits on his tail.

spike weaner

A circle of wire spikes fitted around a calf's nose and serving the purpose of weaning the animal.

spilled

Thrown from a horse.

spinner

A horse which bucks in a tight circle, spinning either to right or left. This type of horse generally does his bucking in a small space, but his actions are so violent as he whirls and bucks with a backward motion as he hits the ground, that the average rider quickly becomes dizzy, loses his sense of balance, and is soon "eating gravel." This type of bucker seldom hurts his rider when throwing him, because he doesn't throw him high. He merely whirls and turns out from under him, letting him down comparatively easy. (Bruce Clinton, "Buckin' Horses," *Western Horseman*, III, No. 3 [May–June, 1938], 10.)

splatter dabs

Slang name for hot cakes.

split

An earmark made simply by splitting the ear midway from the tip about halfway toward the head.

split the blankets

To share one's bed with another.

splitting the tail

It was believed among old-time cowmen that splitting a cow's tail would prevent blackleg.

spoiled herd

One that has acquired the habit of stampeding at every opportunity.

spoiled horse

One abused at the breaking period until he has had his character ruined—a man-made outlaw.

spook

To scare.

spooky

Said of a horse with a nervous temperament.

spool your bed

To roll it up for packing or moving.

spotted pup

Rice and raisins cooked together.

spraddled out

The cowboy's term for being dressed up in his best. Yet it is one of the philosophies of the cowman that, "It's the man that's the cowhand, not the outfit he wears."

spread

A roping term, a ranch, together with its buildings, cattle, and employees.

spread the mustard

To put on airs.

springer

A cow about to calve.

spring roundup

Synonymous with calf roundup, occurring in the spring.

spur buttoning

Sliding the button of the spur along the sides of a bucking horse when scratching instead of turning the rowels against his flesh. This is practiced by some rodeo riders.

spur leather

A broad, crescent-shaped shield of leather fitting over the instep to hold the spur on the foot.

SPURRING

See bicycling, business riding, coasting on the spurs, comb, curry him out, curry the kinks out, gaff, gig, goose, hundred-and-elevens, raking, reefing, scratch, scratching, screwing down, shove in the steel, slick-heeled, spur buttoning, throwing the steel.

spurs

The metal necessities worn upon the cowboy's heels. They are one of the most essential implements of the cowboy's equipment for controlling his horse. He does not wear them to punish a horse as many people think, nor are they on his heels for ornament. He uses them more than he does the reins, but mostly as reminders. They are necessary in helping a horse over rough places he does not want to cross, or in signaling him for turnings and quick starts and stops.

If a cowhand used his spurs to cut a horse up, he would not last long at most ranches, and if the outfit was so short handed it was forced to keep him on, he would likely be given such a rough string, he would be kept so busy trying to hang on he wouldn't have time to use his spurs.

The real cowboy loves his horses, and being cruel to them is farthest from his mind. When he buys a new pair of spurs, the first thing he does is to file the points of the rowels until they are blunt. Sharp rowels keep him from doing good work because they keep the horse fighting and nervous and shrinking from their touch. When he uses them, a mere touch is as far as he goes and sometimes a slight motion of the leg is all that is necessary.

He does not buy a big spur because it looks scary, but because the big one is less cruel. The bigger the rowel and the more points it has the less damage it does. It is the little spur with few points that sinks in. (Will James, *All in a Day's Riding* [New York, Charles Scribner's Sons, 1933], 54.)

The jingle of the spurs is sweet music to any cowhand. It keeps him from getting lonesome when he's riding the range, and as long as he hears the music of the spurs everything is rosy. He rarely takes them off when he is working, and in some sections he loses his social standing when he is caught without them. Many a pair of boots has been worn out without ever having had the spurs removed. Spurs are helpful at night, too, as a bootjack in removing boots.

SPURS

See buck hook, buzzsaw, California drag rowel, can openers, cartwheel, Chihuahuas, danglers, diggers, flower rowel, gad, gal-leg, galves, gooseneck, grapplin' irons, gut-hooks, gut lancers, hooks, Kelly's, locked spurs, petmakers, rib wrenches, shank, spur leather, spurs, star rowel, steel, sunset rowel, tin-belly, wagon-spoke rowel.

square

This word has a broad meaning on the range. A man entitled to such a testimonial to his worth has to possess qualities of unflinching courage, daring, and self-reliance; and in addition to these he has to be ready and willing to "stand by" a brother cowman and to do his duty efficiently in everything that might happen to come up in the work of the day. Moreover, whatever he might have been and might have done elsewhere, he must be truthful, honest, and honorable in all his relations to the outfit as a whole and to each of the men with whom he is associated in taking care of its property. Lying, crookedness, and double-dealing are intolerable offenses in this close-bound life. To say of a man that he is *square* is to pay him the highest compliment. (*Prose and Poetry of the Cattle Industry* [Denver, 1905].)

squat

A bit of land, a claim (as noun); to settle on a claim (as verb).

squatter

One who settles on state or government land.

squaw hitch

A packer's knot.

squaw horse
What the cowboy sometimes calls a poor specimen of horseflesh.

squawman
A white man who marries an Indian woman.

squaw wood
A slang name for dried cow chips; also used in speaking of small, dry, easily broken sticks when used for fuel.

squeeze 'em down
Narrowing the width of a trail herd for the crossing of a river or any other purpose.

squeezers
Narrow branding chutes.

squeeze the biscuit
To catch the saddle horn when riding.

squeezin' lizzie
Holding the saddle horn. One cowhand spoke of another's "hangin' on like an Injun to a whiskey jug" during a ride.

squirrel can
A large can used by the cook to throw scraps into. Whenever anything, from a saddle blanket to a spur, is lost, someone jokingly suggests looking for it in the squirrel can.

stack
Short for *haystack*.

stack it on
To throw a rope upon an animal.

stack-yard
Where hay is stacked for winter feeding of cattle.

stags
Male animals castrated late in life.

staked to a fill
Given a good meal.

stake out
To picket an animal.

stake rope
The Texan's name for the picket rope used to stake horses.

STAKING
See loggin', picket, picket pin, picket rope, putto, stake out, stake rope.

stamp brand
One made with a set branding iron which burns the complete brand with one impression. This iron is only practical when comparatively small brands are used. Modern cowmen use smaller brands since the use of the running iron is unlawful, for large brands ruin the animal's hide for the leather buyers.

stampede
The running wild of cattle or horses from fright. Used both as a verb and a noun and from the Spanish *estampida*, meaning *a general scamper of cattle*; also a loud noise or crash. The term is also used to express the rush of humans to new localities.

A stampede is dangerous both to the running cattle and to the men herding them. The cattle will often run until exhausted, and of course, this is damaging to both their weight and their condition. The fact that the majority of stampedes occur on stormy nights make them more difficult to bring under control and more dangerous for the riders. Many a cowboy has been left in an unmarked grave upon the prairie as the result of a stampede.

Nothing can happen so quickly as a stampede. It is difficult to realize how suddenly many cattle can rise to their feet and be gone. As the cowman says, "They jes' buy a through ticket to hell and gone, and try to ketch the first train." A stampede spoils cattle and makes them nervous and hard to hold for many days. Often many of them are killed or crippled, and others are so scattered they are never recovered.

Anything can cause a stampede. Thousands of causes have been listed by the cattlemen, some of them so simple that they sound ridiculous to the uninitiated. In the trail days the cattle were traveling a country strange to them and were naturally nervous and suspicious. Also at this time the country was full of thieves who often stampeded a herd in the hope of retrieving some of the scattered ones. The old-time cowman called them "stompedes," and his description of one was, "It's one jump to their feet and another jump to hell." (J. Frank Dobie, *The Longhorns* [Boston, Little, Brown, 1941], 88.)

The riders make every effort to gain a position alongside the lead cattle and try to head them into a milling circle. Each rider keeps up his singing or some sort of noise, and if he can hear his partner, he knows he is safe. If he does not hear him, he might be down. Contrary to general belief and popular fiction, guns are rarely fired in front of cattle in an effort to turn them. This would only frighten them the more.

stampeder

A horse easily frightened, which runs away blindly; also a cow or steer which habitually starts the herd stampeding. If there ever is a horse genuinely hated in an outfit it is the stampeder. He is more dangerous than a bucker, because he is generally sort of crazy and does not look where he is going. (Dick Boyd, "The Evolution of a Cowboy," *Cattleman*, XXV, No. 10 [March, 1939], 119–21.)

stampede to the wild bunch

Said of one who has committed a crime and is dodging the law; one who joins an outlaw band. According to Old Man Kip Bronson, at one time in a certain section of the West, the "thieves and killers was so thick y'u'd a-thought they had a bill-o'-sale on the whole damned country."

stand

In the parlance of the buffalo hunter this meant bringing a whole herd to a halt by killing the leading bull, then killing animal after animal that attempted to get to the front of the herd. As a rule buffaloes refused to leave after they smelled the blood of the first one shot, and their slaughter was easy. (W. S. Campbell [Stanley Vestal] to R.F.A.; Sophie A. Poe, *Buckboard Days* [Caldwell, Idaho, Caxton Printers, 1936], 79.)

stand by

To remain loyal.

standing feed

Grass, uncut hay.

standing night guard

Doing guard duty with the herd at night. See *night guard*.

star

A small patch of white in the forehead of a dark-colored horse.

star gazing

A trick-roping term which means to start a body spin and slowly assume a sitting posture, then lie on the back, spinning all the while.

star-pitch

To sleep in the open without covering.

star rowel

A spur with a rowel of five or six points.

star strip

When the white star on a horse's forehead extends below the level of the eyes, it is called a star strip.

startin' the swim

Putting the leaders of a trail herd into the water for a crossing. Getting cattle to take to water often calls for a great deal of patience, a knowledge of cow psychology, and a lot of experience. If the sun shines in the eyes of the cattle, they have difficulty in seeing the opposite bank and will not swim. Sometimes starting the swim is accomplished by keeping them away from the water a day or two and then gradually working them down to an easy taking-off place. Frequently, just as the cattle reach the water's edge, the horse herd will be eased into the river ahead of the lead cattle and started for the opposite bank. Usually the drovers have no difficulty in getting the cattle to follow the horses.

star-toter

A sheriff or deputy.

starve-out

A pasture of very few acres at a permanent camp, usually without water and with the grass used up, into which horses are thrown overnight to avoid having to catch them in the morning.

state's eggs

The cowboy's name for eggs, because in the early days they were all shipped in from the states to the cow country, most of which at that time was in the territories.

stay in one's tree

To remain in the saddle. *Stay in one's pine, stay in one's ellum fork* are variants. These expressions are often used as shouts of encouragement or admonition.

stay out with the dry cattle

To make a night of it, to carouse, to get drunk.

Stay with him!

The familiar cry of the breaking corral and a phrase of encouragement heard at every rodeo when a man is riding a bucking horse.

STEALING

See borrowed, Pecos swap, rustle, rustling, sleepering, swing a wide loop, yamping.

steel

Slang name for spurs.

steeple fork

An earmark made by cutting two splits into the ear from the end, back one-third or halfway toward the head, and cutting out the middle piece, the splits about an inch apart.

steer busting

A popular name for roping and throwing a steer with a rope single-handed. The roper rides as close to the animal as possible before casting his loop. When it is settled around the horns or neck, and has been given a jerk to hold it there, the slack of the rope is dropped just under the steer's right hip-bone and around his buttocks. The rider then reins his horse to the left and braces himself for the shock which is sure to follow. When the slack is taken up, the steer is reversed in midair and slammed to the ground with a force that knocks the breath from him. (John M. Hendrix,

"Roping," *Cattleman*, XXII, No. 1 [June, 1935], 16–17.)

steer horse

A roping horse trained so that he will take up the slack by facing away and pulling forward from the thrown animal.

steer roping

The art of capturing, busting, and hog-tying a range steer single-handed.

step across

Slang for mounting a horse.

Stetson

A name the cowboy often gives his hat whether it is a "genuwine" Stetson or not. The big Stetson hat is the earmark of the cow country. It is the first thing the tenderfoot buys when he goes west, but he never seems to learn to wear it at just the "right jack-deuce angle over his off-eye." One cowman can tell what state another is from by the size and shape of his hat.

It is not altogether vanity that makes the cowboy pay a high price for his hat. He knows he has to have one of fine quality to stand the rough usage it receives. He may throw it on the floor and hang his spurs on a nail, for he knows a good hat can be tromped on without hurting it, while tromping on a spur does neither the tromper nor the spur any good.

You may be surprised to learn that the cowboy's hat has more different uses than any other garment he wears. Often his life depends upon a good hat, for a limber brim of a cheap hat might flop in his eyes at just the wrong time. When he is riding in the scorching sun, the wide brim is like the shade of a tree, and the high crown furnishes space to keep his head cool. The wide brim also shades his eyes so that he can see long distances without getting sun-blinded when a lot depends upon his vision. When the sun is at his back, he tilts his Stetson for neck protection. In the rain it serves as an umbrella and makes a good shelter when he is trying to snatch a little daylight sleep. (Will James, *All in a Day's Riding* [New York, Charles Scribner's Sons, 1933], 15–20.)

The crown makes a handy water bucket if his horse can not get to water, and the brim serves as his own drinking-cup. He starts his camp fire with his hat by using it as a bellows to fan a sickly blaze, and he can use it again as a water bucket to put out that same fire when he breaks camp. In the winter he pulls the brim down and ties it over his ears to avoid frostbite.

His hat is the first thing a cowhand puts on when he gets up and the last thing he takes off when he goes to bed. But during the day there are many times when he may have to jerk it off to use as a handy implement. There are times when its sudden use saves a lot of hard work, a long ride, a nasty fall, or even sudden death. Perhaps he is penning a bunch of snaky critters when the wave of a big hat will turn a bunch quitter and save a long ride. It also comes in handy to turn a stampeding bronc from dangerous ground by fanning its head when reins would be useless. It is useful in splitting a bunch of horses in two when the cowboy is afoot in a horse corral.

A big hat in the hands of a bronc rider can be used like a balancing pole of a tight-wire walker. If the rider loses his hat, he loses a lot of his balancing power.

Perhaps the cowboy is afoot in a branding pen when some old mama cow hears the bellow of her offspring as he is being branded. She comes on the run and on the prod. (Being afoot in a pen with a cow in this mood is, in the language of the cowhand, "more dangerous than kickin' a loaded polecat.") The big hat now comes in handy to throw into her face when she gets too close, making her hesitate long enough to let the cowboy get to a fence.

Most riders decorate their hats with bands, both as ornaments and for the purpose of adjusting the fit to the head. What they use is mostly a matter of personal taste. Some like leather bands studded with silver conchas, some use strings of Indian beads, while others are satisfied with bands of rattlesnake skin or woven horsehair. Whatever is used will likely serve as a storage place to keep matches dry.

See *John B.*

stew ball

A corruption of *skewbald*, meaning a horse spotted with white and any other color except black.

stick horse

One that has to be forced to work.

STICKING

See hang and rattle.

stickin' like a postage stamp

Said of one making a good ride.

sticky rope

A slang name for a rustler. His rope has a habit of "stickin' to other folk's cows."

stiff

Synonymous with *corpse*. As the lifeless body of a human soon becomes rigid, the more easily spoken word *stiff* was substituted for *corpse*, and was later applied in a contemptuous way to suggest worthlessness, or to "dead ones." (Robert M. Wright, *Dodge City, the Cowboy Capital* [Wichita, Kansas, 1913 (reprint)], 163.)

stiff man

A man, who, with wagon and team and a barrel or two of oil or gasoline, drives over the range disposing of carcasses by burning them as he comes across them. It is a better job for a man who has lost his sense of smell.

stiff rope and a short drop

Said of a hanging.

stingy gun

A derringer or bulldog pistol of light weight.

stinker

A word applied to a person held in contempt. The word, originated in this sense by the buffalo hunters, was applied to newcomers on the range who skinned the buffalo that the former had killed, but were unable to secure the hides immediately on account of freezes or other natural causes (Robert M. Wright, *Dodge City, the Cowboy Capital* [Wichita, Kansas, 1913 (reprint], 163).

stirrup leathers

The broad leathers that hang from the

bar of the tree of the saddle and from which the stirrups hang.

stirrups

Foot supports of the saddle, usually made of wood bound with iron, brass, or rawhide, but sometimes all iron or brass. There is nothing the cowboy dreads more than having a foot caught in a stirrup and being dragged to death by a horse.

STIRRUPS

See ación, bulldogs, dog-house stirrups, drop stirrup, eagle-bill, hobbled stirrups, leg jockey, monkey nose, one foot in the stirrup, open stirrups, oxbow, ox-yokes, stirrups, stirrup leathers, tapadero.

stock detective

A man engaged in trying to catch cattle thieves and brand burners, usually employed by a cattle association.

stockers

Cattle acquired for building up a new herd on a previously unoccupied range.

stock horse

Brood mare and colt.

stocking

When the white on a horse's legs extend above the fetlocks, he is said to have stockings.

STOCK RAISER

See cattleman, rancher, ranchero, ranchman.

stogies

The cowboy's name for cheap, hand-me-down boots.

stomach pump

A spade bit, so called because of the piece of flat steel which curves a little and goes up into the horse's mouth.

stomp

A cowboy dance. Most of the boys are timid until the dance warms up. Cochise Jones once said: "They've run in a straight steer herd so long they're shy as a green bronc to a new waterin' trough. Some of 'em dance like a bear 'round a beehive that's afraid of gettin' stung;

others don't seem to know how to handle calico and get as rough as they do handlin' cattle in a brandin' pen. The women would jes' as soon dance with a grizzly as one of them kind, but most peelers go more or less loco when a female's around."

stood up

Robbed.

stool-and-bucket cow

Gentle milch cow.

STORIES

See entries under windies.

straddlin' down the road

A good cowboy description of a bow-legged man walking on high heels.

straight as a wagon tongue

Said of a trustworthy person.

straight bit

A bit made of a straight piece of metal.

straight buck

Said when a horse makes straight jumps without any twists or turns. See buckin' straight away.

straight steer herd

A herd composed of nothing but steers.

strainer

A strip of galvanized iron placed over the middle of the saddletree to cover the open space between the side-boards. Upon this is laid a piece of soft, thick leather fashioned to the form of the rider.

strangulation jig

A hanging. A man being hanged had his hands tied behind him, but his feet were usually free and these kicked about in his death struggle; hence the name.

strapped on his horse, toes down

This meant that the one spoken of had been killed. During range wars many men were sent home in this manner. A loose horse will usually go home of his own accord, and when he carries such a gruesome burden, it serves as a warning to the faction opposing the killers.

straw shed

A winter shelter made of posts and covered with straw.

straw boss
Assistant foreman.

stray man
See *rep.*

strays
A term applied to cattle visiting from other ranges; horses from other ranges are said to be *stray horses*, not merely strays.

stretchin' the blanket
Telling a windy or tall tale, lying.

stretchin' out
When one cowhand ropes an animal by the forefeet, while another one ropes him by the hind feet, thus stretching the brute.

string
Slang for a rope; also a mount of horses. The cowboy's string of horses is carefully made up of the different kinds necessary for his work: circle horses, cutting horses, roping horses, a night horse, and one or two broncs. Once a string has been turned over to him, it is the same as his own as long as he stays with the ranch; and no one, not even the boss, can ride one of the horses without his permission.

Each man is responsible for the condition of his own string, and while the boss never interferes with these horses, he had better not see them abused. A string is never split. If the rider quits or gets fired, the horses in his string are not used until he comes back, or another rider takes his place. A rider taking a new job has a string of horses pointed out to him by the boss. He receives no information concerning them. Information is frequently taken as an offense, as it implies a lack of confidence in his ability. When the boss takes a horse from a rider's string, this action tells the rider more strongly than words that he wants him to quit.

STRING
See cavvy, choosin' match, mount, remuda, saddle band.

stringin' a greener
Playing tricks upon a tenderfoot.

There are many such tricks, and they constitute a favorite sport of the cow country.

strings
Short for *saddle strings*. See *saddle strings*.

string up
To hang.

stripper
A heifer, a cow without milk; also a skinner of buffaloes or dead cattle.

stub-horn
Usually an old bull whose horns were chipped and broken from many fights. He often spent time rubbing these horns on rocks and trees attempting to sharpen them for the next battle (W. S. Campbell [Stanley Vestal] to R.F.A.). Also sometimes applied to a man who has been scarred by many battles.

stuck his bill in the ground
Said when a horse lowers his head between his forelegs to start bucking.

stud bunch
A bunch of mares and colts which a stallion herds and holds in one bunch, averaging about twenty head.

stuff
A common reference to general range stock which might include yearlings, bulls, steers, weaners, cows with calves, and dry cows.

stump sucker
A horse having the vice of biting or getting his teeth against something and "sucking wind."

SUCCESS
See big casino, bonanza, get the bacon.

sudadero (soo-dah-day'ro)
Spanish, meaning *a handkerchief for wiping off the sweat*, or *sweat pad*. The cowman uses it to mean the leather lining of the skirt of the saddle. This term is sometimes incorrectly applied to the *rosadero.*

suggans
Blankets for bedding, heavy comforts often made from patches of pants, coats,

or overcoats. A suggan usually weighs about four pounds, as the cowboy says, "a pound for each corner." Also called *soogans* or *soogins*.

In her recent book, *No Life for a Lady*, Agnes Morley Cleaveland tells a good story about soogins:

"It was a popular joke with us to tell some tenderfoot that we were sorry, but we had to confess that all our beds had soogins in them, and then watch the look of apprehension settle in the visitor's eye.

"One visitor put a certain cowboy properly in his place—an especially ignorant cowboy, I confess, but not too rare a specimen. The cowboy laughed uproariously at the visitor's unconcealed distaste for sleeping in a bed infested with soogins.

" 'You should laugh,' retorted the visitor, 'I happen to know that you slumber in your bed.'

"The cowboy turned purple. 'No man can say that about me and git away with it!' he roared.

"Fortunately he had no gun. We rescued the visitor."

(Agnes Morley Cleaveland, *No Life for a Lady* [Boston, Houghton Mifflin, 1941], 166.)

sugar-eater

A pampered horse.

suicide horse

A blind bucker; a horse that goes insane from fear when ridden and is more dangerous to himself than to the rider, as he is apt to kill himself by bucking into or over obstacles.

sulker

A rodeo contestant is indeed unlucky when he draws a horse of this type. Such a horse will not leave the chute until he is good and ready. He will squat back on his haunches, bunching himself, after the chute gate is opened. No amount of coaxing will make him come out until he is ready to do so of his own accord. Suddenly he will leave with a mighty leap which causes most riders to break their balance across the cantle board of the saddle. Very seldom is the rider ever able to regain his seat and get with his mount. Another cowboy bites the dust, and the crowd gets a good laugh. (Bruce Clinton, "Buckin' Horses," *Western Horseman*, III, No. 3 [May–June, 1938], 28.)

summer name

When a man chose to give a name other than his true one, the West respected a strict code of showing no curiosity about his past. The nearest approach to curiosity would be when he was asked, facetiously, "What is your summer name?"

Sunday-go-to-meetin' clothes

What the cowboy calls his very best raiment.

Sunday horse

One with an easy gait, usually a single-footer with some style, and one the cowboy saves to ride upon special occasions. He is usually a fancy, high-stepping, all-around saddler, but as Whitey Blythe used to say, "He ain't worth a damn—only to ride down the road."

sunfisher

A horse that sunfishes.

sunfishing

A bucking term used in describing the movements of a horse when he twists his body into a crescent, alternately to the right and to the left; or, in other words, when he seems to try to touch the ground with first one shoulder and then the other, letting the sunlight hit his belly.

sun-grinner

Slang name for a Mexican.

sunned his moccasins

Often said when one is thrown from a horse, especially when he lands with his feet in the air!

sunpecked jay

A rustic, a rural resident.

sunset rowel

A spur wheel with many points set close together; also called a *sunburst*.

Supaway John

The expression an Indian used in asking for food when he came to a cow camp.

surcingle
A belly-band.

surface fuel
Dried cow chips.

surly
A slang name for a bull.

swag
Quantity, load, a low place, a coulee.

swallow-and-get-out trough
A hurry-up eating place. There is a story in the West which runs something like this: "When a passenger train stopped at an eating station, an eastern lady rushed from it to one of those railroad swallow-and-get-out troughs. The conductor notified the passengers that they had only about five minutes to eat as the train was late, so the lady just ordered a cup of coffee. When she got it, black and boiling hot, she remarked that she doubted whether she could drink it in time to catch her train. A cowboy sitting next to her wanted to show her true western hospitality, so he shoved her his cup and said, 'Here's one, lady, that's already saucered and blowed.'"

swallowed his head
Said when a horse bucks high and produces a decided curve in his back with his head between his front feet and his tail between his hind ones.

swallow-fork
An earmark made by hollowing the ear lengthwise, beginning halfway back, cutting at an angle of forty-five degrees toward the end. The result is a forked notch in the ear.

swallow-forkin'
Putting on airs, all dressed up in one's best.

swallow-tail
An earmark made by trimming the tip of the ear into the form of a bird's flaring tail.

swamper
The cook's helper, a janitor in a saloon; also a man who handles the brakes and helps the driver of a jerk-line string.

swamp seed
Slang name for rice.

swapping ends
A movement peculiar to a bronc, where he quickly reverses his position, making a complete half-circle in the air.

sweat
To work for one's board without other pay.

sweatin' a game
Sitting around looking at a card game.

swell-fork
A saddle with swells, or projections, in leather on each side of the fork below the horn. The rider can hook his knees under these projections when riding a pitching horse and they help keep him in the saddle.

swimming horse
A horse, selected because of his ability to swim, used in crossing rivers. Not all horses are good or steady swimmers, and during the trail days when there were many rivers to cross, much depended upon a good swimming horse.

swimming the herd
If the river to be crossed is at medium stage and calm, there is usually no trouble in getting the leaders to take the water; but if the river is high and turbulent, much vigorous urging is required. Sometimes a cowboy or two will swim ahead on their horses to show the cattle that there is no danger. Occasionally the horse herd will cross to open the way. If the cattle reach swimming depth, they usually go ahead to the other side unless some floating log or other untoward event causes them to start milling in midstream.
There have been instances when the lead cattle have refused under all urging to take to the water of a swollen river and several days have elapsed before a crossing could be made.

swimming water
Water too deep to cross without swimming.

swing a wide loop
To live a free life, to steal cattle.

swinging brand

One suspended from and connected to a quarter-circle.

swing rider

One of the riders with a trail herd, riding about one-third of the way back from the point riders. See *point rider*.

swing team

Any span of horses in a jerk-line string between the leaders and the wheel horses.

swivel dude

A gaudy fellow. Silk Kutner once said of one, "He's so pretty I feel like takin' off my hat ever'time I meet 'im."

T

"There ain't no hoss that can't be rode,
There ain't no man that can't be throwed"

tack-berry buckle

A cinch buckle carrying two wraps of the latigo and hooking into the cinch ring.

tailing

The throwing of an animal by the tail in lieu of a rope. Any animal can, when traveling rapidly, be sent heels over head by seizing its tail and giving it a pull to one side. This method was resorted to frequently with the wild longhorns, and a thorough tailing usually knocked the breath from them and so dazed them that they would behave for the rest of the day. The act requires both a quick and swift horse and a daring rider. (J. Frank Dobie, *Vaquero of the Brush Country* [Dallas, Southwest Press, 1929], 15.)

TAILING

See bull tailing, tailing, tailing up.

tailings

Stragglers.

tailing up

Lifting weak cattle to their feet by their tails. This method is used primarily after cattle are extricated from bog holes.

tail out

To depart, to decamp.

tail over the dashboard

Said of one in high spirits.

tail over the lines

Said of one hard to control.

tail pulling

The southern cowman lets the tails of his horses grow. Perhaps it is to protect them from flies and insects which are worse on southern ranges, perhaps it is merely a tradition. But since early in the industry, on northern ranges, it has been the custom to make some changes in the horse's tail. It became the practice at the end of the season to cut the tail off close to the bone. By doing this the riders, when they rode out the following spring to roundup the saddle horses, could distinguish them from the wild ones. With the aid of field glasses these riders could see the horses at a great distance, and if the bunch they spied wore long tails, they knew the horses were not the ones they were looking for and consequently were saved a long ride.

But this cutting of the tail made it grow out unnaturally heavy and bushy, giving it an ugly, misshapen appearance. To give the tail a lighter and dressier look, the cowhand began pulling or weeding out the hair. This improved the appearance so much that it became the fashion to pull rather than to cut the tail, and to this day a pulled tail is the sign that its possessor is a broken horse.

When the northern cowboy sees a saddle horse with a tail long enough to drag against his hind hoofs, he figures he belongs to a farmer or a gambler in town. To him, horses with long tails look like brood mares. (Bud Cowan, *Range Rider* [Garden City, Doubleday, Doran, 1930], 24; and J. K. Rollinson, *Pony Trails in Wyoming* [Caldwell, Idaho, Caxton Printers, 1941], 36, 112.)

tail rider
One of the men at the rear of a herd on a drive; also called *drag rider*.

take a run
Means *making for a horse*—to run to and mount one.

take a squatter's right
Often said of one thrown from a horse.

take on
A common reference to cattle's putting on flesh or fat.

take the big jump
To die.

take the pins from under it
To throw an animal by roping it either by forefooting or heeling.

take the slack out of his rope
To defeat one, to place one at a disadvantage.

take to the tall timbers
To run away, to be on the dodge.

take to the tules
Another expression meaning *to run away;* also is used in the sense of being on the dodge.

TAKING A CHANCE
See grabbin' the brandin' iron by the hot end, playin' a hand with his eyes shut.

taking leather
Grabbing the saddle horn when riding a bucking horse.

takin' up a homestead
Said of one thrown from a horse; also taking up land and improving it for a home.

TALKING
See augur, augurin' match, carajoing, chew it finer, chew the cud, Chinook, circular story, comeback, cow talk, coyotin' 'round the rim, cut the deck deeper, dally your tongue, diarrhea of the jawbone, flannel mouth, giggle talk, good comeback, grapevine telegraph, haze the talk, His saddle is slippin'., hobble your lip, leaky mouth, load, make medicine, medicine tongue, mix the medicine, moccasin mail, moccasin telegraph, more lip than a muley cow, mouthy, no medicine, powwow, range word, sign language, talking horse, talk like a Texan, talkin' talents, talk turkey, tie one to that, tongue oil, windies.

talking horse
The favorite subject of conversation with a group of cowmen.

talkin' iron
Slang name for a gun.

talkin' load
Just drunk enough to be loquacious.

talkin' talents
Ability to talk freely.

talk like a Texan
Said of one boastful of his work or accomplishments.

talk turkey
To mean business.

TALL
See built high above his corns.

tallow factory
An establishment where cattle were cooked solely for the tallow they might produce. Places of this sort were established in Texas during the days immediately after the Civil War when cattle were plentiful and there were no markets for them.

tally branding
Taking an inventory of cattle.

tally hand
A man selected to keep a record of the calves branded at the spring roundup. He was chosen for this position because of his honesty and clerical ability, though sometimes because of his physical inability to do more strenuous work. (Philip A. Rollins, *The Cowboy* [New York, Charles Scribner's Sons, 1936], 235.)

tally man

Same as *tally hand*. He was appointed by the roundup captain. He might be an older man, one recovering from an illness, or one hurt in riding a horse the previous day, but he was chosen for his reputation for honesty. He had many opportunities to falsify his records, and upon his count depended an owner's estimate of the season's profit. Yet, through his own honesty and the ethics of the range, these things never entered his head. All the time calves were slithering to the fire, he chanted his tally, and as the number of unbranded calves grew smaller, the lines in his smudged and grimy book grew longer. At every lax moment he took the opportunity to sharpen a stub pencil, which was wearing down rapidly.

tally sheet

The book or paper upon which the tally man's record was kept.

tank

A reservoir made by damming a stream, a reservoir of wood, concrete, or metal (as noun); to cook cattle for their tallow (as verb).

tapadero (tah-pah-day'ro)

From the Spanish *tapaderas*, which comes from the verb *tapar*, meaning *to close* or *cover*. It is a wedge-shaped piece of leather which covers the stirrup front and sides, but is open in the rear. Its literal meaning is *toe-fender*. The word is usually shortened to *taps*. Made from heavy cowhide and occasionally reinforced by a wooden frame, it is used mostly in the brush country to protect the rider's feet and stirrups from brush.

tapaojos (tah-pah-o'hose)

This Spanish word is also from *tapar*, *to cover*, plus *ojos*, *eyes*. A blind or eye-cover for animals. It is a strip of leather about three inches wide, fastened to the headstall of the hackamore and long enough to extend across the brow of the animal. It is used on mean or unbroken horses being mounted for the first time, and also on pack mules when loading, to keep them from getting excited. Americans do not use tapaojos extensively. (Harold W. Bentley, *Dictionary of Span-*

ish Terms in English [New York, Columbia University Press, 1932], 205.)

tarantula juice

A slang name for whiskey. A few drinks of some of it would, in the words of Muley Metcalf, "have a man reelin' 'round like a pup tryin' to find a soft spot to lie down in," or as another said, "knockin' 'round like a blind dog in a meat shop."

tarp

Short for *tarpaulin*. The Westerner's name for any canvas not especially titled either *pack covers* or *wagon sheets*. Usually it refers to the piece of canvas in which he rolls his bed when not in use and with which he covers himself at night.

tarrabee

An all-wood machine, carved by hand from whatever wood the man of the house possesses and used for spinning the threads for making girths. Patterns vary, but all twirlers work on the same principle. All have wooden handles with a hollow toward one end, and near this hollowed end a handle is inset to extend at right angles. The wood of a much used twisting paddle takes on the appearance of satinwood. Contact with oily hair and sweating hands give it a rich brown polish. (Brooks Taylor, "Girt Making," *Cattleman*, XXVII, No. 9 [February, 1941], 73–74.)

tasting gravel

Being thrown from a horse.

tear squeezer

Something sad, a sad story.

techy as a teased snake

Said of one in a bad humor, or one easy to anger.

teepee

Originally an Indian conical-shaped tent made of buffalo hide and used by the Plains Indian, but also an idiom used by the cowman in referring to his home.

Teeth

See nut crackers, smooth mouth, toothing.

teeth in the saddle
Said of a saddle which causes sore backs. More riders have lost their jobs over back-eating saddles than any other one thing. Some of the early-day saddles, as one cowboy said, "could eat out of a wire corral in one night."

teguas (te'gwas)
Rawhide moccasins, ankle high, laced in front and undecorated, yet light and comfortable. Worn principally by Mexicans and Indians.

telegraph him home
Said when a man is hanged by using his own rope and a pole borrowed from Western Union.

tellin 'a windy
Relating a tall tale, telling a lie.

tellin' off the riders
Giving directions to each rider about where to start his drive for the roundup. See *scattering the riders.*

tender
Said of a horse when he shows signs of getting saddlesores or sore feet.

TENDERFOOT
See advertising a leather shop, Arbuckle, early bouten, greener, green pea, Johnny-come-lately, lent, mail-order catalog on foot, mail-order cowboy, Monkey-Ward cowboy, new ground, phildoodle, pilgrim, pistols, punk, savage, shorthorn, skim-milk cowboy, stringin' a greener, tenderfoots.

tenderfoots
The name originally applied to imported cattle, but later attached to humans new to the country; both cattle and humans are also called *pilgrims.*

terrapin
A slang name for a saddle; also, as a verb, it means to travel on foot slowly.

Texas butter
The cowboy's name for gravy. Put some flour into the grease in which the steak was fried and let it bubble and brown, then add hot water and stir until it thickens.

Texas cakewalk
A hanging.

Texas fever
Same as *Spanish fever.*

Texas gate
A makeshift gate made of barbed wire fastened to a pole.

Texas skirt
The style of square skirt used on the Texas saddles.

Texas tie
When a roper keeps the home end of his rope tied hard to his saddle horn, it is often called by this term, because most Texans use this method.

There's a one-eyed man in the game.
One of the commonest superstitions in the West is that bad luck will forever follow a man who plays poker with a one-eyed gambler. The superstition gave rise to this expression and means, "Look out for a cheat."

THIEF
See mavericker, pack rat. See also *entries under* rustler.

thirty years' gathering
What the cowboy calls his trinkets and plunder gathered through the years. Agnes Morley Cleaveland, in *No Life For a Lady,* tells a story of a cowboy on his way to a local roundup stopping at her ranch for a meal. While he was eating, something stampeded his string of horses and with them went the packhorse carrying his bedroll. The man leaped from his chair shouting, "There goes the savin's of a lifetime!"

three-legged riding
This is what a Westerner calls riding with a tight rein and sawing on the horse's mouth with the bit.

three-quarter rig
A saddle having the cinch placed halfway between that of the center fire and the rim fire.

three-quarter seat
Said of a saddle whose leather seat

covering extends only to the rear edge of the stirrup groove.

three saddles

The professional buster considers a horse broken after three rides, or, as he says, three saddles.

three-up outfit

A small ranch which, as one cowboy said, "Don't own 'nough beef to hold a barbecue."

three-up screw

Said of a cowboy working on a small ranch where three horses are considered enough for a mount.

throat-latch

The leather strap fastening the bridle under the throat of the horse.

throat-ticklin' grub

The cowboy's name for the fancy food he never gets on the range.

throw back

When a bucking horse hurls itself backward intentionally, the trick of a killer; also to revert in type or in character to an ancestral stock.

throw down

The act of covering one with a gun, the act of shooting. The high hammer of the frontier six-gun was not designed to be cocked by the thumb tip as are the hammers of modern double-action revolvers, but by hooking the whole thumb over it and simply closing the hand for the first shot. The recoil throws the gun muzzle up in the air, the thumb is hooked over the hammer, and the gun cocks itself by its own weight when level. This is where the phrase *throwing down* originated.

throw dust

To try to cover up, to deceive.

throw gravel in his boots

To shoot at one's feet.

throw in

To go into partnership.

THROWING

See bulldog, bull tailing, bust, calf on the ground, California, dog fall, fair ground, forefooting, hoolihaning, jerked down, rolling a calf, stretching out, tailing, take the pins from under it.

throwing over

Pushing stray cattle of outside brands toward their home range at the end of a roundup.

throwing the steel

Said of one using the spurs freely.

throw lead

The act of shooting a gun.

THROWN FROM A HORSE

See bit the dust, chase a cloud, chew gravel, dirtied his shirt, dumped, dusted, eatin' gravel, flung him away, grassed him, grass huntin', Ketch my saddle!, kissed the ground, landed, landed fork end up, landed on his sombrero, lost his hat and got off to look for it, lost his horse, met his shadow on the ground, pickin' daisies, piled, spilled, sunned his moccasins, take a squatter's right, takin' up a homestead, tasting gravel, turned the pack, unload, went up to fork a cloud.

throw out

To stop a moving herd and move off the trail. The expression is used as "throw out the cattle and build camp"; also an animal cut from a herd. Also sometimes used in referring to a dilapidated human, as I heard one cowman say of such a man, "He looks like a throw out from a footsore remuda."

throw the lines away

To drive a team recklessly.

thumb buster

A name given the old-fashioned, single-action six-gun.

thumber

A type of shooter who removes the trigger and guard from his gun and shoots by raising and releasing the hammer with his thumb. He does his shooting at close quarters and relies upon speed for safety.

thumbing

Jabbing a horse with the thumbs to provoke further bucking.

tied holster

One tied down to the leg of the wearer to facilitate a quick draw, a good indication of a professional gunman. There is a saying in the West, "The man who wears his holster tied down don't do much talkin' with his mouth."

tie-down man

One who ties his holster down to his leg.

tied reins

Bridle reins tied together at the ends.

tied to the ground

Said when the cowboy drops his reins to the ground, knowing that his trained horse will be anchored just as surely as if he were actually tied.

tie-hard

A term frequently used in speaking of a tie-man to distinguish him from a dally-man.

tie-man

One keeping the home end of his rope tied to the saddle horn. Cowboys have scattered so much today that you can find both tie-men and dally men in all parts of the range, but as a rule they tie east of the Rockies and dally west of them. The tie-men use shorter ropes than the dally men and the ranges they ride are open and level. They are usually expert ropers and have complete confidence in their ability to make successful catches.

The Texan ties his rope, and when he ropes anything, he figures on hanging to it. The Californian keeps his rope untied, and when he ropes anything, he has to take a dally around the saddle horn; then if his catch gets him into a jam he can turn loose. The Texan does not say much about this action, but the Californian knows what the Texan thinks, and he does not like those thoughts.

Tie one to that.

A phrase used by western storytellers at the conclusion of a wild tale, as if inviting the next man to tell a bigger one; now commonly used everywhere (W. S. Campbell [Stanley Vestal] to R.F.A.).

tie rope

What the mecate is sometimes called; also a short rope used for hog-tying. See *mecate*.

tiger

The cowboy's name for a convict, because the latter is caged and wears stripes.

tight-legging

Riding with the legs tightly gripping the sides of the horse, a manner of riding which disqualifies a rider under rodeo rules, as he is supposed to scratch his horse with the spurs continuously.

time

Wages.

TIME

See heel-fly time, high-heeled time, mañana.

time judge

The timer for calf-roping and bulldogging contests at a rodeo. In other rodeo events his status is that of a referee at a prize fight.

tin-belly

Slang name for a cheap, inferior spur.

tinhorn

A cheap gambler; also applied to others not proficient in their chosen profession.

tip the hole card

To give one's plans away.

tobiano

Another Argentine word, used as a contrast to *overo*. The color characteristics of this pinto are that the white originates at the back and rump and extends downward, with the borders of markings generally smooth and regular. See *overo*. (George M. Glendenning, "Overos and Tobianos," *Western Horseman*, VII, No. 1 [January–February, 1942], 12.)

Tom Horn

Occasionally used in some sections as a slang name for rope.

tongue oil

Talking ability.

tongue splitter
A rustler who cruelly splits the calf's tongue to keep it from nursing and following its mother.

tonsil varnish
Slang name for whiskey.

too handy with a rope
Said of a rustler.

tool chest
A bit to which contrivances have been added to make it cruel. The man who uses one of these is soon cold-shouldered off the range.

too much spread
Said of one who has the habit of bragging, picking quarrels, or otherwise making himself disagreeable.

too thick to drink and too thin to plow
What the cowboy calls muddy water when he is forced to drink it. He might "have to chaw it 'fore he can swaller it," but if he's thirsty enough it's "damned good water."

toothing
Looking into a horse's mouth to tell his age.

top
The cowboy's idea of the best. The best roper is the *top roper;* the best rider, *top rider;* the best cutting horse, *top cutter;* and so on. Yet the best shooter is called a *crack shot.*

top off
To ride first, to take the rough edges off a horse.

TOPOGRAPHY AND VEGETATION
See arroyo, Badlands, bench, black chaparral, black spot, boggy crossing, bosque, bottom, box canyon, brasada, brush country, buffalo wallow, butte, cactus, canyon, cedar brakes, chaparral, chaparro, cholla, coulee, cross canyon, crossing, cut-bank, down in the Skillet, draw, hogback, llano, mal país, mesa, motte, paso, piñon, pup's nest, Quaker, sag, sendero, swag, tule, tumbleweed, yucca country.

top railer
A man who sits on the top rail of a corral and advises who should do the work and take the risks.

top screw
The foreman.

tornado juice
Another slang name for whiskey.

toro (toh'ro)
Spanish for *bull.* Sometimes used in the cow country.

totin' stars on his duds
Said of the Texas cowman, whose clothing was almost always decorated with stars. An old saying of the range is, "For a Texas puncher not to be totin' stars on his duds is most as bad as votin' the Republican ticket."

touchin' leather
Synonymous with *pulling leather.*

tough lay
Said of a ranch employing a bunch of badmen or gunmen.

TOWNS
See cow town, honkytonk town, pueblo, town with the hair on.

town with the hair on
Said of a wild and woolly or tough town like those at the end of the old cattle trails.

tracker
One expert in tracking or reading sign.

TRACKING
See back trail, blind trail, camping on his trail, cold trail, cut for sign, long-ear, plain trail, readin' sign, ridin' sign, sign, sliding the groove, tracker.

trail blazer
One who goes before, one who marks or blazes a new trail.

trail boss
The foreman of a trail herd. He had to know men and cattle; he had to be aggressive, quick to handle an emergency, and resourceful. It is said that a

good trail boss fed his hands out of his herd, lost a few en route, and yet got to his destination with more cattle than he had when the owner counted them out as they left the home range. He belonged to the class of men who made cattle history in bossing the herds up the long trail north from Texas. The world will never see his like again.

trail broke

Said of cattle after they became used to the trail.

trail count

Counting cattle as they were strung off on a trail drive. After the cattle left the bed-ground in the morning and were strung out in a thin line, the trail boss selected a man to be stationed opposite him on the other side of the passing herd. Both men selected an imaginary line upon which they stationed themselves, and as the cattle passed between them, their forefingers rose and fell as they pointed directly to each animal that passed. As each hundred head was counted, each man dropped a pebble into a handy pocket, tied a knot in his horn string, or used any other counter his individual selection dictated. When the herd had passed, each man counted his counters and announced to the other his tally for comparison. The chances were that their first count checked. If it did not, and there was a very wide margin of difference, they rode to the head of the moving herd and started over again. (Editorial, *Cattleman*, XXI, No. 4 [September, 1934], 26.)

trail cutter

A man employed, usually by stock associations, to halt marching herds and inspect them for cattle which did not properly belong with them.

trail days

The days when long trails were thoroughfares for great herds of cattle. Such a spectacle, as a business, will never be seen in the world again.

trail driver

A cowhand engaged in driving cattle over the long trails, usually one of the interstate trails leading from Texas.

trail driving

The act of moving cattle on the trail. It was called *driving*, but cattle were *trailed*, not driven. Instead, they were kept headed in the direction the drover desired them to go as they grazed. In this manner they would travel ten or twelve miles a day and fatten as they went. The only times they were driven was to get them away from familiar territory when they first left the home range, to tire them down in an effort to avoid stampedes, or to reach food and water in sections where these were scarce.

trail hand

Another name for a man engaged in trailing cattle. Every Texas range-bred boy was ambitious to "go up the trail." It gave him an opportunity to break the monotony of range life and offered a chance to "see the world."

trail herd

A bunch of cattle, guarded day and night, being trailed from one region to another. A trail herd usually traveled in single file, or in twos and threes, forming a long, sinuous line, which, if seen from above, would look like a huge serpent in slow motion.

TRAIL TERMS

See bedding down, big swimmin', bringin' up the drags, cut in, cutter herds, cut the trail, cutting the herd, drag, drag rider, drift, drive, dry drive, eatin' drag dust, excuse-me-ma'am, flank rider, following the tongue, haze, head 'em up, keeping up the corners, layover, lay-up, lead men, lead steer, Little Mary, night drive, over the willows, point riders, pounding 'em on the back, regular, ridin' 'em down, road brand, squeeze 'em down, startin' the swim, swimming water, swing riders, tailings, tail riders, throw out, trail boss, trail count, trail cutter, trail days, trail driver, trail driving, trail hand, trail herd, trail wagon, trimmin' the herd, up the trail, watering the herd.

trail wagon

One fastened behind another wagon in moving camp.

trap

Any freak saddle.

trap a squaw

To get married.

trap corral

A corral for capturing wild horses or cattle. The gate opens easily inward and closes behind so that the animals can not escape.

trapper's butter

Marrow from the bones of a killed animal. Sometimes this was put into a gallon of water and heated nearly to the boiling point, then blood from the animal was stirred in until a thick broth was made.

travels the lonesome places

Said of one on the scout, a man who "ain't on speakin' terms with the law."

tree

The wooden frame of the saddle which is covered with leather. The saddle usually takes its name from the shape of its tree, such as California, Visalia, Frazier, Ellenburg, or Brazos.

treeing the marshal

A common saying in the old days. On their return from a trip up the trail, the cowboys liked to brag about how they made the marshal of the town at the end of the trail "hide out."

tree ring

The metal ring to which the latigo straps are fastened.

trigger is delicate

Said of one quick tempered or quick to shoot over a grievance.

trigger itch

Said of one quick to shoot.

trigueño (tre-gay'nyo)

Spanish, meaning *swarthy, brownish*. The Southwest uses this word to designate a brown horse.

trimmin' the herd

The act of cutting cattle from a herd. The expression is usually employed when a trail cutter cuts the herd.

TROUBLESOME

See cut his wolf loose, hell bent for trouble, hellin' 'round town, hell with the hide off, lookin' for someone, sharpen his horns, tail over the lines, too much spread.

trunk strap

A latigo strap which buckles. Used in the sense of ridicule.

TRUSTWORTHY

See He'll do to ride the river with., measure a full sixteen hands high, square, standby, straight as a wagon tongue, up and down as a cow's tail.

tryin' to chin the moon

Said of a horse standing on his hind feet and pawing the air with his front ones; also said of a high bucker.

tucker bag

A bag for personal belongings. Not a commonly used term.

Tucson bed

Sleeping in the open without cover, or, in the cowboy's language, "usin' yore back for a mattress and yore belly for a coverin'."

tule (tu'le)

In the Southwest the name is applied to the yucca and certain kinds of reeds. When a man "takes to the tules," he goes into hiding or is on the dodge.

tullies

Men or cattle native of the *tulares*, or country of tules.

tumbleweed

A Russian thistle which, when dry, rolls before the wind. These plants roll and jump great distances, scattering their seeds as they go. One old-timer said he "reckoned" the Lord put tumbleweeds here "to show how the wind blows." Also a man with roving proclivities is called a *tumbleweed*.

tumbling brand

A brand leaning in an oblique position.

turn a wildcat

Said of a bucking horse.

turned the cat

When a horse falls after stepping into a doghole.

turned the pack
Said when a horse throws his rider.

turned through himself
Said when a horse stops quickly and turns in another direction.

turning the grass upside down
Plowing.

turn-out time
Time in the spring to turn cattle out to grass.

twelve-hour leggins
Slang name for chaps.

twine
Slang name for rope.

twister
Either short for bronc twister, or another name for the twitch; also a cyclone.

twist-horn
A nickname for the longhorns because of the many different twists and turns of their horns.

twisting down
The act of twisting a steer's neck in bulldogging until it falls upon its side.

twitch
A small loop of cord with a stick through it, used to punish a held horse. The loop is placed vertically around the animal's upper lip and then tightened by twisting the stick. (Philip A. Rollins, *The Cowboy* [New York, Charles Scribner's Sons, 1936], 152.) It is also called a *twister*, and some claim this is where the term *bronc twister* originated.

two-buckle boy
Farm hand.

two-gun man
A man who wears two guns and can shoot with either hand. This species was rare, even in the old West, and exists mostly in fiction. It's a rare case when two guns have any advantage over one. Their chief advantage is that they make a threat of an ace in the hole as a show of force when a lone man stacks against a crowd. The two-gun man, when among strangers, has to be careful with the motions of both hands, thus being handicapped in doing little things other men can do. He is, as a cowhand would say, "dressed to kill."

two jumps ahead of the sheriff
Said of one dodging the law. As one of them told me, he "didn't have to leave Texas. The sheriff come to the state line and jes' *begged* me to come back."

two-up driver
A driver of two spans, or four horses.

two whoops and a holler
Only a short distance.

tying down
Roping and catching an animal and tying it down by three of its feet against time. See *hog-tying*.

tying fast
Using the home end of the rope tied to the horn of the saddle in roping. See *tie-man*.

U

"Tossin' your rope before buildin' a loop don't ketch the calf"

uncorkin' a bronc
Taking off the rough edges.

under-bit
An earmark made by doubling the ear in and cutting a small piece, about an inch, out of the lower part of the ear, an inch in length and usually one-third of that in depth.

under-hack
An earmark made by simply cutting up on the underside of the ear for about an inch.

under-half-crop

An earmark made by splitting the ear from the tip, midway, about halfway back toward the head, and cutting off the lower half.

underhand pitch

This is strictly a heel loop for use on cattle. It can be used on foot in a corral, but is a favorite catch for mounted men working on roundup. It is about the only loop for which it is permissible to whirl while working among cattle and it is whirled very slowly, just enough to keep it moving. The loop is kept in motion at the right side of the thrower in a vertical plane, swinging up. When the object to be roped passes in front, the roper brings the rope around with a snap to give it carrying power and turns the loop loose over the back side of the hand as it swings forward. This pitches the loop, standing up, under the animal's belly so that he can jump into it with his hind feet. The right hand continues to hold the rope, as is the case in most heeling and forefooting throws, and the slack is jerked out at once. (W. M. French, "Ropes and Roping," *Cattleman*, XXVI, No. 12 [May, 1940], 17–30.)

under-round

An earmark made by cutting a half-circle from the bottom of the ear.

under-slope

An earmark made by cutting the ear about two-thirds of the way back from the tip straight to the center of the ear at its lower side.

under-split

An earmark made by splitting the ear from the lower edge to about the center.

underwears

The cowboy's contemptuous name for sheep.

UNDISCERNING

See blind as a snubbin' post, chuckle-headed as a prairie dog, throw dust.

unhook

To unhitch a team from a wagon. The cowboy never uses the words *hitch* and *unhitch*.

unload

Said when a horse bucks off his rider.

unravel some cartridges

To shoot.

unrooster

To take the rough edges off a horse.

unshucked

Naked; when used as a gun term, one is said to have *unshucked his gun*, meaning that he has drawn it from the holster, thus making it a naked gun.

UNWELCOME

See His cinch is gettin' frayed, saddle a dead horse on him.

unwind

Said when a horse starts bucking.

up and down as a cow's tail

Said of an honest and trustworthy person.

up the trail

Driving cattle up the trail. This became a profession during the years between the middle sixties and the eighties, and experienced trail drivers were in demand.

use him to trim a tree

To hang one.

using his rope arm to h'ist a glass

Said of one drinking.

V

"The bigger the mouth the better it looks when shut"

vaca (vah'cah)
Spanish for *cow*.

vacada (Vah-cah'dah)
A drove of cows.

vamoose
Americanized from the Spanish word *vamos (vah'mose)*, meaning *let's go*. The cowboy uses it to mean *get to hell out of here*.

vaquero (vah-kay'ro)
The word comes from the Spanish *vaca (cow)* with the suffix *ero* and means one engaged in working with cows. Although commonly used in the Southwest with reference to cowboys in general, it means more particularly Mexican cowboys.

velvet couch
The cowboy's slang name for his bedroll.

vent brand
From the Spanish *venta (ven'tah)*, meaning *sale*. When used as a noun, it means a brand placed upon an animal that has been given an ownership brand and later sold, and has the effect of cancelling the ownership brand, thus serving as the acknowledgment of a sale. It is usually placed on the same side of the animal as the original brand. As a verb, it means the act of putting on such a brand. See *counter brand*.

vigilantes
From the Spanish *vigilante (ve-he-lahn'tay)*, meaning *watchman* or *guard*. The American pronounces it *vig-i-lan'te* and uses it to mean men who organize themselves to take the enforcement of the law into their own hands; a volunteer committee of citizens to suppress and punish crime when the law seems inadequate.

VIGILANTES
See hemp committee, vigilantes.

visa
Saddle; short for a saddle made on a Visalia tree.

visiting harness
What the cowman sometimes calls his "town clothes."

voucher
What the cowboy calls an Indian scalp.

W

"It's sometimes safer to pull your freight than pull your gun"

W
A throw line tied to the forefoot of a horse, then run up through a ring in the belly-band and back to the wagon; used to break a wild horse to harness. If the horse starts to run away, a pull on this rope will immediately trip him.

waddy
It is claimed by some that *waddy* was created by the cowman from the word *wad*, which he uses to mean one who fills in or rounds out a ranch outfit in busy times (Don, "Vaquero Lingo," *Western Horseman*, IV, No. 2 [March–

April, 1936], 16). In the spring and
fall when some ranches are short-handed,
they take on anyone who is able to ride
a horse and use him for a week or so;
hence the word *waddy*, derived from
wadding—anything to fill in.

Some cowmen used the word to mean
a genuine rustler, or one faithful to his
fellows and his illegal calling; later it
was applied to any cowboy.

wagon, the

The roundup wagon, the cowboy's
home during the roundup; sometimes
called the *works*, *spread*, or *layout*. All
of the various wagons upon the range
are designated by their specific names,
but when the cowman speaks of *the
wagon*, every range man knows he is
talking of the chuck wagon. See *chuck
wagon*.

wagon boss

The man in charge of the roundup.
He stands out above the rank and file.
One who knows the cow country can
ride up on an outfit at a chuck wagon
or in a branding pen, for the first time,
and go straight to the boss, though he
be hard at work and dressed like the
others of the outfit. His appearance and
attitude denote leadership. He is a product of the hard school of the range.
(John M. Hendrix, "Bosses," *Cattleman*, XXIII, No. 10 [March, 1937],
65–75.) He is usually quiet, with a certain measure of reserve, and has to have
a better than average intelligence in
order to understand the nature of the
cowhand. He has to arrange each man's
work and place, day and night, without appearing to give orders; and this
calls for both tact and understanding.
See *roundup captain*.

wagon herder

A sheepherder with a wagon.

wagon manners

A term used to describe good behavior.

WAGONS AND APPURTENANCES

See band wagon, bed-wagon, bitch,
blattin' cart, buckboard, caboose, cake
wagon, calf wagon, Chihuahua cart,
chip wagon, chuck wagon, cuña, democrat wagon, fence wagon, fly, grass train,

groanin' cart, growler, hoodlum wagon,
hook up, holligan wagon, hubbing, jerk-
line, jerk-line string, jewelry chest, maniac den, mess wagon, Mormon brakes,
pie-box, pie wagon, possum-belly, prairie schooner, sheet, shotgun wagon,
throw the lines away, trail wagon, un-
hook, wagon, wagon herder, wheel
house, Which way's the wagon?

wagon-spoke rowel

A spur with an extra-long shank supporting widely spaced rowels about six
inches long and resembling the spokes
of a wagon wheel.

Walker pistol

An early frontier revolver made by
Colt after the suggestions of Captain
Samuel Walker, a Texas Ranger, and
named after him.

walkin' beamin'

The see-saw effect of a bucking horse,
when he lands alternately on his front
and hind feet.

WALKING

See high heel, straddlin' down the
road.

walking brand

One with lower designs like feet.

walking down

A method of capturing wild horses
which calls for following them in re-
lays fast enough to keep them in sight
and give them no chance to rest or eat.
After several days of this chase the mustangs are exhausted enough that the
riders can approach them and begin to
control their turnings in any desired direction. This has been known to have
been accomplished by men on foot.

walkin' sheep

Synonymous with herding sheep; the
term is applied because the work is done
on foot.

walkin' stick

A humorous reference to a horse of a
long-legged puncher.

walkin' the fence

Said when cattle walk continuously up
and down the fence line in an effort to

find a way to break out. Also used in referring to a nervous or impatient man.

walkin' whiskey vat
A heavy drinker.

wall-eyed
Said of a horse with glass, blue, or "china" eyes and with an irregular blaze.

wallow in velvet
To have plenty. Often one hears a prosperous person spoken of as having " 'nough money to burn a wet mule," or, "He had a roll as big as a wagon-hub."

waltz with the lady
A shout of encouragement for the rider to stay with a bucking horse.

wanted
Said of a man desired by the law.

war-bag
The cowboy's sack or bag for personal belongings, in which he keeps all the useless ditties and dofunnies he has gathered through the years. Here he keeps his supply of makin's and cigarette papers, an extra spur, some whang leather, an extra cinch or bit, and perhaps a carefully wrapped picture of a girl or some tattered letters which have brought him news of the outside. Among this plunder, too, there will likely be a box of cartridges, a greasy deck of playing cards, a bill of sale for his private horse, and his low-necked clothes.

warbles
Larvae of the heel fly. The eggs hatch on the hair, and the tiny larvae burrow into the skin, causing itching and discomfort. Also called *cattle grubs* and *wolves*.

war bonnet
A slang name for the cowboy's hat.

war bridle
A brutal hitch of rope in the mouth and around the lower jaw of the horse.

WARN
See cuidado, Go 'way 'round 'em, Shep., moccasin mail, send up a smoke, shook a rope at him, smoke signal.

warps his backbone
Said of a horse bucking with arched back.

washerwoman loop
A big, flat loop.

washin' out the canyon
The cowboy's expression for taking a bath.

wash off the war-paint
To get over an angry spell, to back down from a fight. One cowhand describing such an incident said, "When he looked into the danger end o' that scatter-gun, it didn't take 'im long to pull in his horns."

wasp nest
The cowboy's name for light bread.

wassup
A nickname for an outlaw horse.

waste a loop
To throw a rope and miss the target.

wasted 'er
When a rider dashes off after a cow which has escaped from the herd and fails in his attempt to bring her back he is said to have *wasted 'er*.

watchin' the op'ra
Sitting on the top rail of the corral fence watching a fellow puncher ride a bad horse.

WATER
See beef tea, gypped, too thick to drink and too thin to plow, washin' out the canyon, water hole, water rights, water-shy.

water hole
A place for watering cattle; also a slang name for a saloon.

watering the herd
This means more than herding the cattle toward water and letting them go of their own accord. Watering a trail herd is quite an art. A good trail boss starts slowing his herd up some distance before he hits the river. As he brings them to the water, he spreads them along the bank, heading the lead cattle down-

stream. Thus they get clear water, and as the others come up, they are hazed upstream, so that all cattle, including the drags, get clear water because they drink above each last successive group.

If the cattle were allowed to hit the river in a bunch, the lead cattle would be forced to the other side before they got sufficient water, and all the water would be muddied. As a rule, cattle are watered only once a day, in the evening. Charles Goodnight once said that "the science of the trail is in grazing and watering the cattle, but the watering is the most important of the two."

watermelon under the saddle

Said of a horse that arches his back excessively.

water rights

The right to a "piece of water" by priority of occupation.

water-shy

Said of a person not particular about body cleanliness. Rip Gunter, telling of an unusually dirty cook, who was "considerably whiffy on the lee side" and working with a certain wagon, said, "He's always got his jowls full o' Climax, and ain't none particular where he unloads it, and his clothes are so stiff with beef blood and dry dough y'u'd have to chop 'em off."

We were kidding a certain puncher about being water-shy, and he answered right back: "I ain't afraid o' water. In fact I like a little of it for a chaser once in a while."

water trap

A stout corral built in plain sight and around a spring or watering place. It has a wide gate which is sprung after the animals enter for watering.

wattle

A mark of ownership made on the neck or the jaw of an animal by pinching up a quantity of skin and cutting it, but not entirely off. When the wound is healed, a hanging flap of skin is left.

wave 'round

To wave a hat or other object in a semicircle from left to right, which, in the sign language of the plains, means you are not wanted and to stay away. On the range, when a rustler happens to have a maverick calf tied down at a branding fire and sees a rider approaching in the distance, he jerks his hat off and waves this rider 'round. If his warning is not heeded, he has the advantage of a .30–.30 which he is not afraid to use, and the "whine of a bullet is a hint in any man's language."

WEAK

See His thinker is puny, paper-backed.

weaner

A calf old enough to wean, slang name for a young child.

wearin' calluses on his elbow

Said of one spending his time in a saloon.

WEATHER

See blizzard, blue whistler, Chinook, cow skinner, dry storm, fence lifter, foxfire, goose drownder, gully-washer, hell wind, Idaho brain storm, norther, Oklahoma rain, open winter, pitted, silver thaw, twister.

weaver

A horse that employs a peculiar weaving motion and whose feet never strike the ground in a straight line when bucking. This motion is most disconcerting to a rider.

wedding ring

A trick-roping stunt done by swinging a wide, horizontal loop with the performer in the middle as it swings around him. It can be performed either on foot or on horseback, and takes a strong wrist and arm and above the average skill.

wedgers in

People who come uninvited, meddlers.

weedy

Locoed. Said of an animal addicted to eating loco weeds.

week on the bed-wagon

Meaning that a sick or injured man will not be able to ride again for about that long.

went up to fork a cloud

Said of a rider who had been thrown high from a horse.

wet stock

Cattle or horses which had been smuggled from across the Rio Grande River after having been stolen from their rightful owners in Mexico or Texas. Later the term was used to refer to any stolen stock.

whale line

A slang name for rope.

whangdoodle

A brand with a group of interlocking wings and with no central flying figure.

whang strings

Long strings attached to the saddle for tying on things; another name for saddle strings, especially when made of buckskin.

wheel horse

The rear horse of a jerk-line string.

wheel house

A canvas-covered wagon.

whey-belly

An inferior horse, a pot-gutted animal.

Which way's the wagon?

The old-time trail driver's familiar greeting when he rode upon a trail outfit. The wagon was always the place where he sought company, food, or information.

while the gate's still open

To the cowman this term is synonymous with *opportunity*.

whing-ding

The playful bucking indulged in by both horse and rider in the spirit of fun; also a party or social affair.

whip breaking

Training a horse, usually in a corral, by stinging his rump with a whip or the end of a rope every time he turns from you. In time, from the pain, he will turn toward you, and if you back away each time and drag your whip, he will begin to understand what you want him to do. Very few cowmen use this method. (Will James, *In the Saddle With Uncle Bill* [New York, Charles Scribner's Sons, 1935], 58–59.)

whippin' a tired pony out of Texas

This term became a synonym for *on the dodge*.

WHIPPING

See chapping, clean his plow, clipped his horns, hang up his hide, horns sawed off, leggin' case, puttin' the leggin's, sharpen his hoe.

WHIPS

See blacksnake, bull whip, cow whip, quirt, quisto, romal.

whirling

Whirling the noose of a rope about the head until sufficient spread is developed to make a throw at the object to be roped. The whirl is never used in a corral, especially the horse corral, as it alarms the animals.

WHISKEY

See base-burner, brave-maker, bug juice, coffin varnish, conversation fluid, dynamite, fire-water, gut-warmer, Indian whiskey, neck-oil, nose-paint, red disturbance, red-eye, red-ink, scamper juice, snake-head whiskey, snake poison, tarantula juice, tonsil varnish, tornado juice, wild mare's milk.

whiskey mill

A frontier name for the saloon.

whistle

Slang name for any one young and foolish.

whistle-berries

The cowboy's name for beans.

whistle judge

The man in the rodeo stand who blows the whistle at the end of ten seconds in bronc-riding contests.

white-collar rancher

A nonresident ranch owner.

white-faces

Hereford cattle; also called *open-faced* cattle.

white house

Slang name for the main house of the ranch, or owner's home; the executive office.

white-water bucko

A good river driver.

whittler

Slang name for a good cutting horse.

whittle whanging

Wrangling, quarreling.

whole shebang

A collective whole.

wickiup

An Indian hut of primitive construction made of branches of trees loosely interwoven. Sometimes used colloquially by cowmen in referring to their own houses.

wigwam

An Indian dwelling, generally of conical shape, formed of bark and mats or hides laid over stakes planted in the ground and converging at the top, where there is an opening for smoke to escape. Also used by the cowman in speaking humorously of his residence.

WILD

See snuffy.

wild bunch

An outlaw gang, horses not handled enough to be controllable.

wild cow milking

A rodeo event. A wild cow is turned loose in the arena. Two cowboys dash after her; one ropes the animal, then the other mugs her. After this, the roper runs on foot carrying a pop bottle and tries to obtain about an inch of milk in it. After securing the milk, he runs to the judges to show it. He does all this against time.

wild mare's milk

Slang name for whiskey.

wild, woolly, and full o' fleas

A phrase of the early days which the cowboy created to impress the tenderfoot with his woolliness. The saying became so common that some people actually believed the cowboy had fleas, but actually he has no more love for fleas than any other man. As one said, he had "rather have gray-backs than fleas 'cause after these seam squirrels graze, they bed down, but a flea's never satisfied. After he locates paydirt on one claim he jumps to stake another, and he's a damned nimble prospector."

willow tail

A horse, usually a mare, which has a loose, long, coarse, heavy tail—never an indication of good breeding.

Winchester

An early model repeating rifle named for its maker and still a favorite with Westerners.

Winchester quarantine

A barrier by force of arms. These quarantines occurred many times in the early West, especially on the trail when some group of natives objected to a tick-infested trail herd's passing through their range.

wind-belly

An orphan calf, all belly, or as the cowboy would say, "fat in the middle and pore at both ends."

windbreak

One or more rows of trees, a tall fence, or a natural formation on the windward side providing shelter from cold winds.

windbroken

Said of a horse with a respiratory disease that impairs his breathing.

windies

Cattle that have to be driven out of canyons on to the plains. These cattle are usually contrary and hard to drive, and by the time they have been coaxed out of the canyon, the cattle, the horses, and the cowboys are about exhausted, hence the name; also the name of boastful stories which contain no semblance of the truth.

WINDIES

See corral dust, hassayampa, load, Pecos Bill, peddler of loads, stretchin' the blanket, tellin' a windy, wild, wooly, and full o' fleas, windies.

windmiller

A man who cares for the windmills of the later-day ranch. Only the large ranches hire a man for this special duty. With a helper he is kept busy building new windmills and keeping the old ones in repair.

windmilling

Said of a horse when he is swapping ends.

windmill monkey

A man who oils and repairs windmills, because he has to do considerable climbing to do the job well.

wing fence

A fence on each side of a corral entrance which flares out for many feet to help direct the leaders of the entering herd into the opening of the pen.

winter horses

Horses kept up for use in winter.

winter kill

Cattle which die from the winter cold.

wipes

The cowboy's slang name for his neckerchief. It has more uses than almost anything else he wears and is not merely an ornamental necktie, as many folks think. The rodeo rider prefers bright colors in neckerchiefs as in shirts; but the range man, who wants to dodge the attention of either people or animals, since bright colors advertise him when he is trying to avoid notice, prefers neutral colors.

Folding his neckerchief diagonally, like the first garment he ever wore, he ties the two farthest corners in a square knot and hangs it on the peg he finds handiest—his neck. In this way he is never without it in case he needs it, and he generally does. Mostly he wears it draped loosely over his chest with the knot at the back. If the sun is at his back he reverses it for the protection of his neck. Riding in the drag of a herd, he pulls it up over his nose and mouth so that he can breathe without being suffocated by the dust that is kicked up. It is a protection against cold wind and stinging sleet. Pulled up under his eyes, it guards against snow blindness. (J. Frank Dobie, *Vaquero of the Brush Country* [Dallas, Southwest Press, 1929], 264; Philip A. Rollins, *The Cowboy* [New York, Charles Scribner's Sons, 1936], 107.)

If he is riding in a stiff wind and does not have bonnet strings on his hat, he ties it on with his bandanna; sometimes, when the weather is cold, he uses it for an ear-muff, and when it is hot, he will wear it wet under his hat to keep his head cool. Caught in a country where there is no running water when he is thirsty, he spreads it over a muddy water hole to use as a strainer to drink through.

When he washes his face at the water hole in the morning, he carries his towel with him, tied around his neck. In the branding pen when the sweat is running down into his eyes, this mop is hanging handy, and it also makes a rag for holding the handle of a hot branding iron.

Perhaps he uses it as a blindfold in saddling a snaky bronc, or as a piggin' string when he runs across a calf that has been overlooked in branding. He sometimes uses it to hobble his horse; one end tied to the lower jaw of a gentle horse serves as an Indian bridle that will do in a pinch. It has been used as a sling for broken arms, a tourniquet, and a bandage for wounds. Men have been handcuffed with neckerchiefs and more than one cowboy has been buried out on the plains with one spread over his face to keep the dirt from touching it.

It can be used as a saddlebag, a mosquito net, or a trail marker; it has been used as a flag for signaling, a dish cloth, a recoil pad, a gun sling, a basket, and a sponge; and the highwayman has used it for a mask.

wipin' him out

Quirting a horse.

WIRE

See California buckskin, silk.

wisdom bringer

A schoolteacher. As most of these teachers were imported from the East, the cowman did not have much respect for their knowledge. To him, anyone who did not know cows "couldn't teach a settin' hen to cluck."

WISE

See bone seasoned, hair off the dog, more wrinkles on his horns, out fox, savvy.

wish-book

A mail-order catalog. Many cowboys got their education from one of these wishbooks, and by studying the pictures knew what practically everything on earth was before they ever saw the real article. The women of the ranch did their wishful window-shopping in its pages, and it was not uncommon to see some cowboy thumbing through its thickness, lingering with a lot of wonder on the pages picturing women's personal wearing apparel.

witches' bridle

Tangles in a horse's mane.

wohaw

The first cattle the Indians saw under the white man's control were the ox teams of the early freighters. Listening with wonder to the strange words of the bullwhackers as they shouted, "Whoa," "Haw," and "Gee," they thought these words were the name of the animals, and began calling cattle *wohaws*. Rarely did a trail herd pass through the Indian country on its march north that it was not stopped to receive a demand for *wohaw*. This demand become so common that the cattlemen themselves began to use the word and it became a part of their vocabulary. (J. Frank Dobie, *The Longhorns* [Boston, Little, Brown, 1941], 251; George W. Saunders to R.F.A.)

wolf

Not only a predatory animal of the cattle country, but also what the cowboy calls a cattle grub hatched from the eggs of the heel fly.

wolfer

A man hired by the ranch to trap and hunt wolves on its particular range. He matches wits with this most cunning of animals for the bounty paid, both by the rancher and the county in which he works.

WOMEN

See calico, calico queen, catalog woman, cookie pusher, cow bunny, dulce, heart-and-hand woman, live dictionary, long-haired partner, Montgomery Ward woman sent west on approval, painted cat, puncture lady, runnin' mate, sage hen.

wood

A slang name for the saddle.

wood monkey

A flunky or man responsible for supplying wood for a roundup camp.

wood pussy

A skunk.

wood sheller

Cutter of fence posts and branding fuel.

woolies

A common name for sheep.

wool in his teeth

Said of a person of low principle, implying that he is a sheep-killing cur.

woolsey

Slang name for a cheap hat, usually made of wool. Ross Santee tells a good story of a cowhand named Shorty letting a cow-town merchant sell him a cheap hat so much too large for him that he had to stuff five lamp-wicks under the sweat band to make it fit.

" 'It's pourin' rain when I leaves town, [says Shorty] and the old hat weighs a ton. I ain't any more than started when it's down over both ears, an' by the time I hit Seven Mile it's leakin' like a sieve. I'm ridin' a bronc that's pretty snuffy, an' every time I raises the lid enough to git a little light, I see him drop one ear. I finally decides to take the lamp-wicks out altogether. I'm tryin' to raise the lid enough to see somethin' besides the saddle-horn when the old bronc bogs his head. I make a grab for leather when he leaves the ground, but

I might as well have a gunny-sack tied over my head, for I can't see nothin'. When he comes down the second time I'm way over on one side. When he hits the ground the third jump, I ain't with him. I'm sittin' in the middle of the wash with both hands full of sand. I finally lifts the lid enough to see the old bronc headin' for the ranch. He's wide open and kickin' at his paunch.' " (Ross Santee, *Men and Horses* [New York, The Century Company, 1921], 115.)

wool with the handle on

The cowboy's name for a mutton chop.

wooshers

What the cowboy calls hogs.

Worchestershire

A slang name for the Winchester rifle.

wore 'em low

This expression signifies that the one spoken of wears his gun low where it is easily accessible and that he is willing to stand or fall by his ability to use it. Very often it is used to mean that his gun is for hire, and that he is a professional gunman. Duke Noel used to say of one of them, "That hogleg hangin' at his side ain't no watch-charm, and he don't pack that hardware for bluff nor ballast."

work

A term applied to handling cattle. To round up stock, to brand calves, and to gather beeves is to work cattle.

WORK

See sweat, work.

work horse

One used in harness.

working ahead of the roundup

When a rancher or cowhand drives his cattle on the range ahead of those of the larger outfits and claims all unbranded stock. A herd can be built up quickly in this way. See *Sooners*.

working brands

Changing brands from one type to another through the use of the running iron.

WORKING CATTLE

See chouse, cutting out, cuttin' the herd, gin around, mustard the cattle, pulling bog, tailing up, work, working the herd.

working the herd

Cutting a large herd into one or more smaller lots. The cattle are gathered on circle during the roundup for the purpose of cutting out beef cattle, breeding specimens, or other specific types wanted for other reasons.

work over

To change a brand, to take the buck out of a horse.

WORTHINESS

See he'll do to ride the river with, measured a full sixteen hands high, square.

WORTHLESS

See cull, cultus, peal, plumb cultus, scalawag, scrub, stiff, worthless as a four-card flush.

worthless as a four-card flush

Anything worthless or beyond repair.

WOUNDED

See mining for lead, singed.

wrangatang

An occasional name for the day wrangler.

wrangle

To herd horses.

wrangler

A herder of the saddle horses. It is the duty of this man or boy to see that the horses are kept together and at hand when wanted for the work. The word is a corruption of the Mexican *caverango*, meaning *hostler*.

His job is considered the most menial in cow work and he does not stand very high in a cow camp. He rides the sorriest horse in the outfit and is the butt of all the jokes of a dozen cowhands. Yet his job is a training school, and many good cowboys have gotten their start in a wrangler's job.

By studying the characteristics of the various horses, he saves himself much work and grief. He knows which are apt to be bunch quitters, which are fighters, and which are afraid of their own shadows. The arrival of stray men with their strings adds to his cares, and he has more horses to get acquainted with. Although it can rarely be said, the greatest praise that can be bestowed upon a wrangler is that "he never lost a horse."

WRANGLER
See caverango, cavvy man, dew wrangler, hood, horse pestler, horse rustler, horse wrangler, jingler, jingling, mustangler, night herd, remudero, rustler, wrangatang, wrangler, wrango.

wrango
Short for wrangler.

wrastlin' calves
A common expression for flanking.

wreck pan
The receptacle for the dirty dishes

after a meal in a cow camp. See *round pan.*

wring-tail
A horse of nervous disposition that has been ridden to exhaustion and spurred to make him go, causing him to develop the habit of wringing his tail as he runs. Jerking on the bits also develops this habit. No real cowman likes to ride a wring-tail horse, for it makes the rider nervous.

wrinkled his spine
An expression used when referring to the bucking of a horse.

wrinkle-horn
Cowboy's name for an old steer whose horns have become wrinkled and scaly.

wrinkles on his horns
Said of a person possessing wisdom or having had much experience.

X

"Faint heart never filled a flush"

Xerga (csay'gah)
A saddle cloth placed between the salea and the packsaddle.

Y

"Nobody ever drowned himself in sweat"

yack
A stupid person.

yakima
An Indian pony.

Yaks
A nickname given by the northern

cowboy to the Mexican cattle which went up the trail, because they came from the Yaqui Indian country.

yamping
Ordinary stealing, petty theft.

yannigan bag
A bag for personal belongings.

yearling
   A year-old calf or colt, a child.

yellow bellies
   Cattle of Mexican breed splotched on

flank and belly with a yellowish color.

yucca country
   A general reference to the Southwest.

Z

"Never call a·man a liar because he knows more'n you do"

zebra dun
   A horse of dun color with a more or less distinct dorsal stripe over the entire length of his top line, with often a transverse shoulder stripe and sometimes zebra stripes on the legs.

zorrillas (thor-reel'lyahs)
   Cattle of the early longhorn breed,

called this in the border country from their color, which is black with a lineback, white speckles frequently appearing on the sides and belly. The word is from the Spanish, meaning *polecat*. (J. Frank Dobie, *The Longhorns*, [Boston, Little, Brown, 1941], 24–25.)

Adiós, and may you never get your spurs tangled up

TITLES OF RELATED INTEREST FROM HIPPOCRENE . . .

Dictionaries

NAVAJO-ENGLISH DICTIONARY
165 pages • 5 ¼ x 8 ½ • 9,000 entries • 0-7818-0247-4 • $9.95pb • (223)

COLLOQUIAL NAVAJO: A DICTIONARY
461 pages • 5 x 7 • 10,000 entries • 0-7818-0278-4 • $16.95 • (282)

PSYCHOLOGY OF BLACK LANGUAGE
106 pages • 5 ½ x 8 ¼ • 0-7818-0086-2 • $9.95pb • (387)

Travel

U.S.A. GUIDE TO THE UNDERGROUND RAILROAD by Charles Blockson
This illustrated travel guide and historic reference contains over two hundred landmark houses, institutions, buildings, museums and monuments related to the northward movement of African Americans towards freedom.
380 pages • 5 ¼ x 8 ½ • b/w photos, illus., index, glossary
0-7818-0253-9 • $22.95hc • (108)
0-7818-0429-9 • $16.95pb • (547)

EXPLORING THE BERKSHIRES by Herbert Whitman
This book guides the reader through six comprehensive tours of both the familiar and the unfamiliar.
"This gem of a book [is] aimed at the inquisitive roamer."
—*A Conde Nast Traveler*
168 pages • 5 ½ x 8 ½ • illus. • 0-87052-979-X • $9.95pb • (210)

EXPLORING NANTUCKET by Herbert Whitman
Windswept beaches, lush greenery and lovely historic buildings are listed along with local history and lore.
112 pages • 5 ½ x 8 ¼ • illus. • 0-87052-792-4 • $11.95pb • (46)

EXPLORING THE LITCHFIELD HILLS by Herbert Whitman
Learn Indian legends, history, and curiosities along six roaming tours of Litchfield county.
112 pages • 5 ¼ x 8 ¼ • illus. • 0-7818-0045-5 • $9.95pb • (132)

U.S.A. GUIDE TO THE HISTORIC BLACK SOUTH
by James Haskins and Joann Biondi
"Provides some wonderful reading and inspires tourists to go and explore a part of the South that has not been emphasized in travel." —*Library Journal*
300 pages • 5 ½ x 8 ½ • index, b/w photos • 0-7818-014-0 • $14.95pb • (92)

BLACK FLORIDA *by Kevin McCarthy*
This guide introduces the reader to churches, schools, homes and other significant sites in seventy different towns across Florida, providing information on their historical importance, present condition and availability for visiting.
331 pages • 5 ½ x 8 ¼ • 50 b/w photos • 0-7818-0291-1 • $16.95pb • (84)

BLACK WASHINGTON: Places and Events of Historical and Cultural Significance *by Sandra Fitzpatrick and Maria Goodwin*
Described by the *L.A. Times* as a "thorough and well-organized book," *Black Washington* weaves together history, anecdotes and practical information.
288 pages • 5 ½ x 8 ¼ • b/w photos, maps • 0-87052-832-7 • $14.95pb • (25)

U.S.A. GUIDE TO HISTORIC HISPANIC AMERICA by Oscar and Joy Jones
"Chapters survey museums, historic sites, and Spanish and Indian legends and lore." —*Midwest Book Review*
168 pages • 5 ½ x 8 ½ • b/w photos, maps • 0-7818-0141-9 • $14.95pb • (110)

THE SOUTHWEST: A Family Adventure *by Tish Minear and Janet Limon*
For the family, the Four Corner states are a playground of spectacular national parks, historic sites, and exotic cultures.
440 pages • 5 ½ x 8 ¼ • 27 b/w photos, over 50 line drawings, appendices • 0-87052-640-5 • $16.95pb • (394)

EMIGRATING TO THE USA: A Complete Guide to Immigration, Temporary Visas and Employment *by E.C.Beshara and Richard and Karla Paroutad*
A comprehensive, easy-to-use directory offering a wealth of information on obtaining temporary and permanent U.S. visas.
362 pages • 5 ½ x 8 ½ • drawings and charts • 0-7818-0249-0 • $18.95pb • (133)

Cookbooks

THE HONEY COOKBOOK: Recipes for Healthy Living *by Maria Lo Pinto*
Much more than a cookbook, this indispensable guide shows how honey works as a powerful healer, a tonic, on burns and bites, and with oatmeal as a facial mask. The book features 240 recipes, menus, cooking tips, and substitutions.
174 pages • 5 x 8 ½ • 0-7818-0149-4 • $8.95pb • (283)

A SPANISH FAMILY COOKBOOK, Revised Edition
270 • pages • 5 ½ x 8 ½ • 0-7818-0546-5 • $11.95pb • (642)

ADDITIONAL TITLES
FROM HIPPOCRENE BOOKS . . .

Dictionaries

BEGINNER'S ESPERANTO
400 pages • 5 ½ x 8 ½ • 0-7818-0230-X • $14.95pb • (51)

SPANISH-ENGLISH/ENGLISH-SPANISH CONCISE DICTIONARY (Latin American)
500 pages • 4 x 6 • 8,000 entries • 0-7818-0261-X • $11.95pb • (258)

SPANISH-ENGLISH/ENGLISH-SPANISH PRACTICAL DICTIONARY
338 pages • 5 ½ x 8 ¼ • 35,000 entries • 0-7818-0179-6 • $9.95pb • (211)

SPANISH-ENGLISH/ENGLISH-SPANISH DICTIONARY OF COMPUTER TERMS
120 pages • 5 ½ x 8 ½ • 5,700 entries • 0-7818-0148-6 • $16.95 • (36)

500 SPANISH WORDS AND PHRASES FOR CHILDREN
32 pages • 8 x 10¼ • full-color illus. • 0-7818-0262-8 • $8.95 • (17)

SPANISH GRAMMAR
224 pages • 5 ½ x 8 ½ • 0-87052-893-9 • $12.95pb • (273)

SPANISH VERBS: Ser and Estar
220 pages • 5 ½ x 8 ½ • 0-7818-0024-2 • $9.95pb • (292)

MASTERING SPANISH
338 pages • 5 ½ x 8 ½ • 0-87052-059-8 • $11.95 • (527)
2 Cassettes: 0-87052-067-9 • $12.95 • (528)

MASTERING ADVANCED SPANISH
326 pages • 5 ½ x 8 ½ • 0-7818-0081-1 • $14.95pb • (413)
2 Cassettes: 0-7818-0089-7 • $12.95 • (426)

Proverbs

DICTIONARY OF PROVERBS AND THEIR ORIGINS
250 pages • 5 x 8 • 0-7818-0591-0 • $14.95pb • (701)

INTERNATIONAL DICTIONARY OF PROVERBS
580 pages • 5 ½ x 8 ½ • 0-7818-0531-7 • $29.50hc • (656)

COMPREHENSIVE BILINGUAL DICTIONARY OF FRENCH PROVERBS
400 pages • 5 x 8 • 6,000 entries • 0-7818-0594-5 • $24.95pb • (700)

DICTIONARY OF 1,000 FRENCH PROVERBS
131 pages • 5 x 7 • 0-7818-0400-0 • $11.95pb • (146)

DICTIONARY OF 1,000 GERMAN PROVERBS
131 pages • 5 ½ x 8 ½ • 0-7818-0471-X • $11.95pb • (540)

DICTIONARY OF 1,000 ITALIAN PROVERBS
131 pages • 5 ½ x 8 ½ • 0-7818-0458-2 • $11.95pb • (370)

DICTIONARY OF 1,000 SPANISH PROVERBS
131 pages • 5 ½ x 8 ½ • bilingual • 0-7818-0412-4 • $11.95pb • (254)

Games

THE BOOK OF CARD GAMES *by Peter Arnold*
"A good introduction to many of the most popular card games played in social settings and a very handy reference." —American Library Association, *Booklist*
279 pages • 5 ½ x 8 ½ • illus. • 0-87952-730-4 • $16.95pb • (234)

Travel

LANGUAGE AND TRAVEL GUIDE TO MEXICO
224 pages • 5 ½ x 8 ½ • 0-87052-622-7 • $14.95pb • (503)

HIPPOCRENE INSIDER'S GUIDE TO THE WORLD'S MOST EXCITING CRUISES
510 pages • 5 ½ x 8 ½ • b/w photos, index • 0-7818-0258-X • $18.95pb • (21)

TRAVELER'S IQ TEST: Rate Your Globetrotting Knowledge
194 pages • 24 b/w illus. • 12 maps • 0-87052-307-4 • $6.95 • (103)

TRAVELER'S TRIVIA TEST, Revised Edition
224 pages • 0-87052-915-3 • $6.95pb • (87)

All prices subject to change. TO PURCHASE HIPPOCRENE BOOKS contact your local bookstore, call (718) 454-2366, or write to: HIPPOCRENE BOOKS, 171 Madison Avenue, New York, NY 10016. Please enclose check or money order, adding $5.00 shipping (UPS) for the first book and $.50 for each additional book.

CPSIA information can be obtained
at www.ICGtesting.com
Printed in the USA
JSHW051646250322
24213JS00003B/3